ITALY

A Rand McNally Pocket Guide

Dorothy Daly

Rand McNally & Company
Chicago New York San Francisco

Cover photographs
Italian State Tourist Office, Van Phillips

Photographs
Italian State Tourist Office
p 21, 37, 67, 82, 87, 115

J. Allan Cash Ltd
p 101

Peter Baker Photography
p 76

Van Phillips
p 46, 58, 73

Regional maps
Matthews & Taylor Associates

Town plans
M. and R. Piggott

Illustrations
Barry Rowe

First published 1980
Revised edition 1985
Copyright © Dorothy Daly 1980
Published by Rand McNally & Company
Chicago   New York   San Francisco
Printed in Great Britain
Library of Congress Catalog Card Number: 84-42832
SBN 0-528-84877-1

HOW TO USE THIS BOOK

The contents page of this book shows how the country is divided up into tourist regions. The book is in two sections; general information and gazetteer. The latter is arranged in the tourist regions with an introduction and a regional map (detail below left). There are also plans of the main towns (detail below right). All the towns and villages in the gazetteer are shown on the regional maps. Places to visit and leisure facilities available in each region and town are indicated by symbols. Main roads, railways, ferries and airports are shown on the maps and plans.

Regional Maps

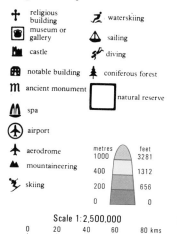

† religious building	⅀ waterskiing
🖼 museum or gallery	⚓ sailing
🏰 castle	🤿 diving
🏛 notable building	🌲 coniferous forest
𝔪 ancient monument	☐ natural reserve
♨ spa	
✈ airport	
✈ aerodrome	metres 1000 / feet 3281
▲ mountaineering	400 / 1312
⅀ skiing	200 / 656
	0 / 0

Scale 1:2,500,000

0   20   40   60   80 kms
0   10   20   30   40   50 miles

Town Maps

† religious building	❀ garden
🖼 museum or gallery	🌳 park
🏰 castle	● railway station
🏛 notable building	🚌 bus station
𝔪 ancient monument	✈ airport
POL police	🏇 racecourse
✉ post office	⚓ harbour
ℹ tourist information	▲ youth hostel
⚒ town hall	🏪 market
📖 library	
✚ hospital	
🎭 theatre	

Every effort has been made to give you an up-to-date text but changes are constantly occurring and we will be grateful for any information about changes you may notice while travelling.

CONTENTS

Regions

1 The Lakes
2 Piemonte and Valle d'Aosta
3 Lombardia
4 Veneto
5 Liguria
6 Emília-Romagna
7 Toscana
8 Marche
9 Umbria
10 Lázio
11 Abruzzi and Molise
12 Campania
13 Púglia and Basilicata
14 Calábria
15 Sicília
16 Sardegna

Town plans

Note on place-names
In this book a stress accent has been used, where appropriate, on place-names as an aid to pronunciation; *eg* Alássio.

A VERY BRIEF HISTORY

Italy as we know it today came to birth on 21 April 754 BC with the founding of the city of Roma (Rome).

At first not much larger than a village, Roma grew within a thousand years into a mighty empire circling the entire Mediterranean, including Spain, France and much of Germany, and stretching up to embrace parts of Britain. The thousand years from its foundation saw the rise and, alas, the fall, of one of the world's greatest civilizations.

In 395 AD Theodore divided the empire into two, the eastern and western empires. During the next 400 years Italy was repeatedly invaded. In return for protection, France was given power of empire over Italy, and in 810 AD Carlo Magno (Charlemagne) was crowned in Roma Emperor of the Holy Roman Empire, and there began the foreign domination of Italy.

Coeval with the invasions was the development of a great chain of monasteries in the country districts. San Benedetto, born in Nórcia in 480, founded the Benedettini (Benedictine Order); others followed. At this time an exodus from town to country is noticed: the monasteries offered protection for those who worked within their territory.

In the 9th and 10th centuries, however, came a return to the cities, to walled cities, high on the hills, far safer against attack than the country monasteries. These cities were more or less uniform in design, each with a large central square, a massive church for devotions, a bell-tower to summon the faithful, a fountain, a huge combined town hall and hall of justice.

Gradually the free *comunes* (city states) evolved, each city having its own form of government, often its own private army and, in the case of marine cities, a private navy as well. All owed allegiance to the central government, but, during the long periods of absentee emperors, each city realized the need for self-reliance and self-protection. Thus grew the spirit of individuality still to be observed in many Italian cities.

Most of these independent cities suffered greatly in the struggles against the German emperors Frederick Barbarossa and Frederick II, but they were the bases of the fabulous principalities such as the Medici of Firenze (Florence), Este of Ferrara and Montefeltro of Urbino, which during the Renaissance gave northern Italy much of the art and architecture we admire today.

From the 15th to the mid-19th century, Italy was fought over and dominated by other European powers. The years after Waterloo saw the Austrians again in Italy but also the rise of a new national spirit; there were unsuccessful revolts between 1821 and 1848, then in 1859 Cavour, with the support of Napoleon III, defeated the Austrians in Lombardia. In the next year Garibaldi took Sicília (Sicily), then conquered Rome after a siege of 25 days. In 1861 Victor Emmanuel became King of Italy; Veneto was ceded by Austria in 1866, and in 1871 Roma once again became the capital of all Italy.

Only in 1946 was the Italian republic of today proclaimed.

ART AND ARCHITECTURE

The earliest examples of art and architecture in Italy stem from Greece and Etruria. Long before the founding of Roma in 754 BC, the central portion of the peninsula was inhabited by the Etruscans, who left splendid examples of wall paintings and funerary monuments in such centres as Tarquínia, Volterra, Cortona and Chiusi, while others may be seen in the museums of Firenze and Perúgia. The Greeks are remembered primarily by temples in Paestum, south of Nápoli (Naples), and in Selinunte and Segesta, Siracusa (Syracuse) and Taormina, the last four all being in Sicília.

As Roman power increased, the architects began to express themselves in great civic buildings and in commemorative arches and columns. In the Foro Romano in Roma one sees the Basilica Julia, built by Julius Caesar (46 BC), later rebuilt by Augustus. The Colosseo, erected in 69 AD under Vespasian, is an

example of Greek architecture adapted to Roman ideas of space. Other examples of Roman art are to be seen in the triumphal Arch of Titus and Trajan's Column, where one notices the cold classicism of Greek portraiture giving place to vivid likenesses of events and people. The Pantheon (18–125 AD) is another fine remnant of Roman architecture. Around 200 AD were erected the huge Terme di Caracalla (baths), which demonstrate the Roman love of spaciousness; a little later came the Terme di Diocleziano. The Basilica di Massenzio in the Foro Romano dates from 306–312 AD.

Painting was confined to wall decorations such as one sees in Pompei and Ercolano, the cities near Nápoli destroyed in the eruption of Vesúvio in 79 AD. One of the finest examples of early statuary is the figure of Marcus Aurelius which now dominates the Piazza del Campidoglio in Roma and which was completed in 176 AD. The art of mosaic was highly developed. Starting as a floor decoration, mosaics came to be used as wall embellishments, as in the Roman villa at Piazza Armerina in Sicília. After the Edict of Milan (313 AD), which gave the freedom of worship to the Christians, mosaics began to appear as decorations in Christian churches. Statuary, too, developed under Christianity.

In the 5th century, Roma ceased for a time to be the capital city, and the centre of activity moved to Ravenna, where a number of magnificent churches were built during the next two centuries, lined with some of the finest mosaics in the world. Ravenna was in close touch with Byzantium, the capital of the eastern Roman empire, and there is a strong oriental influence to be traced.

From the early Longobard period little remains but examples of the goldsmith's art. In the Museo del Bargello in Firenze is a charming 6th-century plaque in copper, showing the Triumph of King Agilupho; the treasury of the cathedral of Monza houses the famous Iron Crown of Monza, with which the Carolingian kings were crowned, so called because lining the gold crown is a band of iron, said to be a nail from the True Cross. Few churches were built during the following centuries, but in about 1000 AD there developed in Lombardia (Lombardy) what later came to be known as the Romanesque style. The church of Sant'Ambrogio in Milano (Milan) is a specially fine example; another is San Michele in Pavia; another the cathedral of Modena, begun in 1099 by the architect Lanfranco. Here, too, are some splendid early bas-reliefs.

Romanesque developed differently in various parts of Italy, while retaining more or less the same basic ideas of blind arches which make the cathedrals of this period so attractive. One splendid development is in Pisa in the Battistero (Baptistery), the Duomo (Cathedral) and the Campanile (Leaning Tower). The cathedral and the church of San Frediano in Lucca have similar ornate treatment. Firenze had its own interpretation, notably in the geometric external decoration of the baptistery and the church of San Miniato al Monte, executed in vari-coloured marbles. Examples in Roma are the campanile (bell-tower) of Santi Giovanni e Paolo and the cloisters of San Giovanni in Laterano. The Basilica di San Marco in Venezia (Venice) is a blend of Romanesque and Byzantine, owing much to the design of the former church of SS Apostoli in Byzantium.

Painting and sculpture were now beginning to lose their Byzantine rigidity, and the mosaics of San Clemente and Santa Maria in Trastevere, both in Roma, offer an interesting parallel development. Two great painters emerge. Duccio di Buoninsegna (1278–1317) was almost the last of the Tuscan painters to reflect the influence of Byzantium, coupled in his case with the meticulous beauty associated with French miniature painters. The Museo dell'Opera del Duomo in Siena houses his magnificent *Maestà*, once a double-sided altarpiece in the cathedral.

Cimabue (1240–1302), a Florentine, worked for a time in Roma, but he is principally remembered for his work in the enormous basilica at Assisi, begun two years after the death of St Francis in 1226. In Firenze, the Galleria degli Uffizi has a *Maestà* by this artist, and in the museum of the church of Santa Croce hangs a wonderfully impressive crucifix – badly damaged in the tragic floods of November 1966. But it is to Assisi one goes to see Cimabue at his finest, and to observe the influence cast by him on later generations of painters. Here were gathered together the leading artists of the period, not merely from Italy, but from other parts of Europe.

With the end of the Middle Ages, Gothic art and architecture began to supersede the Romanesque. Cimabue's pupil, Giotto, ranks as a Gothic painter, and the basilica of St Francis is also basically Gothic. The transition is most clearly marked in the sculpture of Nicola and Giovanni Pisano. In 1260 Nicola executed the pulpit in the baptistery in Pisa, where classical influence is still obvious. From 1266–8 he and his pupils sculpted the pulpit in the cathedral of Siena; later (1276–8), father and son worked on the Fontana Maggiore in the Piazza IV Novembre in Perúgia; in 1298 Giovanni began work on a pulpit in the church of Sant'Andrea in Pistóia, and between 1302 and 1310 he worked alone on the pulpit in the cathedral in Pisa. Here, the Gothic influence in both the architecture and the sculpture of the monuments is clearly visible.

Other great examples of Gothic architecture are the Basilica di Sant'Antonio in Padova (Padua) – a mixture of Gothic and Romanesque – Santa Maria Gloriosa dei Frari, Venezia, and the cathedrals of Siena, Génova (Genoa), Milano. One of Nicola Pisano's pupils, Arnolfo di Cambio, was not only a sculptor but also a notable architect. He was responsible for the cathedral of Firenze – begun 1296, the Brunelleschi cupola added in the 15th century – and conceived the cathedral of Orvieto, completed by Lorenzo Maitano, who sculpted the reliefs of the outer two of the panels dividing the entrance doors.

The first great Gothic painter to emerge is Giotto (1267–1337), a pupil of Cimabue, architect of the Campanile (bell-tower) in Firenze, and painter of a series of frescoes in the upper church of St Francis in Assisi, and of the more mature series in the Cappella degli Scrovegni in Padova. Painting ceases to be the representation of a single moment in time and becomes a living narrative of events. In Assisi, look particularly at the miracle of the peasant drinking from the spring that gushes from the earth in answer to the prayer of St Francis; in Padova note the Kiss of Judas. Other frescoes by this great artist are to be seen in the Bardi and Peruzzi chapels in the church of Santa Croce in Firenze. In the Uffizi, compare his *Maestà* with those of Duccio and Cimabue.

During the 15th century, the great age of the Renaissance, sculptors, architects and artists succeeded in fusing classical ideas with modern. The problem of perspective had been solved by Brunelleschi (1377–1446). In Firenze one should note particularly his cupola of the cathedral, loggia of the Ospedale degli Innocenti and exquisite Cappella dei Pazzi in the grounds of Santa Croce. Other contemporary architects were Alberti (1404–72), designer of the façade of Santa Maria Novella in Firenze, and Agostino di Duccio, architect of the lovely little oratory of San Bernardino in Perúgia.

Leading sculptors included Lorenzo Ghiberti (1378–1455), sculptor of the north and east doors of the baptistery in Firenze, also damaged by the November 1966 floods. In Siena, Jacopo della Quercia (1374–1458) sculpted the Fonte Gaia in the Campo, and a charming funerary monument to Ilaria del Carretto in the cathedral of Lucca. In 1386 was born Donatello who during the 80 years of his life contributed much to Italian sculpture; the *David* and the *St George* in the Museo del Bargello in Firenze, an enchanting panel of child singers in the Museo dell'Opera del Duomo and a feast of sculpture in the Basilica di Sant'Antonio, Padova. The huge equestrian statue outside, representing Gattamelata, one of the great soldiers of fortune, is possibly the finest statue of its kind, comparable only with Verrocchio's *Colleoni* in the courtyard of the church of Santi Giovanni e Paolo in Venezia. Another sculptor to be influenced by Donatello was Antonio del Pollaiolo, whose statue of *Hercules and Antæus* can be seen in the Bargello, his monument of Pope Sixtus IV in the Vaticano.

Painters of this period are too numerous for more than a mention. The work of Masolino (1383–1435) and of Masaccio (b. 1401) is best seen in the frescoes in the church of Santa Maria del Carmine in Firenze – note particularly the drama of the *Flight from Eden*. Outstanding among Florentine artists is the Dominican friar, Beato Angelico (1400–55). A lovely series of his frescoes can be seen in the Convento di San Marco in Firenze; the *Deposition* in the museum gives a fine impression of the spirituality of this magical painter's work. A fine *Annunciation* is in the little hill town of Cortona in Toscana (Tuscany).

Paolo Uccello (1397–1475) is well-known for his battle scenes, of which the Uffizi has a fine example. Another interpreter of the new ideas of perspective was Piero della Francesca (1416–92) – visitors to Arezzo should not fail to go to the church of San Francesco to see his series of frescoes on the Legend of the True Cross. In the Uffizi are his fine portraits of Federigo da Montefeltro and Battista Sforza. Luca Signorelli (1450–1525) is remembered for his series of frescoes in the cathedral of Orvieto, massive figures, no longer veiled with draperies – painters were now beginning to be conscious of anatomy and were not afraid to portray it. And at the height of the Renaissance there comes Botticelli (1445–1510), painter of dainty, aristocratic figures in which one notices a sense of luxury coupled with a curious melancholy and wistfulness; the Uffizi has a splendid collection of his work, including *Spring* and *The Birth of Venus*. The frescoes on the walls of the Sistine Chapel in Roma show a more serious aspect.

One of the great 15th-century teachers of painting was Domenico Ghirlandaio (1445–94), in whose studio the famous Michelangelo was for a time a student. Ghirlandaio painted two fine Last Suppers in Firenze, one in the refectory of the church of Ognissanti, another in San Marco. Perugino (1446–1523) – teacher of Raphael – worked in Umbria. Examples of his work are to be seen in the *Pinacoteca* of Perúgia – splendid, calm Madonnas, with a background of the Umbrian countryside, often including Lago Trasimeno – and in the Collegio del Cambio in Perúgia are some of his finest frescoes. Another Umbrian painter was Pinturicchio (1454–1513), who painted the series of frescoes in the Libreria Piccolomini in the cathedral of Siena. Visitors to the town of Spello, between Perúgia and Spoleto, can see other paintings of his in the church of Santa Maria Maggiore. In Venezia the Bellinis and Carpaccio were enriching the churches. Jacopo Bellini (1400–70) and his two sons, Gentile and Giovanni, had the gift of creating images of alabasterlike luminosity. One of their finest works is the Predica di San Marco in the Palazzo di Brera, Milano; San Zaccaria, Venezia, has a *Madonna and Saints* and the Uffizi the *Sacred Allegory*.

Among architects of this period must be remembered Sansovino (1486–1570), designer of the Loggetta and the Sansovino (or San Marco) Library in Venezia; and Palladio (1508–80), the pure classical beauty of whose designs is to be seen in great profusion in the city of Vicenza, and in the churches of San Giorgio Maggiore and Il Redentore in Venezia. The list of geniuses – men who could express themselves in virtually every medium – from the Renaissance almost to the present day is endless. Leonardo da Vinci (1452–1519), architect, engineer, town planner and great painter: in the Uffizi is

a lovely *Annunciation* (the scene set in the open air), and in Milano the refectory of the church of Santa Maria delle Grazie houses his famous *Last Supper*.

Michelangelo (1475–1564), sculptor, painter, architect, designed the Piazza del Campidoglio in Roma, and was architect of the cupola of San Pietro in Vaticano and of the church of Santa Maria degli Angeli in the midst of the Terme di Diocleziano. In Firenze he designed the façade of the Basilica di San Lorenzo, and the New Sacristy, where are housed the tombs of the Medici family, which he also sculpted. In Roma one can see his *Pietà* in San Pietro in Vaticano, his *Moses* in the church of San Pietro in Vincoli, and in Firenze the much-copied *David* in the Accademia. The ceiling of the Sistine Chapel is the supreme example of his work as a painter, a work achieved after four years of almost superhuman fatigue.

Raphael (1483–1520) follows the rich colourings of Perugino, but adds something of his own which is infinitely greater than anything his master produced. The *Marriage of the Virgin* (Palazzo di Brera, Milano), the *Madonna with the Goldfinch* (Uffizi), the *Madonna della Sedia* and the *Madonna of the Grand Duke* (Pitti, Firenze) are among his finest works. When in Roma do not fail to see the great frescoes in the Raphael Stanze in the Vaticano.

In the Veneto, too, there were splendid painters at this time. Giorgione (1477–1510), by whom there is a lovely *Tempest* in the Accademia in Venezia, and Titian (1477–1576), whose *Sacred and Profane Love* and the smaller *Education in Love* are in the Galleria Borghese, Roma. The Brera, Milano, Uffizi and Pitti, Firenze, also have Titians, and in the Palazzo di Capodimonte, Nápoli, is his portrait of Pope Paolo III. One of his finest works is the altarpiece of Santa Maria Gloriosa dei Frari in Venezia. Tintoretto (1518–98) and Veronese (1528–88) are also well represented in Venezia. The Accademia has several by Tintorétto, including the large canvas of San Marco freeing a slave, and the Scuola di San Rocco has a splendid series which includes the *Crucifixion* and *Christ before Pilate*. Veronese's approach is more florid than that of Tintoretto; more flamboyant figures people his crowded canvases, often giving one, even in his Biblical scenes, a glimpse of the Venezia of his day. The Accademia boasts a large and impressive canvas of *Supper in the House of Levi*, and another of the *Marriage of St Catherine*, while his native city of Verona has a splendid *Martyrdom of St George* in the church of San Giorgio Maggiore.

The 17th century ushered in the baroque period and is particularly associated in Roman architecture with Bernini (1598–1680), and with Borromini (1599–1667). The former, having designed the elaborate *baldacchino*, or canopy, in San Pietro in Vaticano, was later called upon to enrich its façade and to plan the grandiose oval piazza with the double colonnade. He, too, designed the fountain in Piazzo Navona and the Fontana del Tritone in Piazza Barberini. Borromini's designs were even more flamboyantly baroque; visit the church of San Carlo alle Quattro Fontane and the church of Sant'Agnese in the Piazza Navona. The Fontana di Trevi, work of the sculptor Salvi, is another baroque landmark, and in Venezia fine examples are Longhena's church of Santa Maria della Salute, and Ca' Rezzonico. But to see the baroque in its full flowering one should visit the southern city of Lecce in Púglia where Zimbalo produced marvellous buildings in the local yellowish stone. Another great southern exponent was Vanvitelli, architect of the Royal Palace at Caserta, 12km from Nápoli.

In the 18th century the Venetian Tiepolo (1697–1770), much of whose painting is to be found in the Palazzo Labia and Ca' Rezzonico (Venezia), and in the Villa Pisani at Stra on the banks of the Brenta between Venezia and Padova, is outstanding. The Villa Valmarana near Vicenza has a fine series of rustic frescoes. Two extremely popular painters of this century were Antonio Canale, known as Canaletto (1697–1778), and Francesco Guardi (1712–93), both of whom left unforgettable views of the Venezia of their day. Ca' Rezzonico on the Canal Grande has some fine Guardis.

By the late 18th century, baroque had given way to the neo-classicism of such artists and architects as Valadier (1762–1835), who planned the Piazza del Popolo in Roma, and Canova (1757–1822); the latter's recumbent statue of Paolina Borghese, sister of Napoleon, is in the Galleria Borghese, Roma. Out of neo-classicism in painting developed a movement closely resembling that of the French Impressionists. One of its leading exponents was Fattori (1825–1908), many of whose works are in the Galleria d'Arte Moderna, Palazzo Pitti, Firenze.

Of the moderns, one recalls Modigliani's (1844–1920) elongated figures with eyes that seem curiously out of focus; Giorgio di Chiciro (born 1888), painter of splendid horses; the Bergamesque sculptor Giacomo Manzù, sculptor of the new bronze doors of San Pietro in Vaticano, of a fine statue of Cardinal Lercaro in San Petronio in Bologna and of many other works which put him among the truly great sculptors of Italy. Annigoni is known for his portraits of the British royal family and other celebrities, but in the library of the Convento di San Marco, Firenze, is an early *Deposition* which is well worth seeing. The work of the sculptor Marino Marini is equally famous. Finally, the Pirelli building in Milano is one of the most graceful examples of postwar architecture, affirming that the Italian genius is still vigorous.

CURRENCY

The unit of Italian currency is the *lira*. There are notes for 100,000, 50,000, 10,000, 5,000, 2,000, 1,000 and 500 *lire* and coins for 500 ('gold' centre, silver surround), 200 ('gold'), 100, 50 ('silver'), 20 ('gold') and 10 ('silver') *lire*. Since exchange rates fluctuate so considerably at the time of writing, no comparative values are quoted here.

Banks are open from 08.30 until 13.20. They remain closed on Saturdays, Sundays and public holidays (see page 18). There are exchange offices (*cambio*) at all large railway stations. Hotels, too, will change foreign currency and travellers' checks, though at a less favourable rate than banks or recognized offices.

HOW TO GET THERE

Boat and train Most routes from London (Victoria) involved changing in Paris at the Gare du Lyon. Fast express trains serve Génova, Milano, Pisa, Roma, Torino, Venezia and Ventimiglia direct, and there are good train and coach connections to other towns and resorts. Seats, sleepers and couchettes should be reserved in advance. Reductions are available for individuals making extended rail tours, families, children, *etc*. See Useful Addresses (page 19).

Transatlantic routes The main ports of entry are Génova and Nápoli. There are also services to Palermo and Messina in Sicilia. Fairs vary according to class and to the type of vessel. Tips, drinks, *etc* can add considerably to the basic cost.

Air travel Alitalia and British Airways operate services to some or all of the following airports: Génova, Milano, Nápoli, Pisa, Rímini, Roma, Venezia, on direct scheduled flights. Various reductions are available for nights and tourists flights, *etc*, and there are several com-

panies operating charter flights. Further details are available from travel agents and/or the airlines involved (see Useful Addresses).

From America there are direct air services to Roma. Other services usually involve a change in Paris.

Europabus This bus service is operated by the railways of western Europe and provides swift, comfortable travel in air-conditioned buses between many towns on the continent. One can break one's journey at many places en route, but in the peak season it is advisable to plan one's stops and book well in advance.

Full details from Europabus, British Railways Travel Centre, London, SW1, or Europabus (Overseas) Inc., 630 Fifth Avenue, New York 10020, USA.

Internal Communications

Trains There are four different types of trains in Italy:

Rapido; an inter-city express on which a supplement is charged.

Direttissimo; a fast train, but which stops at a few more stations than does the *Rapido*; usually 1st and 2nd class booking is available.

Diretto; fairly fast, but stopping at more stations than the *Direttissimo*.

Accelerato; the slowest type of all, stopping at every station.

In addition to these, there are 'luxury' trains such as the *Trans-Europ Express* on which all seats are reserved and there is a supplement charged over and above first-

class fare. There is also the recently restored and glamorous 'Orient Express'.

Although great efforts are being made to improve services and travelling conditions, it is advisable to travel 1st class and to reserve your seat on most occasions. Second class is always overcrowded, and it is rarely possible to get a seat. Restaurant cars are attached to long-distance trains; some serve a fairly good 'tray' lunch at a reasonable price.

As regards porters, you are advised to use only registered porters, who will wear a badge of identification, and whose charges – moderate – are fixed.

Coaches and buses Local buses connect with every town and village in Italy. There is an excellent network of long-distance buses between all main cities and resorts. (See Europabus, opposite).

Planes Alitalia, Itavia, Alisarda and SAM operate between some 20 towns *eg* Ancona, Bari, Bologna, Bríndidi, Firenze, Génova, Milano, Nápoli, Palermo, Pescara, Pisa, Réggio di Calábria, Rimini, Torino, Venezia and Verona.

Information is available from all tourist offices and from the offices of CIT (*Compagnia Italiana Turismo*) who have offices in 60 major towns and offer a service second to none in Europe.

MOTORING

Documents The only documents required are: the vehicle's registration book, third party (public liability) insurance cover, available in the form of a Green Card from your insurers; a valid driving licence. For British drivers this means your own driving licence accompanied by a translation available free of charge from motoring organizations. American motorists must obtain an International Driving Permit from the AAA.

Ferries Any of the northern cross-Channel routes are suitable, but these are heavily booked up and you are advised to make enquiries well in advance. There are regular sea services from Réggio di Calábria to Messina (Sicilia) and from Nápoli to Palermo and Ischia.

Car-sleeper services operate from Ostend, Boulogne, Amsterdam and Paris to Milano, from Milano to Bríndisi, Roma, Villa San Giovanni and Réggio di Calábria. Although expensive, these services save time, energy, and hotel bills and may be paid for in advance.

Rules of the road Drive on the right, overtake on the left. Before overtaking, you must indicate your intention and sound your horn (at night flash your lights). Unless otherwise indicated, traffic coming from the right always has priority.

Speed limits In November 1977 new speed limits came into force, and heavy fines will be due for any infraction of these rules. Posters with these limits clearly indicated in four languages (English, French, Italian and German) are placed in eye-catching positions at all frontier points, railway stations and airports. It is advisable to acquaint yourself with the Italian Highway Code as regulations are strictly enforced and the police may impose on-the-spot fines. In such cases, it is wise to pay up and forget it.

Fuel and oil All the familiar brands are readily available. Foreign motorists must obtain a *Carta Carburante* from their motoring organizations or at the frontier. This will provide full information regarding the supplies of fuel and oil available, and the length of stay permitted. Fuel coupons may be purchased at the principal banks together with this card, or in Italy at all the offices of the Automobile Club on presentation of this *Carta Carburante*. Remember to cash any unused vouchers at the border on leaving, as they cannot be refunded at home.

Road conditions The *Autostrade* form a magnificent system of motorways which are continually expanding. Although reasonable tolls have to be paid either on entering or leaving them, they save time, fatigue and fuel, and pass through some magnificent scenery. Most of them are equipped with telephone boxes every 2km for use in case of a breakdown.

Other roads are less satisfactory –

crowded, dusty, bad surfaces – and are often cluttered with large trucks towing larger trailers. Many of them are 3-lane, but a sensible system of lane-marking *which must be observed* obviates the worst dangers of this type of road.

Breakdowns In all areas you dial 116 to get in touch with the ACI, which is affiliated to the AA, RAC and AAA, for free assistance. Motorists must carry a triangular warning sign, which may be bought in Britain or hired temporarily at the frontier, to place 50 metres behind the halted vehicle at night or in any other position where parking is not permitted.

Car rental You must have an International Driving Permit and be over 21 years of age in order to rent a car. Cars may be booked in advance at most large railway stations (details from Italian Railways), and the major airlines also offer car rental facilities.

Motels in Italy are excellent. Hachette distribute an official Motel Guide to Europe, which is obtainable at most good bookshops. Information is also available from the ACI provincial offices.

ACCOMMODATION

Hotels are officially classified in five categories: deluxe, 1st, 2nd, 3rd, and 4th class. Charges vary within each class according to the region, situation, season and type of room chosen, but the prices of each establishment are fixed by the government. Do not expect more than you pay for.

If you are considering a package tour, don't automatically plunge for the cheapest offered, or fall for the 'mushroom' agent's silkiest sales talk. Go to a well-established agency and be guided by their advice, then, if you are disappointed, *complain loudly* on your return home; even the best of agents is not infallible, but you will find he welcomes constructive criticism and, when possible, acts upon it.

Hotel charges are not quoted here, but remember that to these prices must be added a 17 percent service charge, plus a possible further 12 percent owing to the introduction of the IVA tax, similar to VAT, or to state taxes in the USA. Wine and coffee are extras, and hotels may also charge for central heating in winter and air conditioning in summer.

Pensions (similar to a comfortable boarding house) are also officially classified in 1st, 2nd and 3rd categories.

Graded lists of hotels and pensions may be obtained from the Italian State Tourist Offices (see Useful Addresses).

Locande (inns), with very few exceptions, are comparable with hotels of the

4th category. On the whole, hotels are preferable as having more facilities.

Alberghi Diurni offer toilet facilities ranging from the simple *gabinetto* (lavatory) without wash-basin, to the luxury of a completely equipped bathroom. In centres such as Firenze, Milano, Roma, there are excellent *diurni* at the railway stations, which feature rest rooms, writing rooms, and *salons*, where one can get a haircut, shampoo, manicure, etc. Prices are shown at the cash register and one pays in advance.

CAMPING

There is an excellent camping guide, *Campeggi e villagi turistici in Italia*, published by the Touring Club of Italy, unfortunately only in the Italian language. If, however, you are not able to read the language, the Ente Turismo, Azienda Autonoma di Turismo, or the offices of the CIT are extremely useful. Usually, at least one member of the staff is multilingual.

Your local tourist agent will also prove helpful, or try the offices of CIT at 256 High Street, Croydon CR9 1LL; 10 Charles II Street, London SW1Y 4AB; 500 Fifth Avenue, New York, 10036; 333 North Michigan Avenue, Chicago, Illinois; 5670 Wilshire Boulevard, Los Angeles, California 90036; the Italian State Tourist Office, 201 Regent Street, London W1; the Italian Government Tourist Office, 630 Fifth Avenue, Suite 1565, New York, 10020; 500 North Michigan Avenue, Chicago 1, Illinois 60611; 360 Post Street, Suite 801, San Francisco, California 94108.

Camps offer a variety of accommodation. Some have tents only, and the sign denoting these is **A** ; others have a combination of tents and bungalows, recognizable by this sign **A E**. There are also some delightful tourist villages, the sign for which is **E E**. Snow camps can be indicated by a white snow-crystal within a dark surround.

Charges are not specified here, as they change so quickly, but the 'tents only' camp is cheaper than the bungalow type, which in its turn is less costly than the tourist village.

It must be remembered that there is a tax (IVA, similar to VAT or state taxes in the USA) to be added to all charges.

Most camps have a provision store and bar and a service station. Many have eating-places, varying from a restaurant with service, to a self-service variety or a snack bar. In most there is a shop where, in addition to staple provisions, one can buy cooking gas in cylinders; but, just in case the cylinder available is not the right type for your particular stove, pack a spare.

In some camps there is an assembly room, where one may chat with friends, dance or listen to impromptu concerts. Many seaside camps have their own private beach, quite a few have swimming pools and, if you are staying on a really luxurious camp site, there may even be a doctor on the site.

If you are taking your dog on holiday, remember that in some camps pets are strictly NOT ALLOWED.

In camping literature – brochures, *etc* – a sign indicates the nearest inhabited place.

The bungalows on camp sites and in tourist villages vary in type. They may be of wood or concrete, and in the really sunny south many have charming conical straw roofs.

For really luxurious tourist village holidays (but by no means the cheapest type) you are advised to try the Club Mediterrane, but here it is advisable to book well ahead, either at the headquarters of the Club at Largo Corsia dei Servi, Milano, or in Viale Europa, in Roma, or through the CIT offices, the Italian State Tourist Office, London, the Italian Government Tourist offices in USA or your local travel agent.

Many sites provide especially for families with children, and in some there are organized games.

As a general rule, camping sites in the north tend to be better and more efficient than those farther south, a fact that reflects the greater prosperity of the northern half of the country.

Near or along the motorways, where demand is greater, the camps tend to be larger and consequently are usually better equipped and better run. Also, the newer the camp, the more efficient it tends to be.

One must not expect too much of a camping holiday, or of the facilities portrayed so glowingly in brochures. So long as one remembers that all camping is bound to be to a certain extent 'roughing it', and doing a holiday 'on the cheap', then the experience will prove rewarding and probably better than one had hoped.

YOUTH HOSTELS

There are over 70 youth hostels in Italy, details of which can be obtained from the Associatione Italiana Alberghi per la Gioventù, Palazzo della Civiltà del Lavoro, Quadrato della Concordia, 00144 Roma (06 5913 02) or from national organizations. The Centro Italiano Viaggi Instruzioni, Via Caetani 32, Roma, will provide information regarding students' hostels.

FOOD AND DRINK

Fish In the coastal centres one can enjoy a variety of fish dishes: scampi, octopus, squid and various shellfish and polypi. There are several unusual white fish which are worth sampling: *San Pietro* (John Dory) are similar to sole, and a Venetian speciality is *coda di rospo*, the tail of the 'frog fish', which has an excellent flavour and texture. A *fritto misto* of fish in any of these regions is an experience not to be forgotten; scampi, tiny mullet, baby octopus, squid, *etc*, are fried in very hot oil, and served piping hot with a slice of lemon and a green salad. In Génova *zimino*, a fish stew, is a delicacy; and *brodetto*, a fish soup, may be enjoyed on the Adriatic. Grilled tuna fish is a high quality in the south and in Sardegna (Sardinia). In the north there is pink-fleshed trout and in Veneto *baccalà* (salt cod) is a splendid winter dish, cooked in milk and oil and flavoured with onion. It may be served with *polenta*, which is a type of pasta made of maize flour.

Pasta is the generic name for any type of macaroni and comes in all varieties, from the long string-like to the *ravioli* or *tortellini* which are small circles or squares stuffed with spinach, *Ricotta* cheese or chopped meat before being served. Plain boiled macaroni or spaghetti are excellent served with a generous helping of butter and sprinkled with Parmesan cheese; a richer variety is *alla Bolognese*, served with a ragout composed of beef, chicken livers, herbs and tomato purée. In the south one's *pasta asciutta* (the name given to pasta not served in soup) often comes with a rich tomato sauce.

Lasagne – green or white – are the large strips of pasta which are excellent when served *al forno*, a kind of savoury first-course pudding cooked in the oven with a combination of Bolognese ragout and béchamel sauce, coupled with generous amounts of grated parmesan. *Cannelloni* is another outstanding variation. There are many varieties of filled pasta which are delicious served as *pasta asciutta* or dropped into a rich, clear chicken soup. *Gnocchi*, which are tiny dumplings of semolina or potato, are similarly treated.

Rice Dishes At one time rice dishes were associated with the north, *pasta* with the south; nowadays the latter is obtainable all over Italy, but the former is still more or less confined to the north. A plain *risotto*, rice cooked in water or white wine, is an excellent dish, served simply with a lump of fresh butter and generous helpings of grated Parmesan cheese (particularly to be recommended for those

recovering from a bout of 'tummy' trouble). But there are more exotic varieties, such as *risotto Milanese* which has beef marrow incorporated in it, and a speciality of the Veneto is *risi bisi*, in which tender green peas are incorporated with the rice. Other combinations are *risotto* with *scampi* or *vongole* (clams).

Soups Apart from the fish soups already mentioned, there are three outstanding soups to be found in Italy: *minestrone*, a thick rich soup of haricot beans, celery, spinach, onions, peas, chopped ham, carrots, cabbage, tomatoes, herbs, and so on, cooked together in meat stock and served with grated parmesan cheese – not unlike a well-made Scotch broth, and similarly almost a meal in itself; *zuppa Pavese* (Pavese soup) is a clear soup with a raw egg dropped into it just long enough to coagulate the white before serving; *stracciatella*, a speciality of Roma, has also a basis of clear chicken soup, into which is whipped, just before serving, beaten eggs combined with grated parmesan cheese.

Meat The raw Parma ham (*prosciutto crudo*) sliced paper-thin and served with fresh figs or a slice of melon makes a delightful hors d'oeuvre, while in Lombardia *bresaola* (dried salt beef) is good.

Veal is excellent in Italy, and when in doubt as to what to order, one cannot go wrong asking for a *costoletta Milanese*, which is a veal cutlet, beaten thin, coated with egg and breadcrumbs and fried in butter; although a speciality of Milano, this can be obtained all over Italy. A richer variety is *costoletta alla Bolognese* with grated Parmesan cheese and Marsala added during the cooking. Again in Bologna one finds *scaloppe farcite*, which are thin slices of veal sandwiched with *prosciutto crudo* and Gruyère cheese and mushrooms, fried and served with a rich sauce. *Osso buco*, another Milanese dish, is a veal shin bone, with the marrow left in, cooked in wine and stock with tomatoes and usually served with a plain white *risotto*.

A great Roman speciality is *abbacchio al forno*, roast baby lamb cooked whole; *capretto* (baby kid), similarly treated, is equally excellent. A delicious summer dish is *vitello tonnato*, thinly sliced roast veal, served coated with a creamy sauce in which is incorporated pounded tuna fish.

The great winter fish of northern Italy is *bollito*, chosen from the trolley which is brought one by the waiter, and on which are displayed beef, calves' head or feet, chicken or turkey, *cotechino* (a rich salted pork sausage), all of them boiled. With this is usually served a piquant green sauce (*salsa verde*). In Nápoli and the south meat dishes are richer and usually served with a thick sauce; *bistecca alla pizzaiola* is a good rump steak, coated with a sauce composed of tomatoes, garlic, green and red peppers, and herbs, cooked together in oil. Where poultry is concerned, in addition to chicken and capon, it is rewarding to try roast *faraone* (guinea fowl), quails, and *uccelletti* (tiny songbirds roasted whole on a spit).

Pizza In Nápoli particularly, but nowadays all over Italy, are to be found *pizze* – open tarts of bread dough baked with any of a number of toppings, the basis of which is usually tomatoes, olives, cheese, but varied at times with anchovies and other additions.

Vegetables can be exotic. Artichokes are cheap and excellent and are served sometimes with olive oil or, when very young and tender, sliced paper thin in a salad, or fried whole. Asparagus is a speciality of the Veneto and of Liguria and is of the large, white variety. *Finocchio* (fennel – rather like a bulbous celery in appearance, and tasting faintly of aniseed) is delicious in salads or cooked and served with butter and grated Permesan. Mushrooms are excellent.

Fruit Apart from the conventional oranges, lemons, apples *etc*, autumn brings persimmons (*kaki*), and pomegranates, both of which are worth sampling. In spring and summer, particularly around Roma, there is an abundance of tiny, wild strawberries.

Cheeses are legion. The north gives one *Taleggio* (at its best not unlike Camembert); *Bel Paese*, *Fontina*, *Provolone*, are all worth trying, as are the *Mozzarella*, made of buffalo milk, and *Ricotta* and *Pecorino* (made of sheep's milk); grated *Parmesan* is widely used as a garnish to hot dishes as it does not coagulate.

Cost of Meals A *ristorante* is often expensive, a *trattoria* less so, and it is wise to choose one that has a priced menu exhibited on the door-post or in the window. To the price quoted will be added a service charge of 10 percent to 15 percent. You should also allow for a cover charge plus IVA tax, similar to VAT or the American state taxes. Wine and coffee are extra. Some restaurants have special tourist menus at fixed prices, but these tend to be a little uninspired – try experimenting with the native food, but only in a restaurant that has the prices indicated on the menu.

If money is running short, a *tosto* (a toasted sandwich consisting of a slice of ham and a slice of cheese between slices of bread) is a good standby with a glass of local wine, and can be obtained in any bar, and a plate of pasta is cheap and not to be despised.

Drinks Usually the local wine, white or red, is pleasant and not expensive. Some of the cruder varieties may need softening down with water. Such wine can be ordered by the carafe, half (mezzo) or quarter (quarto) carafe.

Whisky, brandy, gin and various liquers can be obtained at almost any bar, as can a variety of vermouth appetizers (not least among them Fernet-Branca, that infallible pick-me-up for an upset stomach). If one sits down at an outside table in a smart district, the price soars.

SPORT AND ENTERTAINMENT

Spectator sports The great national sports of Italy are football, basketball, tennis, racing (horses, cars, bicycles), boating, skiing and bobsledding. Golf is played, but not to a great extent. (Further details from the Federazione Italiana Golf, Viale Tiziano 70, Roma). Every town of any size has a football ground, basketball court and racecourse. Games and sporting events are widely advertised and the local Aziena Autonoma di Soggiorno (tourist office) or one's hotel can give full details and supply tickets.

International tennis championships are held in the Foro Romano, Roma, in May; others in Viaréggio at the end of August; in Catánia in Sicilia in mid-March and in Réggio di Calábria in April. In April and May in Roma there is an International Horse Show in the Piazza Siena; Catània has a similar show in October. The main racecourses are in Roma, Faenza, Bologna, Merano and Nápoli. There is car and motorcycle racing at Monza in September; Cortina d'Ampezzo holds an international *Concours d'Élégance* at the end of July, and there is also racing at Caserta near Nápoli in June and at Siracusa in April. A Motor Show is held in Torino in November; an Air Show is held in Génova in the same month.

The international motorboat race *Del Lario* takes place at Como in October; in September there is a sailing regatta at Portofino. International water polo takes place in Roma in May, while during July Ancona holds an international fair of fishing and water sports. Ice hockey championships are held at Cortina d'Ampezzo in August, in Torino – coupled with skating events – in February. From late December to early February the bobsled championships take place in Cortina.

On the less active side, there are bridge championships in Alássio in May and chess championships in Réggio nell' Emilia in December. In July, there is a fashion show at the Palazzo Pitti, Firenze. Venezia holds an International Film Festival in August and September; Cortina has a festival of sports films in March, and there is a Film Review in Roma in September. Every other year, on even years, the Venezia Biennale art exhibition is held from June to October. Both Trieste and Roma have son et lumière (*suoni et luce*) spectacles during the summer evenings, the former at Castello Miramare, the latter in the Foro Romano. These are in a different language each evening, and you should find out when the English version is being held.

Winter sports in Italy

As soon as winter has settled in, almost everyone who can stand up on a pair of skis if off to enjoy the thrills and spills of this exhilarating sport. From early childhood Italians begin skiing, and at most winter resorts there are well-managed ski-schools and practice slopes. In addition to the downhill skiing to which we have become accustomed, great popularity is being gained by cross country skiing (*ski a fondo*).

Even in the hot summer days, ski fans will divide their annual holidays between a few days at the seaside and a few at some high resort, such as the Stelvio, where it is possible and pleasant to ski whatever the season.

Most of the resorts have skating rinks and many have sleigh-rides to tempt visitors; in Cortina d'Ampezzo it is great fun to get into a horse-drawn sleigh and go off, bells jingling, for a ride around the mountain.

There are numerous mountain refuges where the night, or several nights, can be spent. Among the many popular resorts are Cortina d'Ampezzo, San Martina di Castrozza, Moena Val di Fasso, Ortiséi in the Dolomites, and farther west such lovely spots as the Aosta valley.

Even those who do not ski or skate find life in such centres agreeable; the sun is hot, skies are blue, and it is easy to acquire a healthy tan and an even healthier appetite for the plentiful and excellent mountain food, not to forget the mountain *grappa* or hot, spiced wine to warm one up after a spell in the fresh, crisp air.

Music festivals

The following are the more important musical and theatrical events.

Firenze Maggio Musicale, May Musical Festival, 10 May to end June. Summer theatre season, July. **Milano** Opera season at Teatro alla Scala, December–May. Piccola Scala lyric theatre, March–May. **Nápoli** Lyric theatre, Campi Flegrei, July–August. Teatro San Carlo opera season December–May. **Óstia Antica** Performances in Roman Theatre, June–August. **Perúgia** Music Festival, September. **Ravenna** Organ Festival, church of San Vitale July–August. **Roma** Concert season of Accademia Santa Cecilia in the Basilica di Massenzio July–August. Lyric theatre and opera, Terme di Caracalla, July–August. Opera season December–June. **Siena** Music week, September. **Spoleto** Festival of the Two Worlds, June and July. **Venezia** Concerts in Palazzo Ducale, July. Summer season of lyric theatre at Teatro La Fenice, July–August. **Verona** Opera and drama in Roman Theatre and Arena, July–August. **Vicenza** Drama at Teatro Olimpico, September. Further details of all the above events and many others may be obtained from the Italian State or Government Tourist Offices or from the local tourist offices.

GENERAL INFORMATION

Passports and visas All visitors to Italy must hold a valid passport. Visas are not required. Passports may be obtained in Britain. From main post offices where the requisite forms are available, or from the main passport offices (London, Liverpool, Peterborough, Glasgow, Newport (Gwent). Two passport photographs and one's birth certificate are necessary when making application for a passport. The normal passport is valid for ten years. A British Visitor's passport, valid for one year only, may be obtained only at any of the main post offices. A birth certificate or National Health insurance card is necessary for identification.

American citizens should apply in person to the Passport Division, Department of State, in Washington DC, New York, Boston, Miami, Chicago, New Orleans, Los Angeles, San Francisco, or Seattle. If it is not possible to attend any of these offices, personal application should be made before the clerk of any US District Court System. Take along three un-retouched photographs, 6cm (2½in) square, a witness who has known you for at least two years unless you can produce some identification that gives a physical description (a driver's licence will do), your birth certificate or old passport for identification, plus the necessary fee.

A smallpox vaccination carried out within the past three years is obligatory for return to the USA.

Customs Visitors to Italy from Europe may bring in 200 cigarettes or 50 cigars or 250gm tobacco; visitors from outside Europe may bring in 400 cigarettes or equivalent. US Customs permit duty-free $400 retail value of purchases per person, and 1 litre of liquor per person over 21, and 200 cigarettes per person, regardless of age.

smokers can purchase small, cheap *Avanas* or the very strong *Toscanas*, plus a variety of other local and imported brands. Tobacconists (*tabaccaia*) are identified by a large illuminated 'T'.

Postage Stamps may be bought at tobacconists and most other shops where postcards and writing paper are sold. It is essential to remember that the maximum and minimum sizes of letters and cards accepted by the postal authorities are 120×235mm and 90×140mm.

Telephones One can usually telephone from a bar. One buys a *gettone* (token), which is inserted into the slot before dialling. In a city of any size there is a central office, provided with directories covering the whole of the country, from

Duty-free allowances for UK residents *subject to change*		Goods bought in a duty-free shop	Good bought in EEC
Tobacco	Cigarettes or	200	300
	Cigars *small* or	100	150
	Cigars *large* or	50	75
	Pipe tobacco	250 gm	400 gm
Alcohol	Spirits *over 38.8° proof* or	1 litre	1½ litres
	Fortified or sparkling wine or	2 litres	3 litres
	Table wine	2 litres	4 litres
Perfume		50 gm	75 gm
Toilet water		¼ litre	375 cl
Other goods*		£28	£163

* To include not more than 50 litres of beer

US customs permit duty-free $400 retail value of purchases per person, 1 litre of liquor per person over 21, 200 cigarettes and 100 cigars per person.

Electricity in Italian cities is either 125 or 220 volts AC. It is important to check, and bring an adaptor for razors *etc* as points are different from those at home.

Cigarettes British and American cigarettes are obtainable, but they are no cheaper than at home and are usually manufactured in Switzerland or Holland. Of the local brands, *Nazionale* – in various qualities – are quite agreeable. Cigar-

where one can make long-distance and international calls.

Newspapers In any sizeable town or resort, news stands (*edicole*) at the railway station or in the more important squares will carry the best-known newspapers of other countries. The supply is neither great nor regular.

Health As a member of the EEC Britain has an agreement with Italy that medical advice and treatment will be provided on the same basis as for Italian subjects. British visitors must have certificate E111 indicating entitlement to British National Health Service benefits. This certificate is issued by your local Health and Social Security office after you have completed application form CM1. You should ask for leaflet SA28 which gives details of all the EEC health services. If you need medical aid take certificate E111 to the local sickness insurance office (Instituto nazionale per l'assicurazione contro le malattie) USSL. In the provinces of Trento and Bolzano go to the provincial sickness fund (cassa mutua). The USSL office will give you a certificate of entitlement (ask for a list of sickness insurance scheme doctors and dentists). A doctor or dentist will then treat you free of charge. Without the certificate you will have to pay and may have difficulty in obtaining a refund of only part of the costs. Some prescribed medicines are free, others carry a small charge, but you must show form E111 to the chemist.

The doctor will give you a certificate (proposta di ricovero) if you need hospital treatment. This entitles you to free treatment in some hospitals. USSL offices have a list. If you cannot contact the USSL office before going into hospital, show form E111 to the hospital authorities and ask them to contact USSL at once.

American visitors should ensure that their own medical insurance is extended to cover them while abroad. Insurance brokers or travel agents will advise and arrange the additional cover.

Tipping Most hotels and restaurants include a service charge of 10 to 17 percent. This is generally sufficient, but any special services should be tipped for separately. Usherettes in cinemas and theatres should be tipped.

Clothing Great attention is paid to clothing in places of worship. Although there is no longer a strict insistence on a head covering for women their attire should be such as they would wear in a place of worship in their own country.

Papal Audiences Those wishing to participate in a general Papal Audience should apply to the Maèstro di Càmera di Sua Santità, Città del Vaticano, Roma, giving not more than one month's and not less than two days' notice. Roman Catholics are requested to have a letter of introduction from their priest.

Shops are usually open from 08.30 or 09.00 to 13.00; 15.30 or 16.00 to 19.30 or 20.00. Socks, stockings and glove sizes are universal, but dresses, shoes *etc* differ, and it is unwise to purchase a garment without trying it on first.

Public conveniences are few and difficult to find. Use those of filling stations, cafés, bars *etc*. Ladies (*Signore*) may be distinguished from gentlemen (*Signori*) by the last letter – 'e' for 'she'. Some of the larger cities are now installing unisex self-cleaning toilets, said to be the 'last word' in cleanliness, appearance, availability and so on. The price of a visit to this newest member of the public health service at the time of going to press is 300 *lire*.

General behaviour

There has been a considerable slackening of the one-time rigid standards of behaviour, but it is still not considered permissible to wander around churches sightseeing while services are in progress.

As for queueing, disheartening though it may be to be shoved aside by a local, there is always the hope that one day example will prove its worth and we shall gaze spellbound at orderly queues of Italians; till that day dawns, however, it's as well to be philosophical about the custom of the country, which does tend to be 'every man for himself and devil take the hindmost'.

One important thing to remember is that, whatever you may have been taught in your own country, it is courting suicide to stride blindly and arrogantly across a pedestrian crossing. You must be prepared to stand and wait until the accumulation of a fair number of pedestrians has signified to the driver of one of the stream of passing vehicles that it would be courteous to pause and let the humble walkers cross. If, however, you have in your group a mother with a young child, your wait will be far shorter.

And now an unpleasant, but very necessary, caution: do not carry much money around in your handbag. The *scippo* (bag-snatching) is a popular sport these days, and those who play it are expert and ruthless. If you feel a gentle tug at your handbag, it is often wiser to let it go than to enter into combat, unless, of course, you are a karate champion.

Public holidays

Italy used to be notorious for the number of public holidays and consequent long weekends but, as from 1 January 1979 the list is as follows: 1 January – Capodanno (New Year's Day), Easter Sunday, Easter Monday, 25 April – Anniversary of Liberation, 1 May – Festa del Lavoro (Labour Day), Pentecost, 15 August – Assumption of the Virgin, 1 November – Ognissanti (All Saints), 8 December – Imacolata (Immaculate Conception), 25 December – Christmas Day, 26 December – St Stephen's Day.

USEFUL ADDRESSES

In Britain

Italian State Tourist Office, 201 Regent Street, London W1 (01-408-1245). Alitalia, 251 Regent Street, London W1 (01-734-4040). British Caledonian, International Reservations (01-668 4177). British Airways, Dorland Ho., Lower Regent St., London SW1 (01-370 4545). Automobile Association, Fanum House, Stanmore (01-954 7355). Royal Automobile Club, 83-5 Pall Mall, London SW1 (01-930 4343). British Rail Travel Centre, 4 Lower Regent Street, London SW1 (01-283 7171).

In Italy

British Consulates: Via XX Settembre 80A, 00187 Roma (06-4755441); Via San Paolo 7, 20121, Milano (02- 803442); Palazzo Castelbarco, Lungarno Corsini 2, Firenze 1-50123 (055- 212594); Via Francesco Crispi 122, 1-80122 Nápoli (081-209227); Accademia 1051, Venezia (callers), P.O. Box 679, 30100 Venezia (mail), (041- 27207).

American Consulates: Lungarno Amerigo Vespucci 38, Firenze (055-298276); Banca d'America e d'Italia, Piazza Portello 6, Génova (010- 282741-5); Piazza della Repubblica 32, Milano (02- 652841); Piazza della Repubblica, 80122 Nápoli (081-660966); Via V. Veneto 119, Roma (06- 4674); Via Valdirivo 19A, 4th Floor, Trieste (040- 68728); Via Alfieri 17, Torino (011- 543600).

In America

Italian Government Tourist Office, 630 Fifth Avenue, Suite 1565, New York 10020 (245 4822). Alitalia, 666 Fifth Avenue, New York (903 3300). American Automobile Association, World Wide Travel Service, 750 Third Avenue, New York (586 1166).

In Sardegna

Cágliari: Assessorato del Turismo della Regione Sarda, Viale Trento 69, Cágliari. ESIT, Ente Sardo Industrie Turistiche, Via Mameli 95, Cágliari. EPT, Ente Provinciale per il Turismo, Piazza Deffenu 9, Cágliari.
Province of Núoro: Ente Provinciale per il Turismo, Piazza Italia 19, Núoro.
Sássari: Ente Provinciale per il Turismo, Piazza Italia 19, Sássari.
Oristano: Ente Provinciale per il Turismo, Via Cágliari 125/B.

METRIC CONVERSIONS

Shoes

	British	6	7	8	9	10
Men's	European	40	41	42	43	44
	USA	$6\frac{1}{2}$	$7\frac{1}{2}$	$8\frac{1}{2}$	$9\frac{1}{2}$	$10\frac{1}{2}$
	British	4	5	6	7	8
Women's	European	36	37	38	39	40
	USA	$5\frac{1}{2}$	$6\frac{1}{2}$	$7\frac{1}{2}$	$8\frac{1}{2}$	$9\frac{1}{2}$

Dresses

British	10/32	12/34	14/36	16/38	18/40
European	38	40	42	44	46
USA	8	10	12	14	16

Men's Collar Sizes

British/USA	14	$14\frac{1}{2}$	15	$15\frac{1}{2}$	16	$16\frac{1}{2}$	17
European	36	37	38	39	41	42	43

WEIGHT

	($\frac{1}{4}$ kg)	($\frac{1}{2}$ kg)	($\frac{3}{4}$ kg)	(1 kg)
grams	50 100 150 200 250 300 400 500 600 700 750 800 900 1000

ounces	0 1 2 3 4 6 8 12 16 24 32 36
	($\frac{1}{4}$ lb) ($\frac{1}{2}$ lb) (1 lb) ($1\frac{1}{2}$ lb) (2 lb) ($2\frac{1}{4}$ lb)

THE LAKES

Italy has many lovely lakes, and sometimes the combination of natural beauty they offer, together with excellent tourist facilities, makes a greater appeal than seaside or mountains.

Starting up in the Dolomites, well to the north of Belluno, is **Lago Misurina**, pine-clad and a trifle austere when the sun is not shining. One comes upon this lake almost unawares; its azure waters, mirroring the surrounding conifers, give it an other-world quality and one wonders whether fairyland is far away. It is only about 13km/8mi from the winter sports centre of Cortina d'Ampezzo, and is excellently equipped for winter and summer entertainment. Swimming and boating are agreeable in summer and fishing yields catches of pink-fleshed trout; in winter there is skating, also skiing on the surrounding slopes.

The Dolomites have other attractive lakes. Not far from Trento is **Lévico**, a long, fiord-like stretch of water set among wooded hills. Its transparent greenish waters freeze in winter. Only a kilometre away is the small thermal centre of the same name.

Still in the Dolomites, this time in Val Venosta, very near the **Résia** pass leading from the Engadine Valley, is the lake of the same name, the result of the union of two smaller lakes to form a dam. In addition to the attractions of swimming, boating and fishing there is a photogenic subject in the half-submerged church of one of the villages affected by the building of the dam.

On the way from Résia to Merano one passes through many delightful little villages; a particularly interesting one is Sluderno where stands the Castel Churburg (Castle of Coira), interesting for its frescoed cloisters and ancient paintings and sculpture and for a rich armoury, but also for having once been the seat of the Bishops of Chur, a city now included within the confines of Switzerland.

Coming now to the region of Lombardia, first of all one arrives at **Lago d'Orta**, only 3½km/2mi long and 1½km/1mi wide, but one of the prettiest of lakes. The greenish shade of the water reflecting the surrounding wooded slopes make one think of emeralds. There are many holiday centres in this area. Balzac termed the town of the same name *una perla grigia in uno scrigno verde* (a grey pearl in a green casket).

Almost in the middle of the lake is the island of San Giuliano, with a basilica originating from the time when the saint himself was living (390 AD). This is the St Julian of the Golden Legend.

Eastwards from Lago d'Orta is **Maggiore**, 54km/33mi long, never more than 9¼km/6mi wide. It acts as a boundary between the regions of Piemonte and Lombardia and its northernmost point belongs politically to Switzerland. The dark, rocky slopes of the mountains make the northern part grim and almost forbidding, but once past the strait between Cannóbio and Maccagno, the scenery changes; rich green pastureland and woods lead westwards to Monte Zeda, and soon come the real jewels of the lake, Stresa and the far-famed Isole Borromee (Borromean Islands). Behind Stresa rises Monte Mottarone, 1491m/4892ft above sea level, from whose peak can be seen the entire chain of the Alps.

On the eastern shores are numerous little towns, such as Augera, Arolo, Monvalle, Cerro and others. In the last-named is the sanctuary of Santa Caterina, a small 17th-century church and convent that seem to form part of the high rock on which they are built.

On a hill no more than 2km/1½mi from the town of Arona, near the base of the western shores stands a colossal statue of San Carlo Borromeo (1533–1584). The statue, 23m/75ft high, stands on a pedestal 12m/39ft high, and the whole is impressive. Those who wish can climb up inside the statue and emerge at neck level.

Progressing westwards one comes next to **Lago di Varese**, 4km/2½mi from the city of the same name, and excellently served by roads to the main centres. This little lake is very popular for swimming and bathing, though somewhat overshadowed by the nearness of Lago di Lugano, which has the added attraction of being a frontier point between Italy and Switzerland. Tourists who wish to take advantage of this must make sure their passports are valid in both countries.

Lago di Como has the form of an inverted Y. 198m/650ft above sea level, it is one of Italy's loveliest lakes, famous, too, in literature for it is the setting of Manzoni's unforgettable novel *I Promessi Sposi (The Betrothed)*, which opens with a splendid description of that branch of the lake which turns southward between two uninterrupted chains of mountains, growing ever higher, and reflected in the waters.

The town of Lecco stands half-way down the eastern leg of the Y, and is an important tourist centre. The real pearl of the lake, however, is Bellágio at the tip of the peninsula separating the legs of the Y; particularly lovely in summer and autumn, it adds splendid scenery to the more ordinary tourist attractions. Not far away is the Villa Serbelloni, set in a huge park and said to be one of the loveliest villas in Italy.

Como is the capital of the region and has a fine Gothic-Renaissance cathedral and a *broletto* (town hall) which dates back to the early part of the 13th century. Statues of the Elder and the Younger Pliny appear on either side of the entrance doorway.

During the 11th century there originated in Como a privileged group of master-builders, known as the Magistri Comacini. Most of the church building and the characteristic decoration of churches of that period, not only in Lombardia but in other parts of Italy, were the inspiration of these clever master-masons.

Cernóbbio, 5km/3mi away on the western shores, is a well-known resort, with a pleasantly bland climate even in winter.

A tree-lined avenue links Tremezzo and Cadenábbia on the western shore, with views across the water to Bellágio.

Lago d'Iseo, between Bergamo and Bréscia, though small in comparison with Como, is fourth in size of the northern Italian lakes. Surrounded almost entirely by mountains, it offers splendid views, yields a rich harvest of trout, eel and other fish, and is visited by flights of wild duck. Its northern extremity leads into Val Camonica, where there are strange prehistoric designs scratched on the rocks.

Next comes **Garda**, Italy's largest lake covering an area over 50km/31mi long and 17½km/11mi wide, reaching up like a spearhead into the mountains of Trentino/Alto Adige. Its southern shores are relatively flat, but northwards they

Menaggio, Lago di Como

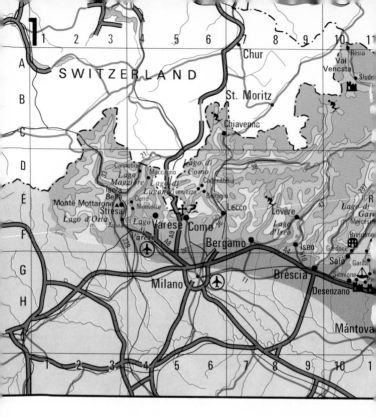

become steeper and at times rise sheer out of the water.

Around the coast there is such a number and variety of holiday resorts that a whole guide book could be devoted to them.

On the south stands Desenzano, very residential nowadays, a pleasant dormitory town for those who work in Verona and even as far afield as Vicenza and Padova. In spite of a large, modern section, a small area of old, arcaded streets remains, wandering at will down to the lake shore, where the remains of a Roman villa can still be seen. Gaily painted handcarts decorated with locally-grown oranges and lemons stand in the narrow streets, with greengrocers' shops where the produce is much fresher than in the modern supermarkets.

Not far away, on a tongue of land to the east, stands the great Rocca Scaligera (Scaliger Castle) of Sirmione (1250). Beyond it lie the ruins of a Roman villa, known locally as the Grotte di Catullo (Grotto of Catullus). It is certain that the poet had a country place at Sirmio, whether at this exact spot or not is a moot point. But of his beloved Sirmio he wrote:

Of all the islands and of all the almost isles
Which Neptune, God of Water, set among clear lakes
And in the vast seas, you, Sirmio, are sole bright gem

(From *Poets in a Landscape*, Hamish Hamilton, 1957, p.40, translated by Gilbert Highet).

Standing near the edge of olive-crowned cliffs on which are the remains of the villa, and looking down at the water washing the vari-coloured rocks below, one is inclined to agree with Catullus, and if, on the way back, one picks a little rosemary 'for remembrance', this shrub is so abundant that one small sprig will not be missed.

If one's feet are protesting after the climb, it is always possible to join the

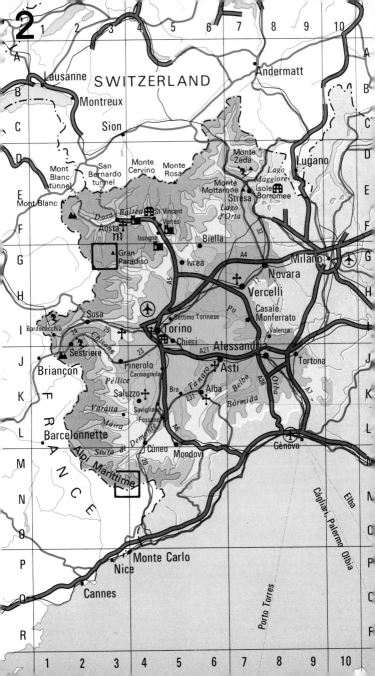

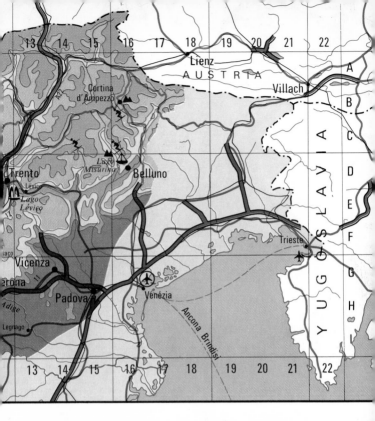

children and return by the little *trenino* that will deposit one near the Rocca Scaligera.

Eastwards from Sirmione is Peschiera, once a fortress town and still possessing the great military fortress built in the 16th century by the architect Michele Sanmicheli. Peschiera, together with Verona, Legnago and Mántova constituted the great Austrian 'Quadrangle'.

Present-day Peschiera offers excellent swimming and boating and lives up to its name as a good fishing centre.

Northwards one comes first to Lazise, with its medieval walls and a castle dating back to 1024, Garda, Punta San Vigilio, Torre del Benaco, Brenzone and finally Malcésine, dominated by the former palace of the Captains of the Lake, now the town hall, and another great Scaliger castle. Even farther north are Tórbole on the east and Riva on the west, where the climate and vegetation are almost Mediterranean.

All these centres provide excellently for tourists and it is possible to take trips on the lake itself, either by steamer or by the swifter hydrofoil.

Along the western shore there is Salò, from which point the Garda Riviera begins; soon comes Gardone of international fame, offering not only some of the finest views of the lake but, in the months of July and August, open-air theatre and ballet in the grounds of Il Vittoriale, the fantastic estate of the late poet, Gabriele d'Annunzio. This is an estate that has to be seen to be believed, with such strange concepts as a ship on land, a circular burial place with the poet's tomb elevated high above those of his friends and a house crammed with *objets d'art*, ranging from the truly beautiful to the utterly worthless.

Working one's way back to Desenzano, every mile or so a fresh expanse of beauty opens up.

(For further information on the lakes, see under regional headings.)

PIEMONTE AND VALLE D'AOSTA

This is the name given to the most north-westerly region and the largest with the exception of Sicilia. The boundary between it and France cuts northwards through the Maritime Alps as far as Mont Blanc (4810m/15,780ft above sea level), Monte Cervino (4478m/14,690ft) and Monte Rosa (4663m/15,300ft), then follows the arc of the Swiss Alps until it reaches the western shores of Lago Maggiore and, descending in a series of curves, arrives at the Ligurian Alps.

Valle D'Aosta, which occupies the northwestern corner, is one of the loveliest valleys in the Alps, ringed around by some of the highest peaks in Europe and including the Parco Nazionale (National Park), the Gran Paradiso. It has been an autonomous region since 10 March 1947.

Deep river valleys alternate with the high mountains, the principal river being the Dora Baltea.

This small area is admirably equipped for tourism. Hotels are excellent, there is a good system of cable railways, there are numerous mountain refuges and guides are available for the more hazardous climbs.

Valle d'Aosta also has much to offer to those interested in archaeology, architecture and art. The capital, Aosta, was an important city in Roman days and has conspicuous Roman remains. The region is rich in castles, one of the most impressive being Fénis between Aosta and St Vincent. Two other interesting castles are those of Verrès and Issogne, both just off the road from St Vincent to Ivrea.

Piemonte lies within an arc of high mountains embracing its northern and western borders, followed by the rounded hills of the Langhe and Monferrato, with an oasis of plainland around Vercelli and Novara.

The climate in the mountains is one of severe winters and mild summers; lower down, though the winters are cold with considerable rain in spring and autumn, summers are hot.

Not only is Piemonte a busy industrial region, it also has many attractions for the holiday-maker, from the well-equipped mountain resorts of Sestriere and Bardon-ecchia in the western Alps to the pleasant western shores of Lago Maggiore and the exquisite little Lago d'Orta.

Nor is architectural beauty difficult to find. There is the 10th century Benedictine abbey, the Sacra San Michele, high on a rocky crest along the motorway running west from Torino. Several cities such as Vercelli, Saluzzo and others have fine Gothic churches and Torino is an exemplar of splendid baroque architecture with a decidedly French flavour.

Festivals May (first Sunday), Fossano (near Cúneo) – Festival of San Giovenale. Portraits or photos of the town's benefactors are displayed on the walls, followed by a procession through the streets. 23 June Torino – Festival of San Giovanni. Huge wooden construction made in Palazzo Castello; on top is mounted a papiermaché bull; all set on fire in the evening. A custom dating from Longobard days to exorcise the ills of the city. September (3rd Sunday) Asti – Palio (horse race) among the various districts of the city, all in costume of the Middle Ages. 23 October, Alba – Fair of the white truffles for which the district is famous, followed by tournament in costume.

Alba   K6

(pop. 27,740) Situated in the Tánaro valley in the province of Cúneo, this small city attracts tourists visiting the Langhe. The seat of a bishopric, its aspect is medieval, even though in recent years industries have been established. It is an important wine-making centre, specialities being Barolo, Barbaresco, Nebbiolo, Barbera and Dolcetto. The city holds a great attraction for gourmets, as the centre of a district where white truffles are found, one of the main attractions of its October Fair.

There is a Gothic cathedral dating from the end of the 15th century, whose inlaid wooden choir is a fine example of the work of Cidonio (early 16th century).

Aosta   F3
(pop. 36,325) This is the capital city of the region of the same name, situated in a wide valley among high mountains. It is a popular tourist centre, placed as it is where the great St Bernard and Mont Blanc tunnels converge.

Founded by the Romans, it still preserves fine monuments: the Arch of Augustus, the Porta Prætoria, a theatre and an amphitheatre.

The collegiate church of Sant'Orso is well worth a visit; externally there is a fine *ghimberga* (high cuspid arch) over the main portal and inside are splendid frescoes – in part ruined by time – of the 11th century; also an excellent wooden choir.

The cathedral, originally of the 11th to 12th centuries, was rebuilt in the 15th to 16th centuries. The interior is Gothic and there is a fine wooden choir.

Asti   J6
(pop. 76,200) This is the seat of a bishopric, the capital city of the province, and is of patrician aspect, with splendid monuments, some from the Middle Ages.

Lying in the middle valley of the Tánaro, it is the centre of a famous wine-producing area, particularly of the famous Asti spumante. Other industries include the production of modern tapestries, wrought iron, pewter and copper.

The cathedral is an impressive Romanesque-Gothic edifice, with three ornate portals and circular openings above; the most interesting of the medieval monuments is the baptistery of San Pietro, dating from the 12th century.

Stresa   E7
(pop. 4739) This town lies on the western shore of Lago Maggiore, one of the most enchanting sites on the lake. Once a mere fishing village, Stresa nowadays is a modern town with numerous well-equipped hotels, elegant villas, and every facility; a rack railway connects with the winter sports centre of **Mottarone**. Stresa has boat services to all the lovely **Ísole Borromee**. Although Ísola Madre is the largest, the one which attracts most visitors is Ísola Bella (Beautiful Island), transformed from virgin rock into a splendid garden surrounding the Palace of the Borromeo family. Ísola dei Pescatori (Fishermen's Island) comes next in attractiveness, with its rustic fishermen's houses. Both of these have hotels. *Milano 90km/56mi.*

Torino (Turin)   I4
(pop. 1,100,000) Torino is regarded by many as the most French city in Italy; much of its culture and many of its

monuments have a strong French flavour. During the Middle Ages it was a Longobard duchy; during the 16th century it became the capital of the French province of Savoy. It played an exciting part in Italy's struggle for independence during the last century, and following the *Risorgimento* was the capital of United Italy from 1861 to 1864.

It is a smart city of gracious squares (166 in all), tree-lined streets and lovely gardens, with elegant bridges over the river Po and its tributary, the Dora. The Via Roma leads from the station to the Piazza San Carlo (tourist information). The Palazzo Madama (off Via Roma) has four turrets, statues on its upper terrace and an imposing façade. This splendid palace is now the home of the Museo Civico d'Arte Antica. In the Piazza Reale is the 17th-century Palazzo Reale, from the balcony of which Carlo Alberto declared the Italian War of Independence on 23 March, 1848. It is now a museum. In the same square the Armeria Reale is celebrated as being second in importance only to that of Madrid. Nearby is the baroque Palazzo Carignano, seat of the Chamber of Deputies 1848–59, now the Museum of the *Risorgimento*. Not far from Palazzo Madama in Piazza San Giovanni are the cathedral and the bell-tower. In a chapel behind the cathedral, designed by Guarini, is preserved the sacred shroud in which the body of Christ was wrapped after being taken down from the Cross. This relic is exhibited only on rare occasions and pilgrims come from all parts of the world to participate in the ceremony. For several centuries the shroud had been in the possession of the royal house of the Savoys. On his death in 1983, the exiled King Umberto left the precious relic to the Vatican, but it will remain in Torino. Porta Palatina, near the cathedral, is a relic of Roman days; beyond it lies the sanctuary of the Consolata.

On the banks of the Po are the magnificent park, the 17th-century Castello del Valentino and the Borgo Medioevale (pseudo-medieval town), erected in 1884 on the occasion of the great exhibition of the same year. Beyond these, in Corso Massimo d'Azeglio, stands the huge, modern palace in which are held exhibitions and international gatherings. On the other side of the Po, visit the hill-top convent, Monte dei Cappuccini, then take a coach or the rack railway to Juvara's masterpiece of baroque architecture, the Basilica di Superga (1717–31), richly decorated and housing the tombs of the Kings of Sardegna and the Princes of Savoy. *Génova 195km/121mi, Milano 140km/87mi.*

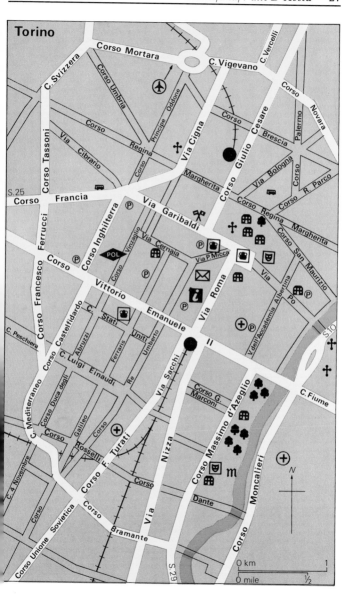

Torino

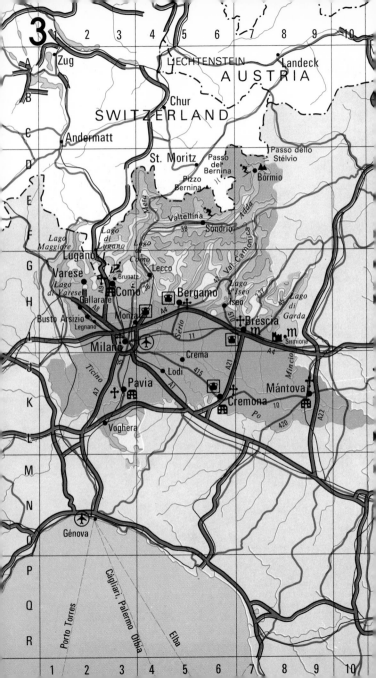

LOMBARDIA

The name of this region goes back to the days of the Longobards, who occupied it from 568–774 AD, making Pavia their capital city. It was first mentioned in the reign of King Alboino, in a diploma dated 30 July 629, as *Longobardia*.

Historical vicissitudes, coupled with its geographical location, have made this the richest and one of the most important regions of Italy. It has direct road, rail and air communications not only within the peninsula, but with the rest of Europe, and is on the main routes between the Mediterranean and the Continent.

Its territory includes the middle section of the Po basin, between the River Ticino on the west and the River Mincio on the east. The southern plain rises to Pre-Alps, then northwards to the imposing chain of the Retiche and Lepontine Alps which divide it from Switzerland. Many of these mountain peaks are over 3000m/9840ft above sea level, Pizzo Bernina rising to over 4050m/13,200ft.

The central section, stretching from Piemonte to the Veneto, is a region of lakes; from the eastern shores of Maggiore, Lugano, Como, Iseo follow in rapid succession until the western shores of Garda are reached.

The climate, thanks to the protection of the northern wall of mountains, is good, particularly in the Pre-Alps. Winters are cold, but not excessively so, summers are agreeably hot. On the plain, winter fogs constitute a driving and flying hazard, and Milano is particularly affected by these.

In both mountains and lakes the scenery is attractive and hotel accommodation excellent. The valleys of the Pre-Alps are dotted with charming small towns and villages; in the higher mountains two of the most popular resorts are Sóndrio in the Bergamasque Alps and Bormio in the high Val Camonica not far from the Stelvio Pass. The lakes of Maggiore, Lugano, Como and Garda are extremely picturesque; around their shores Nature has been helped by the hand of man and there are splendid parks, villas and gardens. Iseo is wilder, more unspoiled.

Lombardia is in the forefront for agriculture. A great series of irrigation canals criss-crosses the plain, and wheat, maize, forage, rice and sugar-beet are cultivated intensively, aided by the most modern mechanical means. The vineyards of the Pre-Alps produce excellent wines, particularly around Garda and Valtellina. Mulberry trees flourish in a few regions where silk is woven.

Industry, helped by rich hydroelectric resources, is developed at a high level: much cotton and wool are produced around Como; metallurgic and mechanical industries flourish in Milano, Bréscia and several smaller centres; production of shoes, clothing, hats and rubber is among the lesser industries of this wealthy, busy region.

Nor are archaeology, architecture or art neglected. Val Camonica has rock-scratched designs depicting life as it was lived twenty-five centuries ago. In the Po Valley evidences have been discovered of *terramare* – dwellings of a pre-Neolithic people. Sirmione on Garda has the imposing remains of a Roman villa; Bréscia has the ruins of the Temple of Vespasian and the ancient jewelled cross of the Longobard King Desiderio. In the cathedral museum of Monza is the famous Iron Crown (see page 7).

Italian Romanesque architecture owes much to Lombardia, and particularly to Como, from which city came the *Magistri Comacini* (master-builders of Como) who, in the early Middle Ages, greatly influenced the development of this style of church building.

Gothic, but of a non-Italian type, is exemplified in the ornate cathedral of Milano, begun in 1386, but not completed until 1887.

In Mántova (Mantua) Leon Battista Alberti's church of Sant'Andrea is a fine example of Renaissance architecture; later came a more elaborate note, as witness the Certosa di Pavia and the Cappella Colleoni in upper Bergamo. Finally comes the neo-classic severity of the Teatro alla Scala in Milano, and the glazed Galleria leading from it to the Piazzo del Duomo, in striking contrast to the city's ultra-modern skyscrapers.

Festivals May (beginning), Bergamo – Amusing rally of 'soap-box' cars. May (last Sunday), Legnano – Procession and race celebrating the victory of the city in 1176 over Frederick II of Swabia. June (early), Milano – Festival dei Navigli (navigable canals). A walk from Piazza del Duomo (or the Arena) for 22km/14mi. In the past this has involved 30,000 spectators or contestants. 7 December Milano – Opening Night of La Scala opera season – tickets are eagerly sought after and difficult to come by.

Bergamo   H5

(pop. 113,500) This city is built on two levels. Lower Bergamo offers wide avenues, lined with trees, elegant mansions, and a wealth of Renaissance and baroque churches, with more than one fine museum. The upper city gives one the feeling of having stepped back into the Middle Ages, even though its architecture ranges from pre-Roman to post-Renaissance.

Little is known of Bergamo outside Italy, yet it is a city that really merits a visit. Under Venetian domination for over 350 years, it has absorbed and retained much of the Venetian atmosphere. Sitting at one of the many open-air cafés surrounding Piazza Vecchia one is reminded of Piazza San Marco in Venezia – there is even the omnipresent Lion of St Mark, embedded in the wall of the Palazzo della Ragione.

After you have sat awhile in this lovely square, go through the archway to the left of the stairs that lead up into the Palazzo della Ragione, and you will see two marvellous buildings. To the left is the cathedral, built in the 17th century on the site of an earlier 6th-century church, rich in frescoes, paintings and with a fine choir.

Facing you is the Cappella Colleoni, the work of Giovanni Antonio Amadeo; inside which is the ornate tomb of Colleoni; to your right is a charming little baptistery, while on the left is the church of Santa Maria Maggiore.

Bréscia   I7

(pop. 180,000) What one first notices about Bréscia are its industries, which pollute the air and darken the stone of the buildings. Once famous for the manufacture of weapons of war, it is not surprising that metal-work still features largely among its products.

However, Bréscia has much to offer other than industry and commerce. Look at the Duomo Nuovo (New Cathedral, 17th century), the work of Lantana and rich inside with groups of marble statuary and other works of art. Then proceed to the old cathedral, popularly known as La Rotonda from its circular shape; it has a

very interesting Romanesque crypt. Nearby stand the Broletto (Court of Justice) and the Torre del Popolo (People's Tower), both Romanesque.

Those who have admired the *Nike of Samothrace* at the Louvre in Paris should make a point of visiting the remains of the Temple of Vespasian, in which is the Museo Romano, with a splendid bronze statue of the *Winged Victory* rivalling that in Paris. There is also the Museo Cristiano, with the presbytery of the one-time church of Santa Giulia where, among other treasures, one can see the famous gold cross of Desiderio, an example of goldsmith's work of the 9th century, breathtaking in its splendour.

Other buildings rewarding to visit are the 9th century Basilica di San Salvatore, the splendid Pinacoteca and the church of San Giovanni Evangelista.

Como   G3

(pop. 76,914) At the base of the western fork of the Lago di Como, this is a delightful spot in which to relax for a few days after the hustle and bustle of Milano (43km/26mi). It has something of everything for the visitor: a zoological garden, water sports, fishing, good theatrical entertainments, steamers to other points on the lake, pullman coach services to Milano and other centres of the province, and a cable railway that in seven minutes conveys one to Brunate on the table-land overlooking the city and lake.

It has several interesting buildings, including the two Romanesque churches of Sant' Abbondio and San Fedele, the cathedral – a jewel of Renaissance-Gothic with a splendid façade – the Broletto or former seat of the *comune*, and the splendid Villa Olmo, adjacent to the fine public park. A pleasant walk from the town is to the 4th-century Basilica di San Carpoforo. *Lugano 31km/19mi.*

Cremona   K6

(pop. 74,275) This might be described as a pilgrimage town for music-lovers, for it was once famous for the manufacture of Stradivarius violins, and both the Museo Civico (collection to be moved to Scuoli di Liuteria in the Palazzo Raimondi) and the Palazzo del Comune have fascinating collections of 'Stradivariana'. Today the city, one of the most absorbing of northern Italy, is celebrated for a gastronomic delicacy – *Mostarda di Cremona* (Cremona mustard). This concoction of whole fruits, cherries, figs, apricots and chunks of melon, preserved in a sweet mustard-flavoured syrup, is delicious with boiled meats.

The cathedral is a splendid example of

Lombard Gothic, with a façade that is a joy to behold – a lovely rose window, delicate colonnades and central portico. Inside there are some fine paintings. The Torrazzo or bell-tower is the tallest in Italy. Other interesting sights include the church of Sant'Agata (19th-century façade and good frescoes), the Loggia dei Militi and the Palazzo Comunale, (both pleasant 13th-century buildings).

After having visited the city, it is rewarding to drive to the church of San Sigismondo on the outskirts. The church, viewed from the outside, is not impressive, but inside are frescoes executed by various members of the Campi family, 17th-century followers of the great Caracci school. Rich in bright colours, these frescoes present a feast of baroque painting at its best.

Mántova (Mantua) K9

(pop. 62,000) Mántova is almost entirely surrounded by the river Mincio which forms, so to speak, three lakes, Lago Superiore, Lago di Mezzo and Lago Inferiore. Originally an Etruscan city, it has passed through many hands during the centuries, but its most flourishing period was during the *signoria* of the great Gonzaga family, starting in 1328 when Luigi Gonzaga was elected Capitano del Popolo, and ending with the death in 1708 of Duke Ferdinand Carlo Gonzaga. The court of the Gonzagas was an important centre of art and culture, and the buildings of Mántova testify to the artistic taste of this great family.

Among the interesting buildings are the Romanesque Rotonda di San Lorenzo (1000 AD) and the magnificent Palazzo Ducale and Castello di San Giorgio, both of the Gonzaga period. The cathedral is an example of Lombard Gothic, but its façade was reconstructed in the 18th century. Nearby is the Cappella dell'Incoronata, while in the church of Sant'Andrea are the tomb of Mantegna and some valuable frescoes. On the outskirts is the stately Palazzo del Te, a pleasure-house designed by Giulio Romano for the Gonzagas.

Seven kilometres from the city is another reminder of the family, the sanctuary of Santa Maria delle Grazie, founded by Francesco Gonzaga and containing good paintings and a gallery of votive statues. *Parma 67km/42mi, Verona 39km/24mi.*

Milano (Milan) I3

(pop. 1,471,471) Now Italy's most important commercial city, busy, bustling, modern, Milano suffered much during the early barbarian invasions until, with the arrival of the Longobards, it became the capital of one of their duchies. With the fall of the Carolingians and the descent of Barbarossa in 1152, the city was destroyed, but rose from the ashes and from 1279 to 1447 was governed as a *signoria* by the Visconti, followed by the Sforza till 1533. It again fell under foreign dominion; Spanish, French, Austrian, until it was created capital of the Cisalpine Republic by Napoleon I, and in 1805 capital of Italy. In 1848 it fell into Austrian hands, but finally achieved freedom in 1860 when it was united with the new Italy.

Milano has some splendid examples of architecture. Probably the finest example of Italian Gothic is the cathedral (1), begun in 1386, with its 135 pinnacles, one over 100 metres high with the famous gilded *Madonnina* (4 metres high) on top. The 'mother church' of Lombard-Romanesque architecture is the lovely Basilica Sant'Ambrogio (2). In the refectory of the church of Santa Maria delle Grazie (3) is the famous *Last Supper* of Leonardo da Vinci, miraculously appearing to extend the length of the room. The splendid courtyard of the Palazzo di Brera (4), seat of Milano's fine art gallery, is the work of the 17th-century architect Riechini; (5) the Castello Sforzesco is another imposing architectural landmark.

Galleria Vittorio Emanuele (6) by the Piazza del Duomo is the great meeting, eating and shopping centre of Milano.

Pavia K3

(pop. 67,960) The capital city of the Longobards who invaded Italy in 568 AD and remained to become absorbed in the civilization of the country, Pavia is an agreeable city with some delightful buildings. The Basilica di San Michele in which the kings of Lombardy were crowned until the 11th century is a splendid example of Romanesque architecture, its façade decorated with cleverly grouped windows, blind *loggettas* and sculpture, and three grand portals, reminiscent of those seen in some of the churches of Provence. Two other interesting churches of the same period are San Pietro in Ciel d'Oro and San Teodoro. The Bramante cathedral is very fine. An ancient bridge over the Ticino was reconstructed after World War II; there are many medieval houses, and some towers remain from the time when Pavia was known as the 'City'of a Hundred Towers.' The university is one of the oldest in Italy, and other interesting buildings are the Castello Visconteo and the Collegio Ghislieri.

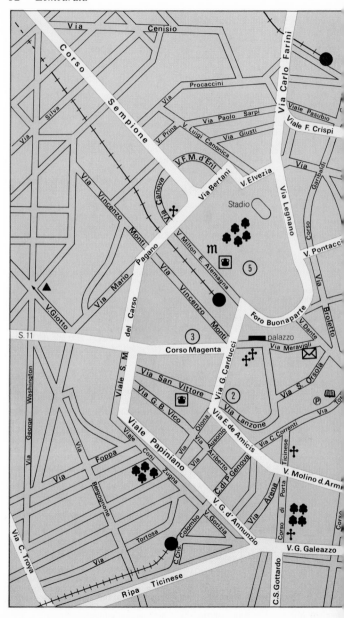

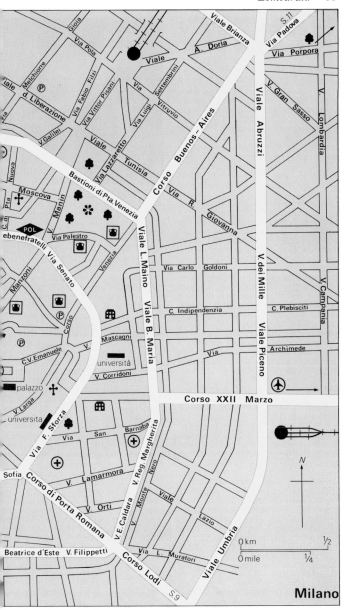

Milano

VENETO

including Trentino/Alto Adige, Friúli/Venezia Giulia

This region occupies the northeastern part of Italy; it is customary to regard the three divisions as individual components of a whole.

Trentino/Alto Adige is the northwestern mountainous region stretching down from the southern Alps to embrace the upper basin of the River Adige and that of the Isarco and Val Sugana on the east.

High mountains alternate with broad, green valleys. The wooded heights favour forestry and cattle-raising. On the less exposed lower slopes are fruit orchards and the vineyards which produce excellent wines. Rich in hydroelectric resources, Trentino-Alto Adige provides about one-fifth of the nation's needs. Paper-making, tobacco-growing, the preserving of fruit and wood-carving are among the industries of the region. Bolzano and Merano have metallurgical and chemical plants. Fishing, too, is important, not only of excellent trout, but in Val Sugana there is considerable salmon-fishing. And one of the great sources of wealth nowadays is tourism, which is well provided for in summer and winter.

The history of Trentino is echoed in its art and architecture. From the time of the Romans it proved a useful passageway between Italy and Germany. The Longobards ousted the Romans and unified the region into the Duchy of Trento, which later became a March under Charlemagne. In the church of San Procolo in Naturno are frescoes dating back to this epoch (8th to 9th century AD). In the year 952 the region passed under Germany, who established ecclesiastical principalities in Trento and Bressanone, from which period remain the Romanesque cathedral of Trento, the abbey of Novacella and the cloisters of the cathedral in Bressanone. In this cathedral can also be seen a fresco featuring San Procolo. At Castel Roncolo near Bolzano, in the imposing 13th-century castle, is a fine series of 15th-century frescoes. The cathedrals of Bolzano, Merano and Vipiteno are splendid examples of the following Gothic period, as is the Castello del Buonconsiglio in Trento with its 15th-century cycle of frescoes of the months of the year. In the little church of Gries, near Bolzano, is a fine altarpiece by Michel Pacher (1471).

Looking at the Renaissance buildings in parts of Trento, one is reminded of the long sitting of the Council of Trent which took place there from 1545–63.

The struggle between Austria and Italy continued, until in 1810 Trentino was declared Italian; but five years later, under the Treaty of Vienna, it was ceded back to Austria, a bitter pill never completely digested by Italy. It was over 100 years before 'Venezia Tridentina' was once again recognized as Italian territory, following a victory which cost many lives, among them those of three patriot martyrs, Cesare Battisti, Fabio Filzi and Damiano Chiesa, remembered today by three flat tombstones in the Martyrs' graveyard at the Castello dei Buonconsiglio in Trento. This was in 1916; following World War II the region took on its present name of Trentino-Alto Adige.

Festivals There is no set date, but during the September grape harvest Merano puts on a colourful parade – decorated carts hung with bunches of grapes, gaily costumed people, music, dancing and an enormous feast. Again with no set date, many villages in Val di Cembra celebrate the *Canta dei Mesi* – groups of youngsters in traditional dress sing songs to a King and Harlequin in honour of the various months. In this region there are numerous fine brass bands and folk song groups, so that music is a frequent accompaniment to a mountain holiday.

The Veneto proper, the middle section, occupies roughly the plain between the rivers Po and Tagliamento, with the former providing a natural boundary on the south, and on the north the upper basin of the Piave River and some of the most spectacular peaks of the Dolomites. Two isolated groups of hills rise on the plain, the Berici near Vicenza and the Euganei not far from Padova (Padua).

Forestry and cattle-raising are the chief activities in the mountainous region, while there is considerable fruit-growing and viniculture on the lower slopes. On the plain the main crops are maize and sugar-beet, with here and there the cultivation of mulberry trees for the not quite extinct silk industry. The Veneto also produces a considerable quantity of tobacco. Fishing is carried on extensively all along the coast and around the reclaimed marshes of the Po valley. The woollen industry is to be found around Verona and Vicenza; Marghera, near Venezia (Venice), is a busy centre for the metal-mechanic industry.

Minor industries are the ceramics of Bassano, Nove and Este and the gold-smithery of Vicenza.

Venezia, with its industrial 'foot on the ground' in Mestre, is one of the main centres of commerce, and its port is of great importance. Verona and Padova are highly industrialized.

Tourism plays a very important part, and the Veneto has much to offer, not only in the beauty of the mountains, the hills and the coastal strip, but also in art, architecture and music.

When, in the year 89 BC, Roma granted Latin rights to the cities of the Veneto, three centuries or more of prosperity ensued, until the barbaric invasions, which finally led to the breaking away of Venezia. Incidentally, this resulted in the establishment of that city as the great independent power she was until the rise of Napoleon in the 18th century signalled the start of a couple of centuries of slow but certain decadence.

The Veneto is rich in architecture of the Roman period; the Arena in Verona is outstanding; and that city also possesses a Roman theatre and two fine gates. In the Arena gardens in Padova are vestiges of another Arena.

The Veneto went through a period of fractioning into Marches and free cities, from which emerged the free *comunes* and later the *signorias*, so that at the beginning of the 14th century power was vested in the hands of the Scaligeri of Verona, the Carraresi of Padova and the Da Camino of Treviso. This was a period of great building activity, during which rose the great Romanesque churches of San Zeno, San Lorenzo and the early part of the cathedral in Verona.

In time this style blended into Gothic of which examples are to be seen in the basilicas of Sant'Antonio in Padova, San Nicolò in Treviso and Sant'Anastasia in Verona, to mention but three of the fine churches of the period, and the various great halls, such as the Palazzo della Ragione in Padova, the Palazzo del Trecento in Treviso and the splendid Scaligeri tombs in Verona.

During the 14th century Padova was enriched by two splendid series of frescoes, those by Giotto in the Cappella degli Scrovegni, those of Menabuoi in the baptistery of the cathedral. A century later Pisanello executed his fine fresco of St George and the Princess in the church of Sant'Anastasia in Verona.

The Renaissance left its mark in the statuary by Donatello in the Basilica di Sant'Antonio in Padova and the equestrian statue of Erasmo da Narni (the Gattamelata) outside. Padova was also fortunate in having a fine series of frescoes by Mantegna in the church of the Eremitani, unfortunately badly damaged during World War II; there is a splendid altarpiece by the same artist in the church of San Zeno in Verona.

Internal wars and rivalries between the various *signorias* gave Venezia the chance to intervene, which she did so successfully that by 1420 she had seized and subdued the whole of the Veneto, a domination which lasted four centuries, a symbol of which is the Lion of St Mark to be seen in many cities of the region. Under the treaty of Campoformio in 1797 the Veneto was assigned to Austria, and this was confirmed in the early 19th century under the Treaty of Vienna. It was not until 1866 that the region was declared Italian.

Not surprisingly the Venetian style in painting spread over the region, which is rich in works by the Bellinis, Vivarini, Carpaccio, and later the great Titian, Veronese, Tintoretto and others, and such Renaissance architects as Sansovino, followed soon by the neo-Classic Palladio. These are but a few of the artists and architects who have made the Veneto a treasure-house.

The islands of the Venetian Lagoon H11

Crossing the long road and rail bridge that links Venezia with the mainland, one is approaching not so much a city crisscrossed by canals, as a group of islands connected by bridges.

After having explored the principal ones, those that constitute Venezia as we know it, it is enjoyable to venture forth to less familiar islands.

Crossing to and from Lido, the steamer passes two hospital islands, San Servilio and San Clemente. Special permission has to be obtained in order to visit these.

There are also two 'monastery' islands; one, San Lazzaro degli Armeni, approachable by steamer from Riva degli Schiavoni, is a tiny oasis of the glorious east once held in fee by Venezia. Formerly an asylum for sick pilgrims, later a hospital for lepers, it was given in 1717 to an

Armenian nobleman, Manug de Pietro, who had fled the Turkish invasion of Modone where he had founded a Benedictine monastery. Having arrived at this island, he founded the institute known as I Padri Armeni Mechcaristi, and later a college for the education of poor orphans.

Today the island is a serious and severe study centre, with a charming little church, a splendid library and a solemnly cordial welcome to visitors.

To reach the other monastery island one goes first to the lace-making island of Burano, and takes a *sandolo* (small type of gondola). The island is tiny, the atmosphere calm but not austere. A mass of cypress trees surrounds the small church and the nearby hermitage with its silent cloisters. Nature has been generous and the beauty and peace of the place give credence to the legend that St Francis of Assisi, on his way back from Soria, put into the island during a great storm, upon which the tempest ceased and the skies cleared. As with many other places visited by Il Poverello (as St Francis was affectionately known), peace and calm have remained as a heritage. The monks living on the island will show you with pride a venerable pine tree said to have developed from the saint's staff which he had plunged into the soil.

Murano, Burano and Torcello can be reached by taking an excursion steamer from Riva degli Schiavoni, but it is cheaper and more adventurous to take a steamer from near Piazzale Roma to Murano, from which it is easy to take a boat to the other two. The routes are Circolare Destra and Circolare Sinistra, both following the same route, but in opposite directions.

On the way to Murano the steamer passes the island of San Michele, the cemetery of Venezia, and it is worthwhile spending twenty or thirty minutes between boats to visit the church and the adjoining cloister. There has been a church on the island ever since the 10th century, when San Romualdo, founder of the Camaldolese Order, is said to have lived there. The present edifice dates back to the Renaissance, and was planned in 1469 by Mauro Coducci. It was the first ecclesiastical building constructed in Venezia during that period and is one of the most beautiful.

The cloisters have not always been reserved for religious purposes. During the last century, in the troubled days of the *Risorgimento*, two patriots, Silvio Pellico and Pietro Maroncelli, were imprisoned there while awaiting trial for having plotted against the Austrian overlords.

Murano is nowadays mainly renowned for the production of glassware ranging from the extremely beautiful to the gaudy. To visit one of the glass factories and watch glass being blown and formed into a variety of shapes is rather like taking a step back in time to the artisans' workshops depicted in ancient prints. Watch the master as he plunges his iron rod into the pan of molten glass in the heart of a fiery furnace, extracts a blob of the incandescent paste and, placing the other end of the rod in his mouth, by sheer lung power converts the blob into a vase, a bunch of flowers, or the figure of a clown. Lung power and a pair of pincers (*borselle*) are the tools of his trade; the results can be seen in the packed showroom attached to the factory. Watch the young apprentices who, while the master is demonstrating his expertise, pick out smaller, cooler blobs and with the aid of spatula and pincers fashion them into tiny horses or birds, which they then try to sell to the spectators.

Murano has long been famous for its glass-making, as can be seen by the exhibits in the Museo dell'Arte Vetraria (Glass Museum). It had, however, an even more impressive past, and from the 13th century to the Fall of Venice had its own local government and its own Golden Book in which were inscribed the names of privileged local men; it also coined its own money, and all this wealth and prosperity were closely linked with the glass-making industry.

Lovers of architecture should make a point of visiting the Basilica di Santa Maria e Donato, one of the most important Venetian-Byzantine buildings of the 12th century, nearly as old as San Marco itself. Externally, it has many features reminiscent of the architecture of Ravenna; inside, there is a stupendous mosaic floor.

Having done this, pause for a drink of wine in one of the many little hostelries, or a meal at one of several excellent eating-houses to be found on the island.

Burano is within easy reach by boat from Murano. On the way the boat may pause at Mazzorbo, which has an interesting small Romanesque-Gothic church and convent. One of the bells in the nearby bell-tower was cast in the year 1318.

In Burano itself we are in the heart of the lace-making industry which, before the fall of the Venetian Republic, brought prosperity to the island. Burano might be said to have introduced the art of lace-making to the rest of the world. Now, thanks to the initiative of wealthy, far-seeing people, the art has been revived, and once again pretty girls are using the *tombolo* (the lace-making pillow) in the lace-making school, and one sees women sitting at their cottage doors working at this delicate task.

Sophistication is far removed from this cosy little island; as you walk around the narrow streets bordering the canals, cottage doors stand open and there are glimpses of interiors not just scrupulously clean, but gay with the colourful gleam of pottery.

On this island one eats well and drinks well. To accompany the wine special s-shaped biscuits are made, intended to hang on the side of one's glass, to be 'dunked' in the drink.

Landing from the boat one may have noticed a group of ancient 'grandfathers' gathered on the quay, one or two of whom will have drawn the craft into the correct mooring position. It is customary to reward them with a small tip, which is accepted with a charming, old-world courtesy.

Torcello, which one approaches from Burano, might well be regarded as a paradise of peace.

It was this island that the fugitives fled from the hordes of Attila in 453 AD. Here they founded a great city.

In the year 638 the Bishop of Altino transferred his seat to the island, and up to the 14th century Torcello continued to grow. In those days it had a fine woollen industry, and was important ecclesiastically. Then came the scourge of malaria and most of its people moved to what is now Rialto; as Venezia rose in wealth and importance, so Torcello declined, its waters silting up, until it became the haven of peace we find nowadays, deserted save for a few little farms and market gardens.

From the landing, one strolls along the banks of a lazy little canal and crosses a bridge into the Piazzetta, on one side of which stands what used to be the seat of the Council and the palace of the Archives, now combined as an interesting Museo dell'Estuario.

On the opposite side of the Piazzetta are two noble buildings, the church of Santa Fosca, and the even more imposing cathedral of Santa Maria Assunta. One should visit both.

After this it is probably time to think of something to eat and drink, and in this connection do not be misled by the humble outward appearance of the *trattoria* (eating-house) of Cipriani, for the humble exterior leads to a hotel and restaurant of prime quality. Prices are high, but the fare is excellent.

Festivals of the Veneto In the little town of Maróstica, some 7km/4mi west of Bassano, the *Cherry Sagra* is held on the last Sunday in May, when the main square is lined with stalls displaying and selling the fine cherries grown in the district. Padova keeps the name day of its patron saint, Sant'Antonio, with a solemn religious procession on 13 June.

One of the great annual festivals is the open-air opera season in the Arena in Verona, to which come visitors from far and wide. Opening night in early August is particularly enchanting, when all lights are extinguished and the overture is played to the light of literally thousands of candles in the hands of the spectators, after which the opera proper begins with a blaze of electricity. Tickets are difficult to get, and very early booking is advisable.

Again in Maróstica, usually on the first Saturday and Sunday of alternate Septembers, there is a delightful festival: a game of chess played with living 'pieces' in the colourful and elegant clothes of the 15th century. There are afternoon and evening performances.

Friúli/Venezia Giulia, the eastern part of the Veneto, stretches more or less from the Tagliamento River on the west to the Isonzo River on the east, and reaches down to include a thin tongue of land as far as the city of Trieste. On the north the Carnic and Julian Alps close the region off from Austria. The coastal strip is interspersed with lagoons, and going inland one finds first a pre-Alpine area soon rising to the high peaks, which appear like a protecting wall. It is an area of great caves, Grotta Gigante near Trieste being one of the largest in Europe.

The name of Friúli is known to many

Venezia, showing the Canal Grande

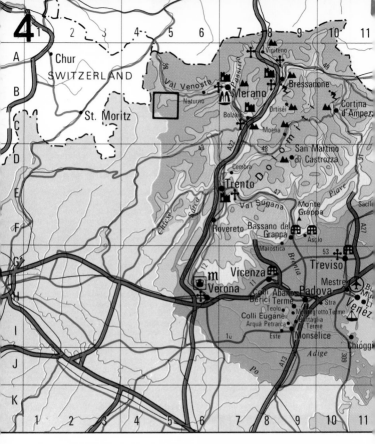

since the disastrous earthquakes of 1976, which took a heavy toll of lives and caused the destruction of many historic buildings.

Mainly an agricultural area, cereals, vines and fruit are grown on a commercial scale. Sheep and pigs are raised on the slopes. It is also a busy industrial area; at Monfalcone, near Trieste, are shipyards and Trieste has a fair quota of metal-mechanical industry, oil refineries, cloth mills and distilleries. Other busy industrial towns are Udine, Gorizia and Pordenone. The finest *prosciutto* (raw ham) in Italy comes from the small town of San Daniele, and among minor industries are the manufacture of furniture and woodwork generally.

Tourism, especially along the coast and in the mountains, is of great importance; during the summer season resorts such as Lignano Sabbiadoro and Grado are crowded, and tourist accommodation is excellent.

Friúli has had an interesting history ever since its Romanization in the 2nd and 1st centuries BC when Aquiléia was regarded as the most important city in the 10th Region. Traces of Roman times can be found in many places – Trieste possesses a Roman theatre, Concordia Sagittaria near Portogruaro offers an interesting group of paleochristian tombs and basilicas beneath the present cathedral, but the great treasure-house is the city of Aquiléia which preserves not only Roman houses, but the Via Sacra following the columned remains of the one-time port, and other relics (see page 40).

Friúli received the full blast of the barbaric invasions, and under the Longobards was divided into two, the Friúli of the land with its capital Cividale, and that of the sea with its centre in Grado.

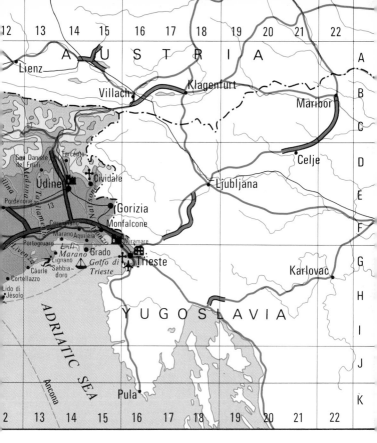

To this period belongs the Tempietto in Cividale and various sculptures in the cathedral of Longobard days.

Before long the Franks superseded the Longobards and the authority of the patriarchs of Aquiléia had increased so that, by the 11th century, it had emerged as the most important ecclesiastic and civil principality of northern Italy, with only the most eastern parts of the region under the Counts of Gorizia – a situation which endured until the 15th century.

Meanwhile, Venezia had been growing more and more powerful, so that in 1420 it annexed Friúli. Up to the advent of Napoleon the region was divided between Venezia and Austria, with Trieste in 1719 declared a free port. In 1815 the whole region passed under Austria and it was not until 1866 that the province of Udine was free to call itself Italian; the rest of the territory had to wait until 1918.

Once it had fallen under Venetian domination, Friúli adopted the Venetian style in art and architecture, a striking example of which is to be seen in the main square in Udine.

Festivals Epiphany in Cividale heralds a celebratory Mass in the cathedral, the Mass of the Great Sword, during which a deacon, wearing a plumed helmet, faces the congregation and, holding an ancient Gospel in his left hand, makes the Sign of the Cross with a huge sword held in his right.

Again at Epiphany, Tarcento celebrates the festival of the *pignarui*, an affair of bonfires on the mountain peaks, accompanied by almost pagan rites.

Sacile, on the first Sunday after 14 August, holds the *Sagra degli Osei*, a bird show which attracts ornithologists from far and near.

Abano Terme   H9

(pop. 11,000) This great thermal centre, about 12km/7mi from Padova, lies at the edge of the friendly little group of hills known as the Eugánei. It is one of the best-known and most frequented spas in Europe for the cure of rheumatic and arthritic complaints. The fame of its curative powers goes back to Roman times.

Huge modern hotels line its streets, many with splendid gardens, several with luxurious swimming pools. Walking along the streets of Abano one notices houses and luxury shops alternating with clouds of acrid-smelling water vapour rising from one or another of the pools of bubbling, gurgling mud.

Like most spas, it is a moneyed town and presents an appearance of comfortable well-being.

Its nearness to Padova makes it possible to visit that city easily; apart from private means of transport, there are frequent and swift local bus services between Abano and the railway station in Padova.

Abano is growing at such a rate that the nearby smaller town of Montegrotto, also a spa town, almost joins it.

Walks and drives into the nearby hills are among the attractions, and a meal in one of the many restaurants or *trattorias* scattered among them is a gastronomic experience not to be missed. The hills are not only beautiful, but friendly, and they have given shelter to more than one famous person in the past centuries. The poet Petrarca lived out the last years of his life in the tiny village of Arquá Petrarca, where you may still visit his cottage; Shelley and Byron once spent a year in the city of **Este**, an event marked by a commemorative plaque on the wall of the Villa Kunkler where they stayed. Abano provides the means for many an excursion into these hills, and one should not miss the opportunity of visiting such interesting little places as **Este**, **Monsélice**, **Teolo**, **Battaglia Terme** and many others.

Aquiléia   F14

(pop. 3500) This is nowadays a village, not far from Udine, the capital of Friúli, but it has had a rich past and is a place to be visited if one happens to be in the near vicinity.

Once an important city and river port under the Roman emperor Augustus, in the Middle Ages it became a patriarchate. There is a lovely Romanesque basilica, originally built around the year 1000, which possesses some of the most wonderful mosaic floors in the world. Aquiléia is rich in memories of Roman days; there is a Roman cemetery; one can still walk along what used to be the banks of the river port and a visit to the Museo Archeologico is exciting. Anyone staying in Udine or holidaying in Grado or Lignano Sabbiadoro should not fail to devote a day to this unexpectedly lovely place.

Bassano del Grappa   F9

(pop. 35,200) This charming little town, lying on the banks of the Brenta not far from Vicenza, is linked with the name of Monte Grappa and the campaigns of the Great War.

It is situated in a picturesque position, characterized by ancient winding streets with porticoes, a number of frescoed houses and an Alpine bridge spanning the river.

It is the centre of a flourishing ceramic industry, and the streets leading to the famous bridge vie with each other in window displays of the characteristic pottery, and also of another Bassano speciality – *grappa*, the fire-water of the Veneto – and, in the proper season, mushrooms. The asparagus of Bassano is also renowned, and in spring one sees great displays of this succulent vegetable.

The cathedral rises within the enclosure of the one-time castle of the Ezzelino family.

One of the best views can be seen by turning left at the entry to the covered bridge and walking along the Viale dei Martiri, where every tree bears a memorial plaque to one of the Alpine soldiers of the city fallen during the Great War.

Within easy reach of such pretty little centres as **Ásolo**, and the **Villa Maser** (frescoes by Paolo Veronese), Bassano can be recommended for a weekend visit.

Bolzano   C7

(pop. 90,000) 262m/860ft above sea level. Not only is this a busy industrial city, but it is a holiday resort much frequented by mountain lovers, and a base for all kinds of truly magnificent excursions to the many mountain centres in the vicinity. It is an elegant city with much in its aspect that reminds one of Austria, which is not surprising when one realizes that for 400 years, until the end of World War I, Bolzano was under Austrian rule.

It has a network of enchanting arcaded streets, shopping facilities are excellent and its open-air fruit market is colourful and appetizing.

Its 13th-century cathedral is well worth visiting, and a bus or tram ride to the suburb of Gries is truly rewarding for there one can see a splendid altarpiece by the Bressanone painter Michel Pacher (15th to 16th century). During winter this church is not used for religious services, and permission to view can be obtained from the caretaker in a cottage nearby.

These are but two of the interesting buildings of Bolzano; walking around the city you will see others, but perhaps you will prefer to spend your time exploring the outskirts of the city, and taking some of the many panoramic walks or drives.

Hotel accommodation is plentiful and good, and the tourist feels welcome.

Bressanone   A8
(pop. 14,000) 559m/1834ft above sea level. Here we have a lovely mountain city in the upper reaches of Alto Adige, an excellent winter sports centre and with numerous architectural beauties such as the 13th-century Romanesque cathedral, frescoed by the Unterberger family, with two bell-towers and a beautifully frescoed cloister. The castle of the Bishop-Princes was built during the 13th and 14th centuries, and the church of San Giovanni Battista is also worth visiting.

Not far from Bressanone is the 12th-century abbey of **Novacella**, a very important group of buildings with a most interesting chapel, that of San Vittore.

The monks of Novacella are great wine-makers and their wines are deservedly popular. One can taste samples, served by the monks, in a cellar whose dim pervading light gives one the impression of having stepped into a painting by Avercamp. It is a truly fascinating place to visit. There are rumours one hopes unfounded, of modernization of the cellar.

Cáorle   G13
(pop. 11,500) This was originally merely a little agricultural and fishing village, but the modern trend for seaside holidays and its fine stretch of sandy beach have combined to turn Cáorle of recent years into a flourishing resort with numerous excellent hotels and restaurants to suit all tastes.

Cáorle is thought to have been originally a part of the one-time Roman city of Concordia Sagittaria.

There are two seashores at Cáorle, the eastern and the western, divided one from the other by a dyke on which stands the little church of the Madonna dell'Angelo. Near the apse of this church a sandbank cuts off a part of the eastern shore that sweeps around in a curve, and there one can see the characteristic *bragozzi*, the fishing boats of the Venetian lagoon. Nearby is a small harbour with accommodation for about 800 tourist craft.

The old part of the town is fascinating and is dominated by a lovely 11th-century cathedral which has a cylindrical bell-tower, one of only two examples in the Veneto, of the type found in Ravenna.

Cáorle has good road and rail communications with Venezia and the inland towns and is altogether an excellent centre for a holiday.

Cividale   E14
(pop. 10,790) This little city, within easy reach by road or rail from Údine, is one of the most interesting in Friúli; at present a busy commercial and agricultural centre, in the past it was the seat of one of the duchies of the Longobards and capital of Friúli.

Lying in a picturesque position on the banks of the swift river Natisone, its central square, Piazza del Duomo, was once the forum of the city in Roman times. The cathedral, in Venetian Gothic style, was begun in 1457 by the architect Bartolomeo delle Cisterne, and completed in the 16th century by P. Lombardo. It is rich in treasures; in the chapel of San Donato is the *Last Supper* by Palma the Younger, and an *Annunciation* by Amalteo. Over the main altar is a fine embossed silver altarpiece of the early 13th century; in the Chapel of the Holy Sacrament *Noli mi tangere* by Pordenone and the *Martyrdom of Santo Stéfano* by Palma the Younger.

From the right-hand nave one enters the part now used as a museum of objects connected with Christianity, one of the great treasures of which is the octagonal baptistery of Callisto, and another the altar of Duke Ratchis (both of the 8th century). There is also a patriarchal chair and there are frescoes from the Longobard temple.

The Tempietto (Little Temple) stands in the medieval part of the city, on the edge of the steep banks of the River Natisone, and is a most interesting monument with a barrel-vaulted roof, Byzantine style frescoes, Gothic choir stalls and stuccoes of the 18th-century – something not to be missed.

While in Cividale one should not fail to taste the typical spiced bread of the region, *gubana*, made throughout Friúli, but at its best in its native city of Cividale.

Cortina d'Ampezzo   B10
(pop. 6967) One of the busiest tourist and winter sports centres in the Dolomites and one of the loveliest. The Winter Olympics of 1956 prompted the building of the huge Olympic Ice Stadium, with two enormous skating rinks. For the winter sports enthusiast, Cortina offers every facility, but in summer it is equally delightful. There is a wide range of accommodation; restaurants, tea shops and coffee bars abound. Excursions to several interesting centres are available and one of the most attractive

is to the lovely **Lago Misurina**, a short drive away, lying in a crown of the Dolomites. *Venezia 160km/99mi.*

Grado   G14

(pop. 10,000) This is a favourite holiday resort, standing on one of the islands in the Golfo di Venezia, linked to the mainland by a traffic bridge 5km/3mi in length. It has a long stretch of sandy beach and a considerable number of excellent hotels.

The modern part of Grado has a fine array of public parks and gardens and bathing establishments. Fishing and nautical sports are well catered for.

The older quarter is typical of Veneto marine centres, but also offers treasures for lovers of architecture and ancient history, for back in Roman days, Grado was the fortified outpost of the once-famous river port of Aquiléia, and when in the 5th century AD Aquiléia fell, Grado inherited much of that city's importance.

The 5th-century church of Santa Maria delle Grazie is in the form of a basilica and is built largely of material from Roman and Byzantine buildings. The cathedral is even earlier, 4th century, and its treasures are a splendid mosaic floor, a fine pulpit and some valuable frescoes. The 6th-century baptistery has a very interesting font.

From Grado one may make an excursion by boat to the small island of **Barbana**, where there is a Byzantine Madonna in wood. Pilgrims visit this little shrine in July and in mid-August.

Lido di Jésolo   H12

(pop. 4500) This resort, a bare 30km/19mi from Venezia, situated between the Port of Cortellazzo and the mouth of the River Sile, with a long, wide stretch of fine, white sand and excellent communications by land and sea, is popular not only with Italians of the north, but also with British, German and other visitors.

Excellently equipped with hotels and with a wide variety of restaurants to suit all tastes and pockets, it seems to offer everything needful for a really wonderful seaside holiday.

Be a little careful when booking a holiday here, and impress upon your agent that you would prefer one end or the other – preferably the end nearer to Punta Sabbione rather than the middle section – for, among Jésolo's entertainments for tourists, the centre proliferates with those of the noisier kind. You have been warned; if you take notice of the warning, you may expect to spend a truly marvellous holiday here, and you will be sufficiently near to Venezia to visit it more than once.

Lignano Sabbiadoro   G13

(pop. 1180) This deservedly popular resort lies at the tip of a promontory jutting out into the Laguna di Marano, almost midway between Cáorle and Grado, and is linked with Lignano Pineta and Lignano Riviera, the three making one large and very lovely expanse of seaside holiday terrain. Within easy road and rail reach of Venezia and Trieste, they are all excellently equipped with hotels and restaurants to suit numerous tourists of varying tastes.

There is a large dock at Sabbiadoro, well-protected, and able to accommodate a considerable number of all kinds of boats.

In the pinewoods are little cottages and bungalows which can be rented, and where one can feel really in touch with lovely nature.

Lignano Riviera has a spa open for cures from June to September.

Merano   B7

(pop. 29,850) 323m/1060ft above sea level. This is one of Italy's strikingly picturesque cities, gifted with a perfect climate for holidays both in summer and in winter, and wonderfully well-equipped in the way of accommodation and places to eat.

A tributary of the River Adige runs through Merano, crossed by several bridges and with delightful walks on either side.

Standing at the head of the lovely Val Venosta, the surrounding mountains make a lovely frame for a charming city. Although of ancient origin, its great development as a holiday and thermal centre began during the last century, and so the 'new' town has an air of elegant dignity and unity.

In the medieval part stands the ancient castle of the 15th century, the 14th-century cathedral where one finds a curving nave, reminiscent of that of Quimper in Brittany, said by some to be the result of an architectural miscalculation, but thought by many others to have been intentional and to represent the bowed form of the crucified Christ.

There are characteristic little streets in this older part, and famous walks, the *Tappeiner* and *d'estate* and *d'inverno*.

A city of lovely public and private gardens and of enticing shops, Merano also offers hunting in the nearby hills, and fishing in the Passirio and Adige Rivers. There are many enticing excursions to be taken, and whether one fancies an energetic or a lazy, relaxing holiday, Merano provides for both, and moreover offers good camping facilities. There is a well-patronized racecourse and horse-racing is one of the many popular sports. Frequent folklore spectacles take place and altogether Merano seems to offer something of everything enjoyable.

Padova (Padua)   H9

(pop. 194,706) Padova has the second oldest university in Italy, nicknamed Il Bo, founded in 1222. This was where Galileo Galilei held the chair in Mathematics (1592–1610), where the poet Tasso studied law and the playwright Goldoni took his degree in jurisprudence, where Oliver Goldsmith spent a little time during his wanderings. Padova holds a magnetic attraction for Catholics in the huge Basilica dedicated to Sant'Antonio

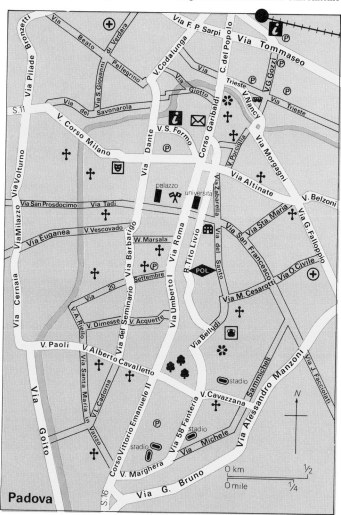

Padova

of Padova, whose tomb is the object of many pilgrimages. This magnificent basilica (off Via M. Cesarotti) is a treasure-house of sculpture and painting – Donatello, Sansovino, Menabuòi are but three of many artists whose work is to be found there. Externally it has a striking aspect with its ornate façade and its minarets and domes reminiscent of a mosque rather than a European church. At its side is the famous equestrian statue of Erasmo de Narni (The Gattamelata) the work of the Florentine sculptor Donatello. Nearby are the Oratorio di San Giorgio with fine frescoes by Altichieri and Avanzo, and the Museo Civico with paintings by Bellini, Titian and Giorgione.

Take Via Belludi from the Piazza del Santo to another huge open space, Prato della Valle, in the centre of which is a patch of green, shaded by trees and surrounded by a circular moat crossed by four stone bridges, then surrounded again by a circle of statues of men who have been famous in the history of the city. On the wall of a palace is a plaque bearing a sonnet by the poet d'Annunzio lauding its quiet and peace – times have changed. In a corner of this huge square is the church of Santa Giustina (14th century) which has an interesting altar picture by Paolo Veronese, and the tomb of St Luke the Evangelist.

Of the three market squares (between Via Dante and Via Roma), the large busy Piazza delle'Erbe, with a corner devoted to flowers and a delightful fountain, and the remainder filled with stalls of fresh vegetables, is the most absorbing. The enormous Sala della Ragione, a huge hall decorated with frescoes, houses at one end a large wooden horse reminiscent of the Gattamelata that stands outside the Basilica. At one end of the Piazza dei Signori stands the Palazzo del Capitano, with an interesting, ancient clock which tells not only the hours but the date.

Facing the university is the Caffè Pedrocchi, famous ever since the Italian *Risorgimento*. Past Pedrocchi, towards the railway station, on the right can be seen the Arena Gardens, with the Cappella degli Scrovegni, housing the famous series of frescoes painted by Giotti at the height of his powers (1303–5). Padova's new museum is on the left, proceeding towards the great church of the Eremitani (hermits). Inside the church are the remains of splendid frescoes by Mantegna (1431–1506) and others.

If you are in Padova long enough to drive along the road to **Teolo** or any of the towns in the charming Euganean Hills, visit the **abbey of Praglia**. The monks are pleased to show people around, and a pleasant liqueur is brewed there; honey may also be purchased.

Trento   E7

(pop. 91,700) This city, capital of Trentino/Alto Adige, is a city of truly noble aspect. The River Adige runs through it, and high mountains surround it. Seat of a bishopric, it was the scene of the famous Council of Trent, which lasted from 1545–63.

The cathedral, a severe example of Romanesque-Gothic architecture, presides over the monumental centre of the city, Piazza Duomo. Nearby is the Palazzo Pretorio, the Torre Civica and two picturesque frescoed houses.

Via Belenzani, which leads off Piazza Duomo, is one of the city's loveliest streets, rich in Renaissance houses with a strongly Venetian air.

The Castello dei Buonconsiglio was in ancient times the residence of the Bishop-Princes. Surrounded by a wall with here and there low towers, it consists of several different edifices. To the north is the cylindrical Great Tower, the battlemented Castelvecchio; in the centre rises the portion known as Giunta Albertina, dating from the 17th century, to the south the Renaissance Magno Palazzo, erected in 1526 to the order of the bishop Bernardo Clesio.

There is much to see in the complex forming the castle, and one sight not to be missed is the splendid series of frescoes of the months in the Torre dell'Aquila. As one enters the castle one passes near the tombstones marking the graves of the three martyred patriots, Cesare Battisti, Damiano Chiesa and Fabio Filzi, who met their deaths in 1916.

Across the river, on a height which can be reached by a *funivia*, stands the memorial erected in honour of Cesare Battisti; from that point there is also a splendid view of the city.

Treviso   G10

(pop. 91,000) This charming little city merits a visit from anyone spending a holiday in the Veneto or in Venezia itself. It is a city of many waters; the River Sile laps its walls and there are numerous canals. It has interesting monuments of medieval and Renaissance origin.

Piazza dei Signori is in the centre of the city and is very medieval in aspect with the huge Palazzo del Trecento which dates back to the beginning of the 13th century, the Palazzo del Podestà with the high tower and, on the west side, the ancient Palazzo Pretorio.

The cathedral, originally medieval, has

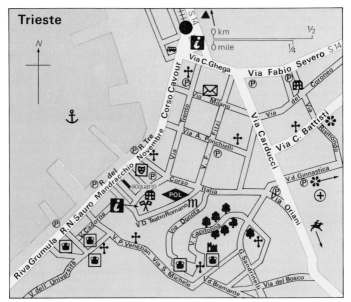

Trieste

had many restorations, even to an elegant neoclassic entrance porch. Less remodelled is the Romanesque baptistery on the left.

There is a fine *Annunciation* by Titian in the Chapel of the Annunciation, and there are various examples of the Renaissance sculpture of the Lombardo family. The crypt of the 11th and 12th centuries, with its forest of supporting columns, is well worth a visit.

The church of San Nicolò is a large Gothic edifice of the 13th and 14th centuries, all in brickwork, with extremely tall single-mullioned windows along the sides and in the three apses.

Inside there is a fine organ, and an interesting, very large 15th-century fresco of St Christopher. The Onigo tomb is also of considerable interest, the sculpture being the work of Antonio Rizzo, the painted sections by Lorenzo Lotto.

The severely plain church of San Francesco is interesting from a literary point of view, for here are buried Francesca, daughter of the poet Petrarch, and Pietro, son of Dante Alighieri.

The gates of the city are beautiful, in particular that of San Tomaso.

Another interesting point of the city is the Peschiera, the little island which is the scene of a lively fish market; nearby is one of the old-time hostelries, La Colonna (in Piazza Rinaldo), where it is still possible to drink the rough local wine, Clinto, which is drunk from a cup without a handle, *not* a glass.

Trieste   G16

(pop. 282,776) Trieste is off the beaten track, but it is a delightful city, and during one's drive from Venezia (150km/93mi) it is worthwhile branching off at Cervignano to **Aquiléia** (see page 40).

From 1382 Trieste formed a part of Austria, returning to Italy only in 1954, and its way of life offers a mixture of Austrian and Italian customs. There is good bathing and pleasant walks in and around the city. The Arco di Riccardo dates back to the time of the Emperor Augustus. The cathedral (near the castle), an amalgamation of two 11th-century buildings – the Basilica dell'Assunta and the little church of San Giusto – is a fine example of Romanesque art, with 14th-century frescoes, a 9th-century font and a painting by Carpaccio. Other interesting churches are Santa Maria Maggiore and Sant'Antonio. The palaces of the *Commune* and the *Governo*, and the *Palazzo della Borsa* all merit a visit. A spacious square near the Stazione Marittima is the Piazza dell'Unita. On the left of this square is the Peschiera, with a fine aquarium. About 7km/4mi back along the coast is the beautifully situated castle **Miramare**, where there are *son et lumière* performances in summer. Try not to visit Trieste on a windy day, as the *bora*, from the mountains to the north, can be savage. *Údine 75km/46mi.*

Údine   E14

(pop. 100,770) This seat of a bishopric, also the capital of Friúli, is a peaceful city with many fine monuments. In olden days it was the capital of the patriarchy of Aquiléia and as such assumed great importance, until the subjugation by Venezia in 1420.

Gondolier

The Castello towers over the city on the remains of the earlier castle of the bishops of Aquiléia. At present it houses the local Galleria d'Arte Antica e d'Arte Moderna and the Museo Civico, with many fine exhibits.

The city centre is in the monumental Piazza della Libertà at the foot of the hill on which stands the castle. Surrounded by elegant buildings, it is strongly reminiscent of Venetian architecture, a remark which applies particularly to the Palazzo del Comune, known as the Loggia del Lionello, a fine building erected in the 15th century to the design of the architect Lionello.

The cathedral preserves part of its 14th-century Gothic Romanesque structure, but was modified in the 18th century. On the 1st altar to the right, and the 2nd and 4th on the same side, are fine altarpieces by Tiepolo.

Other frescoes by G. B. Tiepolo are to be found in the 18th-century Oratorio della Purità on the right of the cathedral.

An interesting excursion from Údine is to **Passariano** to visit the most splendid villa in all Friúli, the **Villa Manin**, which belonged to the last Doge of Venezia, Ludovico Manin, and where Napoleon stayed in 1797 for the period of the signing of the Peace of Campoformio, which marked the end of the Venetian Republic.

Venezia (Venice)   H11

(pop. 346,735) A city founded on fear. When the Huns of Attila came storming into northeastern Italy in the 5th century, many of the inhabitants fled to the lagoon for greater safety. Their first place of refuge was Torcello, where they established a thriving colony and built an imposing cathedral with wonderful mosaics and the octagonal church of Santa Fosca. Then came malaria, Torcello was deserted, and only the two churches, a handful of houses and now Cipriani's, the restaurant beloved of Hemingway, remain. The inhabitants moved to the Rialto district, and from that small nucleus Venezia grew into a powerful coastal city. Separated from the rest of Italy until the building of the causeway across which road and rail traffic now travel, it was very much a city apart, prosperous, independent, elegant, more than slightly eastern in some aspects. During the Middle Ages, indeed, Venezia was a bridge between east and west, and during the Crusades she established small marine colonies along the Dalmatian coast and even farther afield. The head of the city was the Doge; later came the Great Council who nominated a smaller Council of Ten which worked in secret. One of their organs was the group of three Inquisitors of the State, denunciation to whom could mean death. The yawning letter box into which secret denunciations were dropped can still be seen in the Palazzo Ducale (1). The might and power of the city declined after the discovery of America, but Venezia remained rich, colourful, gay, a city of extravagance of every kind.

The great houses along the Canal Grande, Ca' d'Oro (2), built in 1421 for the Contarini family, Ca' Rezzonico (3) where Robert Browning lived (now a fine museum), Palazzo Ducale (15th-century Gothic with a Renaissance courtyard by Rizzo), and other Renaissance buildings such as the Palazzo Vendramin (4), the churches of San Zaccaria (5) and San Michele in Isola, Sansovino's Palazzo Corner (6) and lovely *loggetta* of the Libreria di San Marco, all testify to the wealth and extravagant taste of the city. The Basilica di San Marco (7) holds a curious blend of Byzantine and Romanesque art. It became the treasure house of the city, as can be observed from its wonderful mosaics, the celebrated Pala d'Oro and the two twisted semi-transparent columns behind the Pala, which are said to have formed part of Solomon's Temple. The four bronze horses on the terrace above the façade of the basilica came from Constantinople, but some believe that they were originally part of the statuary group of which only the

Charioteer remains at Delphi in Greece. The spacious and elegant Piazza San Marco has been called 'the finest drawing-room in Europe'. The Torre dell'Orologio (8), the two Moors striking the hours, appears in many an 18th-century painting, but the bell-tower is a faithful copy of the original, which collapsed in 1902.

If one stands on the embankment in front of Piazza San Marco one's eye is caught by the splendidly ornate church of Santa Maria della Salute (9), on the opposite bank of the Canal Grande. This church, consecrated in 1687, was built to commemorate the end of a plague epidemic. During the *Festa della Salute* (21 Nov.), a bridge of boats is cast across the Canal Grande and worshippers walk back and forth to pay their respects to the Saint. Farther across the lagoon can be seen the austere beauty of the church of San Giorgio Maggiore (10), built by Palladio in the 16th century, and if one crosses to the island and proceeds back along the embankment one comes to another Palladian church, that of Il Redentore. On 16 July a bridge of boats is built from the Zattere embankment to this church. There are also colourful regattas at the end of June and early in September when the Canal Grande is cleared of traffic to make room for gondola races, with the crews in period costume.

Venezia's eastern connections are reflected in the floridity and richness of her painting. Canaletto and Guardi give one a faithful picture of what the city and its life were like in the 18th century but colours glow almost like mosaics in Titian's great series of paintings in the church of Santa Maria Gloriosa dei Frari (11), in the Accademia delle Belle Arti (12) and the Palazzo Ducale. Colours glow richly, too, in the Tintorettos in the Scuola di San Rocco (13), and what a mirror of 16th-century Venetian life are the splendid paintings of Paolo Veronese in the Accademia, in San Giorgio Maggiore, in the Anti-Collegio and the Sala del Collegio in the Palazzo Ducale. Among other treasures in the upper floors of Ca' Rezzonico is a series of charming paintings of Venetian 18th-century life by the younger Tiepolo.

Apart from the **Lido** – crowded but excellent beach, and one of Venezia's two casinos – visit the islands of **Murano** (the island of fire), and **Burano**. The former has a number of glass factories where one can see the molten glass blown and fashioned into intriguing shapes and where there is a fine 7th-century basilica with a precious mosaic pavement. The latter is famous for its lace. Another pleasant trip

is by boat to **Chioggia**, a picturesque fishing town. Buses leave from Piazzale Roma for **Padova** and **Stra**, one of the many lovely villas on the Brenta, set in a charming park, with twin spiral stairways leading to a belvedere overlooking the road, a maze and a lake.

Verona   H6

(pop. 232,280) This is not just an agricultural and industrial centre, but a city that has much to offer by way of art and architecture and cultural attractions. Driving from Vicenza to Verona one sees in the hills the two castles of Montecchio and Cappelletti, where, according to the legend, lived the families whose history gave rise to the story of Romeo and Juliet. In Verona one can visit Juliet's tomb, her balcony, Romeo's house; if one is fortunate enough to be in the city during July or August, one may very well see a performance of *Romeo and Juliet* in the huge Roman Theatre.

The River Adige describes a double loop in its passage through Verona, on one of which stands the impressive Castelvecchio (1354–75), now the home of the Museo Civico with a fine collection of paintings by Veronese, Tiepolo, Guardi, the Bellinis, Titian and other artists of the Veneto. From this castle the Ponte Scaligero crosses the river; it has been rebuilt in its original form, following its destruction in World War II. Nearby are the 16th-century Palazzo Canossa and the 12th-century church of San Lorenzo. In the Corso Cavour which runs northeast from the castle are the Palazzo Bevilacqua and the 1st-century Porta dei Borsari; nearby is the picturesque Piazza delle Erbe, with its market column and fountain, where sellers of fruit and vegetables protect their wares under huge, colourful umbrellas. Verona rose to great importance during the Middle Ages under the *Signoria* of the Scaligeri. Near Piazza delle Erbe in Piazza dei Signori are the impressive tombs of the Scaligeri, the Loggia del Consiglio, and a monument to Dante who dedicated *Il Paradiso* to the Scaligeri. Still in the same district are the 17th-century Palazzo Maffei and the Palazzo Emilei (now the home of the Galleria d'Arte Moderna and the Museo del Risorgimento), and the church of Sant'Anastasia with paintings by Mantegna and Pisanello and two interesting holy water stoups supported by dwarfs. The 12th-century Romanesque cathedral has a fine Titian. Across the river are two other churches, the 12th-century Santo Stefano, and the 15th-century San Giorgio in Braida, which contains paintings by Tintoretto and Veronese.

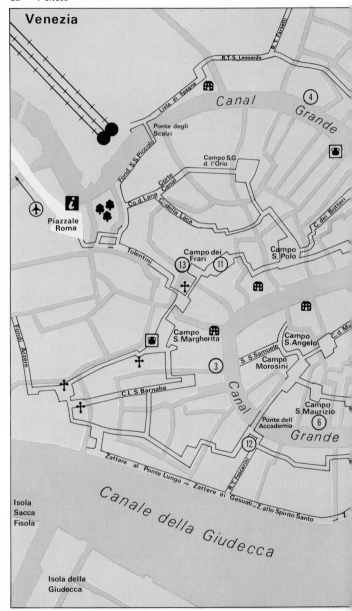

Venezia

R.T. Tassetti

R.T.S. Leonardo

Canal

Grande

④

Lista di Spagna

Fond. S.S. Piccolo

Ponte degli Scalzi

Campo S.G d. l'Orio

Corte Canal

Co. d Lana

C. della Laca

C. dei Botteri

Piazzale Roma

Tolentini

Campo dei Frari

Campo S. Polo

⑬ ⑪

Campo S.Margherita

Campo S.Angelo

C. d. Ma

S. S.Samuele

Campo Morosini

③

C.L.S.Barnaba

Fond. Arzere

Campo S.Maurizio

⑥

Ponte dell Accademia

Grande

⑫

Zattere al Ponte Lungo — Zattere ai Gesuati Z. allo Spirito Santo

R.T. Foscarini

Isola Sacca Fisola

Canale della Giudecca

Isola della Giudecca

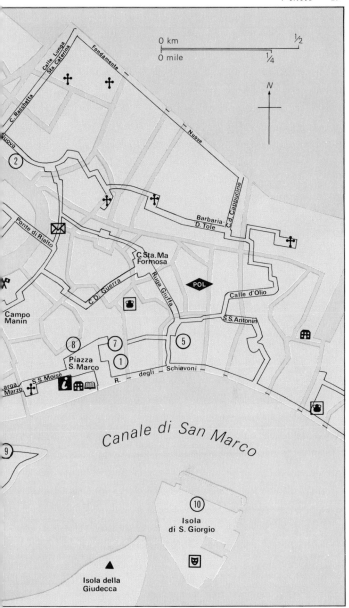

0 km ½
0 mile ¼

N

Calle Lunga
Sta Caterina

C. Racchetta

Fondamente

Nuove

C. d Cappucine

Nuova

②

Barbaria
D. Tole

Ponte di Rialto

C Sta. Ma
Formosa

POL

C. D. Guerra

Ruga Giuffa

Calle d'Olio

Campo
Manin

S.S. Antonin

⑧ ⑦ ⑤

Piazza
S. Marco ①

arga
Marzo S.S. Moisè

R. degli Schiavoni

Canale di San Marco

⑨

⑩

Isola
di S. Giorgio

▲

Isola della
Giudecca

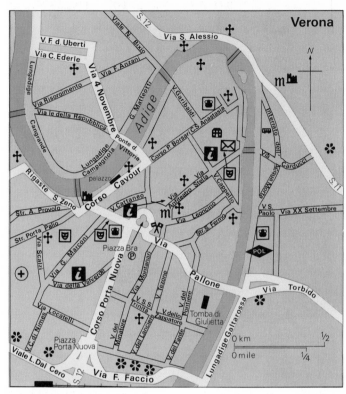

The church of San Zeno is a fairish walk from Piazza Bra along Via Roma and Rigaste San Zeno. This 12th-century Romanesque church has a delightful façade with bronze doors dating from 1100, illustrating in their many panels the Old and New Testaments and the story of the Patron Saint. Inside, the church has a wooden ceiling in the form of the reversed keel of a boat, and slender columns alternating with robust pilasters. There is a precious altarpiece by Mantegna and a charming statue of the smiling Saint 'Zeno.'

Vicenza   G8

(pop. 102,670) The two great architects of the late 16th and early 17th century in this part of Italy were Palladio and Scamozzi, and Vicenza has many examples of their work, the most famous being the Teatro Olimpico, said to have been the first covered theatre in Europe when it was built in 1580–82, and still used to this day. Its stage is a masterpiece of perspective. The Palazzo della Ragione (1549–1614), the Loggia del Capitano, the Palazzo Festa, the house of Palladio himself, the Palazzo Chiericati (1566), now the museum with some fine paintings, are only a few of the many lovely buildings to be seen in this city. On the outskirts are the Villa Valmarana, with a splendid series of frescoes by Tiepolo, and the Villa Rotonda (1570) begun by Palladio and finished by Scamozzi. The Basilica del Monte Berico stands high on a hill as one approaches the city from the south. In the church are a 15th-century statue of the Madonna and a *Pietà* (1500) by Montagna. *Padova 31km/19mi, Verona 51km/32mi.*

LIGURIA

Apart from the Valle d'Aosta, this is the smallest of the regions of Italy. It consists of an arc of mountains, the Maritime and Ligurian Alps, framing the bay of Génova (Genoa) and stretching from the mouth of the River Magra on the east to Cape Mortola on the west. The hills rise up sharply from the sea, leaving only a narrow coastal strip. Liguria is noted for its wonderful land- and sea-scapes, to which this sudden contrast of sea and mountain contributes.

The city of Génova forms a point of division between the two Rivieras, Levante and Ponente, and both together constitute one of the most popular tourist areas in Italy. All along this coast hotels proliferate and are mostly excellently equipped; there are also several good camping sites.

Vegetation is semitropical – mimosa blooms around Christmas-time, followed soon afterwards by bougainvillea; aloes line the coastal roads. From San Remo westward there is intensive cultivation of flowers, mainly carnations, which are sent to the markets of all Europe. Olives and vines grow well.

Génova is Italy's most active port for both passenger ships and freighters; La Spezia is one of Italy's two naval bases, the other being Táranto in Púglia.

The arc of mountains protects the coast from the bitter north winds and consequently winters are agreeably mild, another element which attracts visitors.

Fishing is carried on all along the coast, and excellent oysters, mussels and *datteri di mare* (similar to mussels) are to be had in the area around Portovénere.

There is considerable industry carried on in Liguria, particularly in large cities such as Génova, Savona and La Spezia.

Inhabited in ancient times by the Liguri, the region fell under Roman domination in the 1st century BC. The Longobards occupied it during the Middle Ages, followed by the Franks.

Ventimiglia near the French border and Luni near Sarzana possess the finest Roman remains in Liguria. Paleochristian art is manifest in the baptistery at Albenga.

Under feudalism, Liguria was split up into various counties and marches. It began to make itself felt as a sea power from the 11th century onwards, but it was not until the end of the 14th century that Génova gained control of the whole region. Wars ensued between Venezia and Génova for supremacy at sea, then later

the region became subject first to France and later to Spain. In 1528 the great Admiral Andrea Doria succeeded in re-establishing its independence.

Architecturally, the period which has left most examples is that of Romanesque-Gothic (11th to 14th centuries); then, towards the end of the 16th century, the influence of baroque is observed. Albenga, San Fruttuoso, Génova, Portofino and Lavagna are among the centres where examples of this style may be seen.

The early period of the Renaissance is exemplified in the work of sculptors such as Gaggini and Civitali, particularly in the chapel of San Giovanni in the cathedral of Génova.

In the 16th century Génova was in the vanguard of the world of art, and exercised considerable influence over the art and architecture of the rest of the region.

Under Napoleon, Liguria fell under French domination in 1805 but in 1814, after the Congress of Vienna, it was added to Piemonte.

It must not be forgotten that the discovery of America owed much to Christopher Columbus, born in Génova in 1451.

During the *Risorgimento*, two men who played leading parts, Mazzini and Garibaldi, were both Ligurians.

The region has always attracted many English and American visitors, among them the poet Shelley, who met his tragic death by drowning in the Bay of Spezia in the year 1822. Another was the late Ernest Hemingway, who spent much time in Alássio.

Festivals Good Friday, Savona – A solemn procession through the city in which huge groups of wooden sculpture exemplifying the Passion of Christ are borne through the streets. May (2nd Sunday), Camogli – The festival of fried fish; immense quantities of fish are caught and

then fried in *Il Padellone*, a huge frying pan, then distributed to the spectators. August, Alássio – This is the month of the *Muretto*, which is a wall faced with porcelain tiles bearing the signatures of illustrious visitors to the Café Roma; during August this *Muretto* is the scene of popular beauty contests.

Alássio   J3

(pop. 11,000) This resort has for years been beloved by English visitors, and combines excellent hotel accommodation and restaurants with an air of great elegance. It possesses a fine esplanade with splendid sands, lovely gardens, and from Alássio one can take walks around the richly cultivated hills that rise behind and around it. It attracts tourists of all types, not stopping short of 'jet set' millionaires.

During *Ferragosto* (the Italian mid-August holiday) it is the scene of numerous festivities, and for this period its local traffic police are supplanted by the most glamorous bathing girls who regulate traffic, duly equipped with helmets and batons.

The tower of Adelassia at **Vegliasco**, 4km/2½mi away, has an amusing legend attached to it. It takes its name from Adelassia, the charming, beautiful, but alas, greedy wife of Aleramo, the First Marquis of Monferrato.

This good lady, having betrayed her spouse, was imprisoned in the tower. Bored with her enforced confinement, she gave herself over to an over-indulgence in the pleasures of the table. One day came an opportunity to escape, and Adelassia decided to take advantage of it, but unfortunately, she had by this time become so fat from over-eating that she stuck in the doorway. Her husband took pity on her, and not only eased her out of the door, but took her back as his devoted wife, and also named after her the town we now recognize as Alássio.

True or false, if you look at the coat-of-arms of Alássio, you will observe the device of a tower with a barred door.

Among the more recent visitors to Alássio were the late Sir Winston Churchill and the late Ernest Hemingway. It was a favourite spot for the late Italian poet Eugenio Montale and still is for notabilities such as the actress Sophia Loren, among others.

Tiles reproducing the signature of such well-known people are set into a famous little wall in Alássio – the *Muretto*.

Festivals and sporting events proliferate here, and among the town's gastronomic delicacies are little pastries known as *baci* (kisses) of Alássio.

Albenga   I3

(pop. 16,000) Albenga is one of the many lovely seaside resorts fringing the coast of the Italian Riviera, a city with many facilities for the delight of tourists who want sea air, bathing and boating, but also an important agricultural centre for the surrounding fertile hills, rich in the cultivation of flowers and fruit which go to supply the markets of the north.

The little city had ancient roots, going back even before written history, into the era of mythology – it is said to have been founded by Albion, son of the sea-god Poseidon.

Back in the 6th century BC it was the capital of a tribe of navigators, the Liguri Ingauni, subdued only after a long and bloody war fought against them by the Roman Consul, L. Emilio Paolo, in the year 181 BC. First a Roman and later a Byzantine city, Albenga was destroyed in the 5th century AD by the barbarian hordes, and later rebuilt by the Longobards. In the 12th century it became an independent marine city and the seat of a bishopric, and its inhabitants sent war ships to take part in the Crusades. It had excellent commercial dealings with the Florentines, until Pisa became allied with Génova and Albenga was attacked and destroyed. Late in the 12th century we see Albenga under the domination of Génova. In 1863 it was incorporated in the province of Savona.

Not surprisingly, the historical centre of the city has a wealth of interesting monuments. The cathedral of San Michele dates back to the 5th century AD, as does the adjoining bell-tower. But even older are the Roman aqueduct and the remains of the Roman Amphitheatre. In the 5th-century baptistery are wonderful mosaics and the remains of a font in which baptism by total immersion was practised.

The Museo Navale Romano has a rich collection, including a considerable number of amphora, bronze helmets and other military equipment recovered from the bed of the sea by the ship *Artiglio* as recently as the year 1950. Divers still explore the waters offshore, hoping to recover further treasures.

There are numerous medieval houses still standing in the historical centre, and many lovely mansions.

Those who care to climb the tall, 14th-century tower of the Palazzo Vecchio del Comune will be repaid by the stupendous view from its summit.

The privately-owned island of **Gallinara**, 1500 metres offshore, can be visited by boat. Once the site of an early Benedictine monastery, only a single tower remains to mark the site. On the same island it is possible to visit the Grotto of St Martin, where the saint is said to have sought refuge from Arian persecution back in the 4th century, when he was Bishop of Tours.

The modern part of Albenga is well-equipped with tourist facilities, and altogether it is a town worth visiting.

Bordighera   K1

(pop. 10,949) Celebrated even on the Riviera for the mildness of its climate, for its lovely and abundant Mediterranean vegetation, for its palms. The palm leaves which are blessed in San Pietro in Vaticano on Palm Sunday come from Bordighera. And there is a reason for this 'concession'. In the days of Pope Sixtus V, in the year 1586, the great obelisk was being raised in Piazza San Pietro in Roma, when the ropes heated from friction and seemed about to burst into flame. It was a man from Bordighera, a certain Bresca, who saved the situation by shouting *Acqua alle corde* ('throw water on the ropes'). In gratitude the Pope granted to him and his family in perpetuity the privilege of supplying these emblems of Palm Sunday.

The old city, high above the sea, dominates the bay of Ospedaletti on the one side, while on the other the view extends almost to Monte Carlo.

Coming down to modern Bordighera from this old part of the town one sees the tiny church of Sant'Ampeglia, built over the cave in which the saint once lived. The church is at the beginning of the modern town itself, which is reached along a lovely esplanade stretching far beyond the centre of Bordighera almost to **Vallecrosia**, where, incidentally, there is a delightful Flower Show around the beginning of the year.

Many famous people have lived in Bordighera. One can still see the villa of Queen Margaret of Savoy, to whom a monument has been erected; another interesting villa is that of Garnier, architect of the Opera House in Paris and the Casino of Monte Carlo. Walking towards Ospedaletti, one passes the little house where Katherine Mansfield lived. Bordighera has all the usual Riviera facilities. *Monte Carlo 25km/16mi, San Remo 17km/11mi.*

Camogli   H7

(pop. 9000) Camogli is justly regarded as one of the pearls of the Ligurian coast. Situated in the curve of an enchanting bay, it has a tradition as a fishing centre that goes back to the Middle Ages. The houses here seem to rise sheer out of the water; olives and citrus fruits flourish.

It is said that the mariners of Camogli taught the art of sailing to the whole of Europe. Be that as it may, King Louis Philippe hired the fleet of Camogli when he proceeded to conquer Algiers. Not much more than a hundred years ago, the sailing fleet of this little town was larger than that of Hamburg. Then came the employment of steam-powered vessels and the importance of Camogli declined, so that the medieval city, with its charming little port and its 17th-century quay, is now just a fishing village, though an important one.

In spite of its decline, Camogli boasts the most important Nautical Institute in Italy, the Cristoforo Colombo.

Picturesque and other-worldly, Camogli is a delightful holiday centre. It has several hotels of various grades, and some excellent little restaurants where freshly-caught fish can be enjoyed. It offers opportunities for many pleasant walks, strenuous or not-so-strenuous, to nearby **Portofino, San Fruttuoso** and **Punta Chiappa**.

Chiávari   H7

(pop. 24,000) Chiávari lies across the pleasant River Entella from the popular seaside resort of Lavagna, and is on the direct railway line between Génova and La Spezia. It is a city of considerable culture, a fact that is suggested as soon as one approaches it by its neatly arranged, tidy streets, the flower beds bordering its wide avenues.

Behind it rise slopes where luxurious orchards vie with acres of hothouses for pride of place.

Chiávari has a long tradition of wealth and prosperity. Many of its families can trace the source of their fortune to dealings with South America, with which the town has had close links in the past. It was a Chiávari family who built the railways of Peru. In the museum in Chiávari can be seen a collection of priceless relics of Inca civilization, for it was that same family who, during the last century, instigated investigations into the origins of that far-off civilization.

Chiávari was the birthplace of the fathers of two great Italians, Mazzini and Garibaldi.

Through the centuries the town has given great encouragement to art and literature. In 1791 was founded the Economic Society, the aims of which were the promotion of industry, agriculture and knowledge. Every two years there is an Industries Fair.

Furniture-making is the principal industry, and a close second is slate carving.

Walking around this elegant little town,

one gets an impression of the character of its inhabitants, industrious, elegant and interested in the aesthetic things of life.

The Citadel, behind which lies the old town distinguished by its narrow arcaded streets, was built in the 13th century. In the square in front is a monument in memory of Mazzini, and if we go along the arcaded Via Vittorio Emanuele II as far as Piazza XX Settembre, we find one erected in memory of Garibaldi.

The cathedral, originally built in 1613, has a neoclassic façade in imitation of the Pantheon in Roma. In the parish church of San Giovanni Battista are interesting frescoes by the Carlone family, Coppola and Pinelli.

Accommodation is good in Chiávari, and there are numerous restaurants where one eats well. It is not, however, a town where one can expect to spend an inexpensive holiday.

Génova (Genoa)   H6

(pop. 819,500) Génova, the great port of Italy, and an important industrial and commercial centre, is the scene of many trade fairs. In October is held the Nicolò Paganini Violin Competition, for the celebrated violinist (1784–1840) was a native of the city and his violin is preserved in the Palazzo Doria Tursi. Génova is best approached by sea, for it occupies a delightful position on the Golfo di Génova and is within easy reach of the many charming resorts of the Riviera.

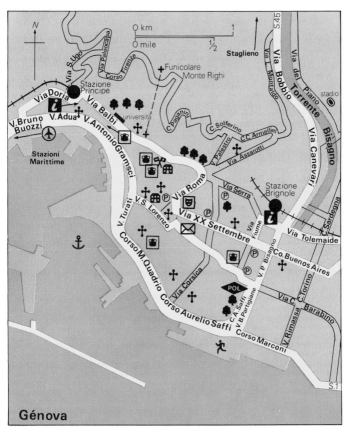

Génova

In Roman days it was a flourishing municipality, and it has continued to grow in importance through the centuries. During the Crusades its power expanded throughout the Mediterranean; it became a free *comune*, then a marine republic until 1805 when it was annexed by France. Ten years later, under the Treaty of Vienna, it became part of the Kingdom of Sardegna. It was the home of Christopher Columbus who is honoured by a striking monument in a square near the main railway station. Off Via Corsica is the church of Santa Maria Assunta in Carignano, from whose dome one has a splendid panoramic view over the city and its surroundings. Two of the great figures of the *Risorgimento* – Mazzini, who was born in Génova in 1805, and Garibaldi, who set forth for Sicilia with 1000 Redshirts in 1860, an expedition which was to lead to the conquest of Nápoli and the south – testify to the independent spirit of the city.

The older part of Génova, west of the central Piazza de Ferrari (junction of Via Roma and Via XX Settembre), dates back to the Middle Ages. Here is the cathedral of San Lorenzo, consecrated in 1118, with three impressive Gothic doors. Here, too, are the churches of San Donato, of Santo Stefano where Columbus was baptized, San Matteo and Sant'Agostino, and the mansions of the famous mercantile families of the Middle Ages, the Doria, the Spinola and the Grimaldi, many constructed in the black and white marble typical of Genoese architecture. In the newer part, slightly farther north, are impressive Renaissance palaces such as the Palazzo Doria Tursi now the seat of the *comune* of Génova, the Palazzo Bianco (1565) and the Palazzo Rosso (1677), both now picture galleries with splendid collections of paintings by Veronese, Rubens, Dürer, Teniers and Caravaggio.

Local specialities include *trenette col pesto* (sphaghetti served with a sauce that includes garlic, basil, Sardinian cheese and olive oil), exquisite candied fruit and a rich, fruity bread (*pan dolce*). Information offices at main station and 11/14 Via Roma.

One visit that is essential is to the impressive cemetery of **Staglieno**, easily reached by local transport, and lying on a hillside with a charming view. The statuary in this vast cemetery is stupendous, and among the interesting tombs is that of Mazzini. Another fine view is from **Monte Righi** (cable railway), from which one can also see the system of defensive forts on the surrounding hills. *La Spezia 112km/70mi, Savona 46km/28mi.*

Impéria   J3

(pop. 36,500) This city, with nearby **Oneglia**, is yet another city of the Italian Riviera that merits a visit. The two centres are linked by the extremely panoramic Corso Matteotti. The River Impero which divides them gave its name to the present city.

San Maurizio, slightly to the west, knew its moment of fame under the Benedictines in the 10th century. It has the characteristics of many of the primitive Ligurian towns and is presided over by an ancient castle.

The famous Admiral Andrea Doria was born here in Oneglia in the year 1466, as was Edmondo de Amicis (1848–1909) the author of *Cuore (The Heart)* a story beloved by Italians who were children in the early part of this century.

The walk up the slope from the village of San Maurizio to its neoclassic cathedral is rewarding for the number of splendid views one can see en route.

The idea of uniting San Maurizio and Oneglia to form the present Impéria came from Mussolini, but the name, as mentioned earlier, came from that of the river.

Not only is Impéria the chief town of the rich district surrounding it, it is said to be the chief producer of the spaghetti so beloved of Italians.

Like most towns along this coast, Impéria is well equipped to provide for tourists, and also offers camping facilities.

La Spezia   I9

(pop. 125,925) La Spezia lies on a lovely bay, backed by hills, with excellent communications by road, rail and sea. It offers a particularly pleasant climate, plus delightful scenery. The city stretches along the sea with lovely gardens, rich in palm trees, pines and plants of many kinds. It also has a busy mercantile port and is a naval base. The city was founded in the 12th century and has an interesting cathedral, with a splendid terracotta by Andrea della Robbia; there is a fine library with an excellent collection of illuminated manuscripts. La Spezia is a good centre for walks into the hills or to the remote villages of the Cinqueterre. One worthwhile excursion is to **Lérici** along the coast for memories of the poet Shelley. *Génova 112km/70mi.*

Lavagna   H8

(pop. 11,000) Lavagna, lying almost midway between Génova and La Spezia, is fortunate in possessing a long stretch of sandy beach, which for many years has attracted visitors. Recently it has enlarged considerably its port facilities for private yachts, and seems bent on attracting even more holiday-makers.

It is well equipped to deal with tourists,

and in addition to a number of good hotels has camping facilities.

Lavagna has the added advantage of being easily accessible by road or rail from Génova. It is within easy walking distance of the next town, Chiávari, and behind Lavagna rise hills dotted with small, picturesque settlements. One very rewarding walk is up to the little village of **Cogorno**, the centre of the slate-quarrying industries from which Lavagna takes its name, *lavagna* being Italian for blackboard and, as we know, all the best blackboards used to be made of slate.

From the town below one can see the very interesting little church of Cogorno, that of San Salvatore, Romanesque and interesting to visit.

In the town itself stands a really imposing church of the 18th century, with twin bell-towers and an elaborate double flight of steps typical of the somewhat pretentious architecture of the period.

The old part of Lavagna offers many a pleasant stroll.

If you are in Lavagna on 14 August you will be able to enjoy the festival of the *Torta Fieschi*, which ends in a splendid parade and the distribution to all around of slices from an immense cake said to weigh 15 quintals (well over a tonne). One wonders where such a cake might be baked.

Le Cinque Terre
(The Five Lands) I8

Between Portovénere at the western extremity of the bay of Spezia, and the seaside towns of Sestri Levante, Lavagna and the city of Chiávari, nestle the five little fishing villages of Monterosso, Riomaggiore, Vernazza, Corniglia and Manarola.

Until very recent years the only means of approach to these enchanting little spots was by sea, train, or very cautiously along an extremely poor road. Gradually things are improving for travellers by car, and alas, one can see the day coming when these may have developed into just five more of the many tourist resorts of Italy.

The villages are dotted along about 15km/9mi of rugged, rockily coastline, so steep that even the birds seem to find difficulty in flying over the towering cliffs. Barren in appearance, these rocky steeps are terraced in vineyards and the light wine of Le Cinque Terre has been highly esteemed through the centuries; even Boccaccio, in the 14th century, praised it in his lyrics. Often, when it is time to harvest the grapes, it is necessary for the harvesters to be let down the cliff-side on ropes. Wine and fishing constitute the means of livelihood here.

Now and again one comes across streets so steep as to be interspersed with flights of steps. In the microscopic squares in the centre of each little town, women sit outside their rough medieval cottages, their lives punctuated by the comings and goings of the fishing fleets.

Monterosso is the largest and the one that, in addition to the old medieval houses high above the level of the sea, has some attractive modern dwellings on the shore. On a neighbouring hill stands an ancient Capuchin monastery; there is a 13th-century black and white church, there are the remains of a 16th-century fortress, a splendid view, and nothing more, save for a beauty of atmosphere rarely encountered in modern times.

Monterosso was the birthplace of the late poet, Eugenio Montale.

Next comes **Vernazza** with 2000 inhabitants, rugged and medieval with no concessions to modernity. Until it was destroyed during World War II, there used to be a medieval castle; now only a couple of fortresses remain, high on the cliffs above. Here, too, there is a Capuchin monastery, and westward of it, a 14th-century dark stone church.

Corniglia, with its fine Romanesque church, stands perched on a plateau, the sides of which rise sheer from the sea; this is the only one of Le Cinque Terre not actually washed by the waters of the sea.

Hotels are lacking, but nearby there is a tourist village of about 30 pre-fabricated bungalows, with a restaurant.

Manarola, with only 900 inhabitants, consists of a handful of dark little cottages perched on a cliff of dizzy height. If you live in Manarola, your only means of contact with the less-secluded world is along a little cliff path, *Via d'Amore*, leading down to **Riomaggiore** (3000 inhabitants), which is built around the mouth of a mountain torrent that rushes into the sea at this point. Houses rise in tiers on either side of the main – and only – street, and on the heights above are the ruins of a 14th-century castle, now transformed into what can only be termed a 'filing cabinet' cemetery, where the graves rise one above another.

There are no big hotels, no smart restaurants in Le Cinque Terre, but at least you will find one or two small eating-houses where a risotto of seafood, or *gamberoni* (larger than the largest Dublin Bay prawns or scampi) are excellent, washed down with some of the local wine. This makes an excellent finish to a day spent in something like fairyland.

Lérici I9

(pop. 13,600) This little town has particular associations for English visitors, for it was near here that the poet Shelley lived in 1822, the year of his death. It was on the beach at Lérici that his body was washed ashore a few days after his boat had overturned during a squall in the Bay of Spezia, and here on the beach was held the ceremony of his cremation, in the presence of his friends the poet Byron and the novelist Trelawny.

Lérici today is a popular seaside resort, well equipped with hotels and restaurants, and with good bathing facilities.

The town is dominated by the huge pentagonal castle of the 13th century, and the beach below is noted for its ivory-white fine sand.

Legend has it that one of the houses in Piazza Garibaldi is haunted by unquiet spirits from the past; as hauntings are not frequent in Italy, this is a novelty.

The hills surrounding Lérici are dotted with elegant villas. Nearby are less well-known beaches such as **Fiascherine** (3km/2mi) and **Tellaro** (4½km/3mi), which is picturesque with its church rising on a tall cliff that dominates the little seashore village.

Another interesting excursion is to *Sarzana*, 11km/7mi away, from which it is a short distance to the remains of the Roman city of **Luni** (see SARZANA).

Portofino   H7
(pop. 1035) Portofino, lying on a promontory jutting out into the Golfo di Génova, is not only beautiful but has an agreeably mild climate throughout the year. There is a small natural harbour with a colourful little square, and on each side gaily tinted old houses. There are delightful walks as far as **Punta del Faro** and excursions to **Portofino Vetta** (possibly the finest viewpoint of all Liguria) and boat trips to the enchanting village of **San Fruttuoso**.

Accommodation is varied but good. A development of modern hotels and villas has been proposed for Portofino, but at the time of writing this has not been implemented. Hopefully, Portofino will remain as charming and unspoiled as it is today.

Portovénere   I9
(pop. 5300) On the western edge of the Bay of Spezia and about 13km/8mi from that city lies the interesting seaside town of Portovénere. Its origin goes back many centuries; not surprisingly it was once a favourite haunt of pirates; today its main industry is fishing.

Its ancient buildings are sited in a picturesque position on the high cliff at the far end of the town, where stands the church of San Pietro, dating back to the 13th century, behind which is a tiny inlet with the Grotto Arpaia, known locally as Byron's Cave, from which it is said the poet used to bathe.

The whole town is inviting, with its tall, multi-coloured houses around the little port.

It is possible from Portovénere to take boat trips to the nearby islands of **Palmária**, **Tino** and **Tinetto**, and further to **Le Cinque Terre**. The scenery that unfolds before one's eyes as the boat churns onward is charming; rocky vine-clad slopes rise out of the water, and it is not unusual for passengers to be entertained by the frolics of a passing shoal of dolphins.

The local food is appetizing and interesting; try, for example, the famous 'Sea Date Soup' – you won't regret your choice.

Rapallo   H7
(pop. 20,000) Rapallo is beautifully situated. An enchanting little port, delightful walks in the town and in the surrounding hills, and all the good organization necessary to make a seaside holiday a joy, account for its popularity. The Collegiata dei Santi Gervasio e Protasio with an interesting bell-tower, and the 16th-century church of San Francesco in which are paintings by Borzone, an artist of the district, and a picturesque 17th-century castle, enhance its attractions. Among excursions is a visit to the **Sanctuary of Montallegro**, by road or by cable railway; another to the picturesque bay of **San Michele di Pagana** where, in the parish church, is a painting by Van Dyck. *Génova 33km/20mi*.

Portofino

San Remo   J2

pop. 60,000) San Remo, capital of the
Riviera of Flowers, is one of the most
famous tourist resorts of Europe, with
over 200 hotels and pensions, more
lovely villas and delightful walks. Just
outside the city is the Pian di Poma, where
every year there are international shooting
competitions; on the left is the road leading to the racecourse; then comes the
famous promenade round the north of the
city, presenting panoramas of great
beauty, and passing through parks and
gardens. In the 15th-century sanctuary of
the Madonna della Costa are paintings by
Fiasella and sculpture by Maragliano, and
the old town is a web of narrow streets full
of interest. The other great promenade is
that of the Empress, along the sea front,
flanked by giant palms. Here is the Rus-
sian church, recognizable by its dome and
its gilded cross. There are elegant shops,
and many interesting buildings to be
visited.

From the centre of the city a cable
railway leaves for **Monte Bignone**,
crossing the only 18-hole golf course in
Liguria. *Ventimiglia 17km/10mi.*

Sarzana   I10

pop. 17,000) Going inland, at a distance
of 7km/4mi from Lérici lies the interesting city of Sarzana, rich in fascinating
buildings such as the *pieve* (parish church)
of Sant'Andrea, mentioned in history as
far back as the 12th century, the medieval
fortress of a famous soldier of fortune,
Castruccio Castracani, the 15th-century
cathedral and the church of San
Francesco.

There is a tradition in Sarzana that
during religious processions the figure of
Christ is borne facing backwards, which
has given rise to a not very complimentary
rhyme on the part of those who dwell in
the nearby section of Falcinello, to the
effect that the inhabitants of Sarzana can
have no fear of God since they carry his
image backwards in processions.

Tradition apart, Sarzana offers other
interests; it is an important commercial
centre, and every year holds an exhibition
of small antiques.

Nearby can be seen the ruins of the
ancient Roman city of **Luni**.

Those who have visited Lucca will
probably have seen there in the cathedral
the very ancient wooden statue of Christ,
which is carried through the streets every
year on the occasion of the festival of the
Volto Santo (Holy Face). It was the old
city of Luni that set up a counter claim for
possession of this image when it was first
observed floating in the sea, and the choice
of Lucca as its eventual resting place was

determined by placing the statue on a cart
drawn by a team of oxen, and leaving to
the beasts themselves the choice between
Luni and Lucca – as we know, Lucca was
the favoured city.

Ventimiglia   K1

(pop. 23,000) Here we have the gateway to
France and many of the advantages (and
disadvantages) of a frontier town, the
Customs offices, to mention but one.

Buses ply through Ventimiglia on their
twice- or thrice-daily journey to Monte
Carlo and Nice; the route is along the
coastal road and reveals lovely panoramas
with every turn.

We are on the Floral Coast, and the
hillsides are lined with greenhouses in
which grow the carnations and other
lovely flowers which go to enrich the
markets of northern cities. The Flower
Market in Ventimiglia is universally well-
known; the 'Battle of the Flowers' that
takes place each year on the second Sunday in June is colourful and exciting.

The wide mouth of the River Roja
divides the newer part of the city from the
old, perched on a hillside and reached
across a bridge. At the mouth of the
Nervia, the city's other river, is the well-
preserved Roman theatre dating back to
the 2nd century AD.

In the village of **Mortola** (300 inhabitants), just before one reaches the French
border, is the once-famous Giardino Han-
bury (garden), at one time among the
loveliest in Europe. Reduced to a ghost of
its former splendour, it still repays a visit.
In the grounds can be seen a stone plaque
bearing Dante Alighieri's words (true to
this day) about the stretch of the old
Aurelian Way that borders part of the
garden, and the steep course it follows.

Down at sea level are what are known
locally as *I Balzi Rossi*, a sinister group of
nine caves in which have been found
Paleolithic remains, animal bones of the
Neanderthal epoch and statuettes thought
to have been the work of men of the Cro-
Magnon era.

Ventimiglia has many attractions for
the holidaymaker, and is also a good
starting-point for various interesting
excursions. It has numerous good hotels
and some excellent restaurants.

EMÍLIA-ROMAGNA

These two territories, always associated, form one of the largest regions in Italy, bordered on the north by the River Po, on the east by the Adriatic, on the south and west by the Apennines. The Roman-constructed Via Emilia, running north-west from Rimini through Forli, Faenza, Bologna, Modena, Réggio nell'Emília and Parma to Piacenza, divides the region neatly into plainland to the northeast, mountains to the southwest. On the plain lie Ferrara, Ravenna and the reclaimed marshes and wet valleys culminating in the low-lying city of Comácchio.

In one of the rich, green valleys of the Parma Apennines are the much-frequented thermal spas of Salsomaggiore and Tabiano whose various mineral waters are effective in the treatment of arthritis, bronchitis and other ills. Not far away is the hill town of Castell'Arquato, a charming medieval enclave in the modern world.

From Comácchio to Rímini seaside resorts follow one another so closely as to seem one uninterrupted stretch of fine sand, offering excellent bathing and hotel accommodation to suit all pockets. Between Ravenna and the coast is one of the best-known pinewoods of coastal Italy, much visited by holiday-makers.

Agriculturally this is a wealthy region. The high mountains are given over largely to forestry and pasturage; from the vines cultivated at a lower level come the pleasant wines of Lambrusco, Sangiovene and others. Tomatoes grow here in ever greater quantity than in the south. The plain produces wheat, hemp, sugar-beet and fruit, especially the cherries of Vignola. Large numbers of pigs and cattle are raised, giving rise to the dairy and delicatessen products for which Emília-Romagna is noted. This is a region where it is considered no sin to 'live to eat'!

The area is rich in methane and there are also deposits of oil.

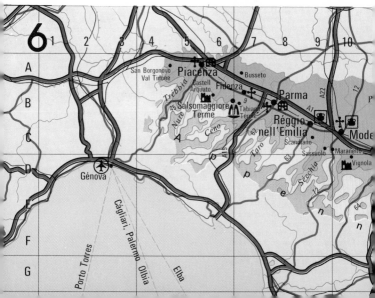

The Ferrari and Maserati luxury cars are built at Maranello near Modena. Ravenna, apart from its history and mosaics, is well known for the production of synthetic rubber; Faenza and Imola for ceramics, and in particular the true faience. Parma is noted not only for its splendid cheese and ham, but also for the perfume of Parma violets, still produced in large quantities.

In Emilia Romagna the march of history is signalized by many monuments.

The Museo Archeologico Nazionale de Spina (on the main floor of the Palazzo di Ludovico il Moro) in Ferrara houses a valuable collection of treasures from Spina, one of the necropolises of the Etruscans who dominated and brought prosperity to the region from the 6th to the 4th century BC.

The end of the second Punic War saw the arrival of the Romans who, among other achievements, built the Via Emilia and left conspicuous monuments, such as the Arco d'Augusto and the Ponte d'Augusto in Rimini.

Under the Romans Ravenna became an important city; then followed periods under the Ostrogoths and the Byzantines, after which Ravenna sank more or less into obscurity.

Following the Longobard and Frank invasions, the rest of the region was under episcopal domination until the 12th century and the epoch of the prosperous free comunes. Early in the 13th century the University of Bologna was officially founded. Now came the building of the great cathedrals of Modena, Parma, Fidenza, Piacenza, Ferrara and the Abbey of Pomposa, linked with such names as Lanfranc and Wiligelmo in Modena, Antelami in Parma. To this period belongs the Castello Estense in Ferrara. Examples of the Gothic that followed are to be seen in the Palazzo del Comune in Piacenza, the church of San Petronio in Bologna.

By the 14th century the comunes had given place to the signorias, the overlordship of great families, the Este in Ferrara, Modena, Réggio nell'Emilia, the Malatesta in Rimini, the Farnese in Parma and Piacenza, the Bentivoglio in Bologna, until the second half of the 16th century the region was divided up into three great states, the Farnese, the Este and the Church. In this period of Renaissance splendour Leon Battista Alberti designed the Tempio Malatestiano (see page 68) in Rimini; Rossetti the Palazzo di Schifanoia, the Palazzo dei Diamanti and the Palazzo di Ludovico il Moro in Ferrara, and Giambologna designed the statue of Neptune one admires in the centre of Bologna.

In more recent days came the Napoleonic campaign, and on his defeat Parma and Piacenza were ceded to his widow, Maria Luigia, who in her 32 years as Grand Duchess of Parma did much for

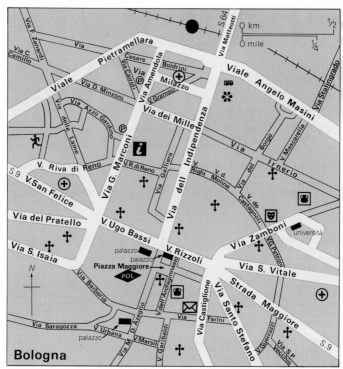

Bologna

that city, including the building of the Teatro Regio, still regarded as a testing-ground for opera singers the world over.

Emilia-Romagna has produced many great figures. The end of the 14th century saw Bologna and Ferrara vying with each other in the world of art. In the former the influence of the brothers Caracci was great on painters such as Guido Reni, Guercino and others; Costa left evidence of his talent in the frescoes decorating the Palazzo di Schifanoia in Ferrara. Correggio and Parmigianino both worked in Parma. In our own days, Minguzzi, sculptor of the last of the bronze doors of San Pietro in Vaticano in Roma, was born in Imola.

Verdi was a native of Busseto, near Parma; Toscanini is another whose name is linked with that city. Marconi was born near Bologna in 1874.

The Italian poets Ariosto and Tasso spent much of their time at the court of the Este in Ferrara, Carducci and Pascoli in turn held the Chair of Literature at Bologna University.

These are but a few of the men and monuments whose names have brought honour to this region.

Festivals Last Sunday in June, Faenza – *Festa del Niballo* – a tournament of 'knights' who attack the image of the Saracen, which is later burnt.

Cesena (no set date) banquets in honour of *Il Passatore* (The Ferryman) who used to rob the rich to aid the poor.

Bologna   D11

(pop. 441,145) This Etruscan and subsequently Roman city has long been one of the most important towns of northern Italy. During the Middle Ages it was a thriving *comune*, memories of which linger in two of its great buildings, the Palazzo del Podesta and the Palazzo Comunale, which now houses an interesting collection of pictures. Early in the 13th century the University of Bologna, the oldest in Europe, was officially established; Bologna had been recognized as an important seat of learning for a considerable time prior to this.

There is an air of prosperous efficiency about Bologna, the gastronomic capital of Italy. Strings of sausages – *mortadella*, *salami* and a thousand others – cheeses of a variety that beats description, tempt one into the numerous delicatessen shops. As one walks through the porticoed streets one gazes in amazement at delicacies being consumed to the accompaniment of coffee or an apéritif: a simple *granita* (frozen black coffee, chipped, piled into a dish and topped with thick whipped cream) becomes a dish for the gods in Bologna.

Architecturally the city has much to offer. Two leaning towers in the Piazza di Porta Ravegnana (junction of Via Rizzoli and Via Zamboni) make a useful focal point. Nearby is the Gothic church of San Petronio, facing the Piazza Maggiore and Piazza Nettuno. Michelangelo worked on a bronze statue of Pope Julius II for this church, but this was unfortunately destroyed. In one of the chapels off the north aisle is a modern statue by Manzù which is well worth pausing to admire, and on the pilasters of the main door are some interesting reliefs by Jacopo della Quercia. Also near the towers is the Palazzo della Mercanzia, a building of the late 14th century, and three tiny churches, all that remain of the former group of seven known as the Basilica di Santo Stefano in Via Santo Stefano. The Pinacoteca (Picture Gallery) near the university has a fine collection of paintings by Titian, Tintoretto, Giotto, Raphael and others, and the city also contains several interesting churches.

Castell'Arquato   B6

(pop. about 6000) A turning off the motor road leading from Piacenza to Fidenza brings us to a little hill town that is extremely interesting from an architectural point of view, and very panoramic.

It goes back to the 8th century AD, but its special interest lies in the tiny square and the buildings around it, the *collegiata* (collegiate church), an early Romanesque fabric of the beginning of the 12th century, with interesting frescoes of the 15th and 17th century and a 14th century cloister which houses a fine collection of paintings and embroidery. There is a town hall of the late 13th century and the Visconti stronghold of the 14th century – nothing more, but all arranged around the square in such a way as to offer architectural perfection, and when one has enjoyed this and the view to the full, there is a welcoming little bar where one may stop before going down the hill once again to more level ground.

Cattólica   F16

(pop. 12,000) This is a busy commercial and fishing centre but also, thanks to its position along the sandy shores of the Adriatic, it is a thriving and well-equipped holiday resort. It stands on a charming bay, surrounded by hills.

The beach of clean velvet-smooth sand is 3km/2mi in length and slopes gently into the sea. During the season, which extends from April to October, there are numerous entertainments, cultural, artistic and sporting.

Excellently served by road and rail, one is within easy distance of the mountain republic of **San Marino**, and of two other hill towns, Gradara with its legendary castle in which was enacted the tragic love story of Paolo and Francesca, and San Leo, the impregnable fortress where for a time the arch-imposter, Cagliostro, was imprisoned.

Among the many entertainments Cattólica provides for visitors is the Sea Carnival held on 15 August of every year, which attracts visitors from far and wide.

Cérvia   D15

(pop. 20,000) This has been a popular resort since it was founded in the 17th century. It has an excellent climate, a fine beach and pinewoods, and is well equipped with hotels and holiday attractions.

The town itself is interesting; the cathedral and the Bishop's Palace merit a visit. A pretty little canal runs through the town, and one can, if one wishes, be ferried across this.

There are many pleasant walks around Cérvia, and altogether it is an agreeable place for a holiday.

Cesenático   E15

(pop. 16,000) This is another of the many popular seaside resorts along the Adriatic coastline. It lies midway between Rimini and Ravenna, road and rail services are excellent, and the town is well equipped with hotels and diversions for holiday-makers.

Back in the 14th century, Cesenático was the port for the city of Cesena.

It is possible to take interesting walks in the area and among the attractions held out to tourists are pigeon-shooting, mini-golf, fishing and, naturally, sea-bathing.

Cesena   E14

(pop. 86,000) This busy commercial centre situated in the heart of Romagna is the seat of a bishopric, and during the 15th century was the seat of the *signoria* of the Malatesta family.

One of the most interesting buildings is the Biblioteca Malatestiana, the oldest and best preserved of all the convent libraries of the era of Humanism. It was erected thanks to the munificence of Novello Malatesta in the convent of the Franciscans in 1451; as a building it is of great interest, its contents, moreover, are even more worthy of a visit from all who love books, illuminated manuscripts and the like.

The Malatestian stronghold, Rocca Malatestiana, can be reached via the picturesque Piazza del Popolo, and is a fine example of a 15th-century fortified dwelling.

Comácchio   B14

(pop. 16,883) This interesting little town is built on a group of 13 islands intersected by canals and bridges. A peculiarity is the 16th-century *treponti*, a construction of five flights of steps forming an arch over the intersection of various canals.

There is an interesting 17th-century cathedral, with an uncompleted baroque bell-tower.

The town is a centre of eel-fishing, which is carried on in the hinterland of salt marshes.

Not more than 6km/4mi away is the necropolis of **Spina**, a city first of all Pelasgic, then Etruscan and finally Roman, before it became buried by the silting up of the marshes. Excavations, begun in 1922 and still going on, have revealed several thousand tombs from the 6th to the 4th century BC, and in the Museo Archeologico in Ferrara it is possible to see numerous vases and other treasures brought to light during these excavations.

Comácchio is very near the stretch of coast known as the Lido di Ferrara, 20km/12mi east and north of the Valli di Comácchio and lying partly in luxuriant pinewoods. Of fairly recent formation the seven lidos (**Lido di Spina, Lido degli Estensi** (the best-equipped), **Porto Garibaldi, Lido degli Scacchi, Lido di Pomposa, Lido delle Nazioni** and **Lido di Volano**) offer possibilities for a delightful seaside holiday within easy reach of such interesting places as **Ravenna** and **Ferrara** and the **abbey of Pomposa** (see FERRARA).

Faenza   D13

(pop. 50,830) This is a place that should be visited by anyone interested in ceramics, for this is the city once so famous for its majolica that it gave its name to the faience so particularly sought after and highly valued in the 15th and 16th centuries. The industry is still kept alive, thanks to able craftsmen and the activities of the Museo Internazionale delle Ceramiche (Ceramic Museum), and other interested organizations. Faenza is still of great importance in the world of ceramics and is the seat of the annual International Show of Ceramics of Contemporary Art, with an annual competition open from the end of July to the end of September.

The Renaissance cathedral (1474–early 16th century) was designed by Giuliano da Maiano.

In the Pinacoteca are paintings by artists of Romagna from the 14th to 17th century; there is also a fine wooden statue of San Girolamo by Donatello and a marble bust of San Giovannino by A. Rossellino.

Ferrara   B12

(pop. 153,393) This is an industrial city in the Po valley, but it is also a city with strong literary associations. Founded by the Romans, the city became a Longobard duchy after the Longobards invaded northern Italy. It was subsequently part of the Church State, then, in the 13th century it became the seat of the great Este family, who established an influential court in the huge moated castle that still dominates the city. Ludovico Ariosto (1474–1533) was at one time secretary to Cardinal Ippolito d'Este, but the Cardinal travelled far too much for his secretary's liking, and he eventually returned to Ferrara, bought a modest house, which can still be visited, and there wrote one of Italy's great works of literature, *Orlando Furioso*. A generation or so later, Torquato Tasso, the author of *Jerusalem Delivered*, another of the glories of Italian literature, was under the protection first of Cardinal Luigi d'Este and later of Duke Alfonso II d'Este.

In the palace of Schifanoia (the name approximates to *sans souci*) once the home of Duke Borso, can be seen the remains of a striking series of frescoes by Cosmé Tura, Foppa and Cossa.

The cathedral of Ferrara has a striking façade, that merits much more than a casual glance. Inside there is a Byzantine baptismal font, and valuable paintings; among the treasures in the adjacent museum are some particularly fine stone carvings representing the months of the year, the work of an unknown 13th-century sculptor. The picture gallery is housed in the Palazzo dei Diamanti and includes works by Carpaccio and local painters. The Museo Archeologico Nazionale has several Etruscan exhibits. In the Chiesa del Corpus Domini are to be found the tombs of the Este family and that of Lucrezia Borgia. Ferrara is noted for its excellent bread, and it also specializes in a semi-spherical dark brown cake with an unusual chocolate-nutty flavour, *panpepato*.

About 40km/25mi east on the estuary of the Po, near the small town of Codigoro, is the magnificent **abbey of Pomposa**, with a fascinating basilica of 8th- to 9th-century origin and an elegant 11th-century bell-tower. The nearby monastery has chapter-house and refectory decorated with frescoes of the Bolognese school, and there is an 11th-century Sala della Ragione (Hall of Justice).

Fidenza   B7

(pop. 20,370) Within 10km/6mi of the thermal resorts of Salsomaggiore and Tabiano lies this important agricultural and industrial city, which merits a visit for its very lovely Gothic-Romanesque cathedral, its majestic façade flanked by two imposing towers, and with three interesting portals.

Internally the cathedral is in three naves and there is a fine series of 14th-century frescoes showing the Last Judgement.

15km/9mi away to the northeast is the little town of **Busseto**, where it is possible to visit the house where the composer Giuseppe Verdi lived.

Forli   E14

(pop. 104,900) This is one of the principal centres of the province of Romagna, lying on the plain and along the Via Emilia, surrounded by a richly agricultural region. It is also a busy industrial and commercial city.

Originally Roman, it became a free *comune* in the Middle Ages, then fell under Church domination until its integration within the Kingdom of Italy during the last century.

The cathedral, of medieval origin, was rebuilt in the 19th century. It should be visited for the sake of two interesting chapels, that of the Holy Sacrament in the right-hand nave and that of the Madonna del Fuoco in the left. There is also a fine Romanesque crucifix.

In the 12th-century church of San Mercuriale, with its bell-tower of the same epoch, is the fine sculptured tomb of Barbara Manfredi.

The local Pinacoteca has paintings by Melozzo da Forli, Guercino and others.

There is also the Rocca di Ravaldino, the stronghold wherein Caterina Sforza strongly resisted the assaults of the notorious Cesare Borgia.

Modena   C10

(pop. about 130,000) This busy agricultural and commercial centre is said to have been originally Ligurian. In the year 189

BC it became a Roman colony and knew a period of great prosperity, which had a temporary lull during the Barbaric invasions of northern Italy. In the 9th century AD, however, it became powerful once again, and so it remained through the centuries right up until the French Revolution, after which, in the general share-out of northern Italy, it was ceded to Austria. In 1859 it became a part of the newly united Italy.

Apart from agriculture and commerce, Modena is rich in art and architecture. Its cathedral is one of the outstanding Romanesque edifices of Italy. There had been two previous cathedrals on the same site, but the building we see today goes back to the end of the 11th century, when the Countess Matilda of Canossa approved the idea of building this great temple, worthy to receive the remains of Geminiano, the patron saint of the city.

Lanfranc, the greatest architect of the times, was commissioned to design and supervise the building; the stone carvings are the works of Wiligelmo.

At the side of the cathedral rises a famous bell-tower, Torre Ghirlandina, partly Romanesque, partly Gothic, in which is housed a famous bucket, which, stolen from Bologna in 1325, sparked off an inter-city war and has been rendered immortal to Italians by the celebrated poem by Tassoni, *La Secchia Rapita* (*The Stolen Bucket*).

Walking around Modena one encounters smartly-attired students, the scholars of the Accademia Militaire, housed in the 17th-century former ducal palace. In the Palazzo dei Musei, the Galleria Estense has a fine collection of paintings by such masters as Tintoretto, Veronese, Velasquez, Correggio and others.

There are other fine and interesting churches, such as San Giovanni Battista where one sees other terracotta statuary groups by Begarelli.

Altogether a fascinating provincial city and, moreover, one where eating is a pleasure, and where the local sparkling red wine, Lambrusco, gives a satisfactory fillip to the excellent food.

Parma   B8

(pop. 155,000) Parma is a provincial city situated in a fertile plain; a busy agricultural centre, it is also an industrial town.

It is of ancient origin and was one of the northern Italian provincial centres that in the year 183 AD became a Roman province. The Barbaric invasions brought about a temporary break in its prosperity, but in the 11th and 12th centuries it was a flourishing *comune*, and in 1303 began various periods of splendour and importance under, successively, the Da Correggio, the Visconti and the Sforza families. From 1545 to 1860 it was the capital of the independent duchy of Parma and Piacenza. After the fall of Napoleon, his widow, Marie Louise (Maria Luigia to the Parmesans), was given this duchy, and established herself in the Farnese palace (*La Pilotta*), with a summer court in nearby Colorno, the setting for Stendahl's novel *La Chartreuse de Parme*.

In spite of her reputation of being rather too fond of the opposite sex, it was Maria Luigia who did much for the city, building roads and bridges, orphanages and other public institutions. She it was who founded the picture gallery that one sees today in *La Pilotta*. This gallery, and the private theatre of the Farnese family, are well worth a visit. Incidentally, the Farnese palace is known by this nickname because in Renaissance days the game of pilotta – which resembles tennis – was played in its courtyard.

But the name of Parma is familiar to us for things other than Napoleonic associations. Our grandmothers valued highly the perfume made from its famous violets, which is evidently still one of the city's best-selling tourist products, though nowadays the faint, musky odour of violets is less popular. And, coming to another of the five senses, there is the famous Parmesan cheese.

One of Parma's glories is the Romanesque cathedral and its baptistery.

The baptistery is the work of Benedetto Antelami, who was not only the architect but the sculptor of the reliefs one admires inside and outside the building. This building, of the late 12th century, merits a lengthy visit, but the cathedral, too, is a treasure-house, for here we are looking at the architecture of the 11th-century Comacine master-builders; then, adding beauty to beauty, here and in the church of San Giovanni Evangelista are frescoes by Correggio, while the work of Parmigianino is to be seen in the nearby church of Santa Maria della Steccata.

Incidentally, behind the cathedral is a fascinating old-time chemist's shop, and if one wants to take home the fragrance of Parma violets, a little shop to the left of the cathedral is well stocked with the perfume.

In Parma one can eat excellently, and the hard, sharp-flavoured cheese is at its best. Don't regard this cheese as merely something to be grated over pasta, eat a chunk of it as you would eat other cheese – you will enjoy it.

A worthwhile trip from Parma is to the nearby town of **Fidenza**, 20km/12mi distant, where stands yet another splendid Romanesque cathedral.

Piacenza   A5

(pop. 84,500) This busy agricultural, industrial and commercial city is situated in a fertile plain. In its earliest days its inhabitants were successively the Liguri, the Etruscans and the Gauls. Its situation made it an important colony for Roma, and the rectangular streets of the centre echo Roman town planning. Later came the Goths, the Byzantines and the Longobards, followed by the Franks, and around the year 1000 the city ranked as a free *comune* – the twisting narrow streets one finds between the heart of the city and the 16th-century bastions, and the splendid Gothic town hall of the 13th century stand as reminders of that period. Various *signorias* followed the *comunes* then, for 200 years, the city became a duchy under the Farnese. After this it passed to Marie Louise, wife of Napoleon, and later to the Bourbons, forming a part of the Grand Duchy of Parma. In 1859 it became part of the United Kingdom of Italy.

The cathedral (1122–1233) was designed by the Comacine master-builders, who had considerable influence over Lombard-Romanesque architecture. The bell-tower is of the 14th century. The interior of the dome was frescoed by Guercino in the 17th century. The 11th century church of Sant'Eufemia merits a visit, as does the richly frescoed sanctuary of the Madonna di Campagna and the 11th-century church of Sant'Antonio, at the side of which is a Gothic atrium (1350) known as *Il Paradiso*, and attached to which is an interesting little museum of illuminated manuscripts and church vestments.

The splendid Palazzo Farnese is of the late Renaissance (1558), begun by the architect Paciotti and from 1564 onwards continued by Vignola. Nearby are the remains of the 14th-century Visconti stronghold.

Interesting excursions can be made to the **Collegio Alberoni**, which possesses a fine collection of tapestries, and to **San Borgonovo Val Tidone**, where the collegiate church of Santa Maria Assunta has a fine polychrome wood altarpiece.

Ravenna   D14

(pop. 120,000) An important Roman city as early as 90 BC, Ravenna rose to much eminence during the great days of the Empire, becoming in 404 AD the capital of the western Roman empire from Classe – now several km inland – as its port. Then came the Ostrogoth invasions, and in 476 AD Ravenna became their capital under

Odoacer and Theodoric. In 535 Justinian, emperor of the eastern Roman empire with its capital at Byzantium (Istanbul), declared war and in 20 years drove out the Ostrogoths; Ravenna once again became a Roman capital, under the aegis of the Byzantine empire. In 568 the Longobards invaded northern Italy and established Pavia as their capital. Ravenna sank to the level of a provincial city, but its magnificent buildings with their unique mosaics recall its former glory.

One of the earliest is the 5th-century Mausoleo di Galla Placidia, tomb of a romantic and powerful Roman matron, at whose death it is said that a long funeral cortège travelled the width of Italy, from Roma across the Apennines to Ravenna. Her name is remembered today not only in the mausoleum but also in the nearby pine forest. The Orthodox baptistery was erected a little later; in both the mosaics dazzle with their rich and varied colouring. In the time of Theodoric, the Basilica di Sant'Apollinare Nuovo was an Arian church, but after the Ostrogoths had been destroyed, it became a Catholic church dedicated to San Martino; in the 9th century the relics of Sant'Apollinare were transferred to it from their previous resting place, Sant'Apollinare in Classe. The basilica is one of the most striking in Ravenna with a broad central nave and Corinthian columns; the apse is semicircular inside, but covered by a polygonal shell; the 6th-century mosaics of the nave depict the Procession of Virgins on the left, that of the Martyrs on the right; above the windows, other mosaics show the story of Christ.

The greatest complex of architecture and mosaics is the octagonal church of San Vitale, consecrated in 547 AD by Archbishop Maximian. The decorative capitals of the columns, the marble *transenna* (low partition dividing the presbytery from the body of the church), the *matroneo* (ladies' gallery), and above all the splendid mosaics showing scenes from the Old Testament and the Courts of Justinian and Empress Theodora are incredibly beautiful. Visit also the strange and impressive Mausoleo di Teodorico (Tomb of Theodoric), its cupola a monolith brought from Istria, and the tomb of Dante, who, exiled from Firenze, died in Ravenna in 1321. The 6th-century **Basilica di Sant'Apollinare** in Classe (5km/3mi) stands in open country and again has magnificent mosaics. The surrounding pinewood and the Corsini Canal, which start in Ravenna, are additional attractions of this town so close to many Adriatic resorts. *Rímini 52km/32mi, Ferrara 74km/46mi.*

Réggio Nell'Emília   C9

(pop. 128,844) This is an important industrial and agricultural centre, with narrow streets in the centre that betray not only its medieval importance but, by their rectilinear plan, the city planning of the earlier Romans who established the city in the 2nd century BC.

Among its many monuments of artistic value is the Romanesque cathedral, originally erected during the 11th century, then rebuilt in the 13th century.

The church of the Madonna della Ghiara, in late Renaissance style, has frescoes by Guercino and others.

The 18th-century Palazzo del Comune is imposing, and going around the city one notices statues erected in honour of Boiardo and Ariosto (born in Réggio in 1474), both highly regarded at the court of the Este *signoria* in Ferrara.

The Museo Civico has a fine collection of mementos of the *Risorgimento*, and in the civic gallery are interesting collections of jewellery, costumes of foreign countries, paintings, sculpture and furniture.

In the public gardens can be seen a Roman tomb.

3km/2mi away stands the **Villa Mauriziano** where the poet Ariosto lived.

Riccione   F16

(pop. 23,000) This large holiday resort on the popular Adriatic coast of Italy has grown up within the past fifty years around a one-time tiny village, a mere

Mosaic, church of San Vitale

halting place for pilgrims before crossing the high mountains on their way to Roma.

There is no sport beloved of seaside visitors that Riccione does not provide for. There is an airport at nearby Miramare, and between Riccione and the equally popular Rimini there is a regular trolley-bus service.

In addition to numerous hotels there is a good camping site, and food, as everywhere in Romagna, is excellent, as are the wines – Albana, Sangiovese and Vino Santo. Small wonder that this town attracts visitors from far and wide. Philatelists should put Riccione on their list of places to visit, for every August an exhibition of stamps takes place here.

Rímini   F16
(pop. 98,675) This is not only a vast tourist centre, with hotels and *pensions* stretching far and wide along the coast, but also a busy agricultural and commercial centre. It has a splendid beach, and an excellent climate, but apart from its seaside attractions, there is much of interest in the older part of the city. From Roman days it has the impressive Arco d'Augusto, the Ponte d'Augusto, completed by Tiberius, and the ruins of an amphitheatre; but one of Rimini's richest treasures is the Renaissance Tempio Malatestiano, a masterpiece of the architect Leon Battista Alberti, reminiscent, on the outside, of Roman triumphal arches, and with internal decorations by Agostino di Duccio. In the choir of the church of Sant'Agostino are charming frescoes by an unknown 14th-century artist. In the church of San Giuliano is a painting by Veronese, and the city possesses a fine art gallery, housed in the Biblioteca Gambalunga, with works by Giovanni Bellini, Ghirlandaio and many others. *Ravenna 52km/32mi, San Marino 24km/15mi.*

Salsomaggiore and
Tabiano Terme   B6, B7
(pop. 17,300) and (pop. 1000) These two well-known and very beautiful thermal centres, both 160m/525ft above sea level, lie in a green, hilly region, 30km/19mi or so from Parma.

Let us look first at Salsomaggiore, renowned for the curative properties of its saline springs. Splendidly equipped as a holiday centre, it provides – particularly in the panoramic section known as Poggio Diana, every kind of amusement one could wish for, including a good theatre and a ballroom.

Nearby Tabiano Terme is frequented particularly by those suffering from bronchial ailments, its waters being strongly sulphuric. Around the thermal zone a protective belt of trees has been planted of a type that do not bear pollen-laden flowers so distressing to those suffering from hay fever.

From both these centres it is possible to take delightful walks, short or long depending on one's wish and capabilities.

Vignola   D10
(pop. 14,500) Vignola is a tiny provincial city, but one worthy of a half-day visit if one is in nearby Modena, especially if one's visit takes place at 'cherry blossom time' for Vignola is the heart of a cherry-growing district, and its firm, sweet fruit (*duroni*) are in great demand. At blossom time (La Fioritura) folks come from far and wide to enjoy the spectacle of acres and acres of flower-decked trees.

The city is the birthplace of the architect, Jacopo Barozzi (1507–1578), known as 'Vignola'. His one-time home is now converted into a bar and billiards parlour, but beyond the bar one comes upon a splendid helical staircase.

Vignola also boasts a castle of the 10th century and a charming parish church, and here, as in nearby Modena, it is possible to enjoy that delicious, sparkling red wine, Lambrusco.

SAN MARINO

San Marino, a mountain city of 3500 people, is the capital of an ancient independent republic. It has its own government, army, coinage and stamps, and preserves diplomatic relations with several European countries and with America. It is one of the earliest republics in the world, going back, it is said, to the 4th century AD. Its earliest statutes date from 1263.

In 1797 Napoleon recognized the independence of San Marino; later it was confirmed at the 1815 Congress of Vienna.

The ruling body, the Great and General Council, consists of 60 members, renewed at each sitting of the legislature. The two Reigning Captains have the mandate of representation and are elected every six months.

The picturesque little city climbs up a hill and down, then up and down again, and has marvellous views all around. There are three fortresses, Guaita, Fratta and Montale, and in the Basilica di San Marino are the niches where the saint used to sleep. San Marino's lovely situation and its Ruritanian air attract hosts of visitors. There are several good hotels, and countless small restaurants and souvenir shops. *Rimini 26km/16mi.*

TOSCANA

Toscana extends over the northwestern section of the peninsula, the Apennines forming its northern and eastern boundaries, the Tyrrhenian Sea marking its long, southwestern coastline. The two main chains of the Apennines are divided by a series of natural basins – those of the Magra, the Garfagnana, the Mugello and the Casentino. Mainly hilly, the region is relieved by a series of lovely valleys, Val di Chiana and that of Chianti. There is little real plainland, and that mainly along the coastal strip. Off the coast lie the very popular island of Elba and the lesser islands of Giglio and Montecristo.

The highest regions of the interior and the mountains around Monte Amiata in the south are thickly wooded, with a preponderance of chestnut groves; here, too, is ample pasturage for cattle and sheep. The lower hills produce olives and vines, from the latter of which come some of the best-known wines of Italy, in particular Chianti; other areas famous for viniculture lie around Val d'Elsa, Siena, Montepulciano, the Mugello and Val di Sieve. Cereals and forage are the main products of the plains.

The soil is rich in minerals. The iron mines of Elba have been famous since Etruscan days; around Grosseto iron pyrites is mined; Monte Amiata is rich in deposits of mercury; Volterra specializes in the mining and working of alabaster; the marble quarries of Carrara, from which Michelangelo personally selected marble for some of his finest sculpture, seem inexhaustible.

There is a fair amount of chemical industry, particularly at San Giovanni Valdarno, Arezzo and Pistóia; Prato has long been renowned for cloth weaving, and Tuscan products in straw have worldwide fame. Another peculiarly Tuscan craft is the working of leather.

This region has long had a magnetic attraction for tourists, be their interests in historic cities, art and architecture, or just the enjoyment of natural beauty as provided by hills and coastline. Not surprisingly, provision for tourists has reached a high level, though Toscana is so popular that early booking of accommodation is essential.

As far back as the 9th century BC Toscana was occupied by the Etruscans, and even then was highly civilized and well organized, so that when, in the 3rd century BC, the Romans came and added it to their 7th Region under Augustus, the ground was already prepared for administrative unity.

There are many evidences of Etruscan civilization. The stretch of land between Cortona and Chiusi is rich in tombs, and both have fine museums; Volterra has an Etruscan arch and possibly the finest Etruscan museum in the peninsula, and these are merely the best-known centres of that civilization.

The Romans left a fine theatre at Fiésole, amphitheatres in Arezzo and Lucca.

Like other regions, Toscana suffered under the Barbaric invasions, until the arrival of the Longobards, under whom Lucca became the centre of a duchy, then later, under the Franks, first a county and then a march.

The *comunes* came into being during the 11th century, and for a time there was bitter inter-city rivalry involving Pisa, Lucca, Pistóia, Siena, Volterra, Firenze and Arezzo, during which time Pisa assumed importance as a naval power.

Throughout this period Firenze had more or less taken the lead, gradually asserting its superiority over Pisa, Arezzo and Pistóia. Later, when the great Medici family had taken over the reins of the *signoria*, we see the conquest of the proud city of Siena (1570).

During the 18th and 19th centuries Toscana made enormous progress economically and in the field of art, for after the fall of Constantinople in 1453, the Greek scholars who had fled persecution found a ready welcome awaiting them in Firenze, where the Renaissance and the doctrines of Humanism knew a flowering that no other city enjoyed.

This period of brilliance was interrupted only slightly under Napoleon, and when the *Risorgimento* movement took over, once again Toscana was in the vanguard. When, in 1860, it was joined to

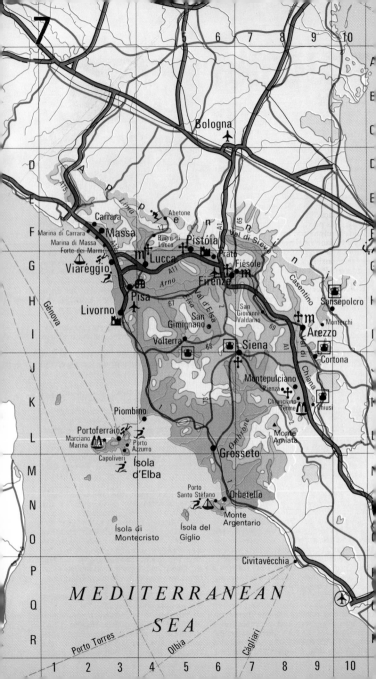

the Kingdom of Italy it was a keypoint of economic progress, and from 1865 to 1871 Firenze enjoyed the honour of being the capital.

From the 11th century onward, Toscana vied with the Veneto in Romanesque architecture, of which Toscana has a special, easily recognizable variety, with black and white or coloured marbles alternating, sometimes in stripes, sometimes in geometrical designs. Examples can be seen in the cathedral in Firenze, topped by Brunelleschi's famous cupola, and the cathedrals in Lucca and Pistóia. In the Piazza del Duomo (or dei Miracoli) at Pisa there is a complex of Tuscan-Romanesque at its best, with many-galleried façades and elegant decoration. During this period Toscana had a galaxy of fine sculptors; Arnolfo di Cambio, Andrea Pisano and the famous father and son, Nicola and Giovanni Pisano, who were responsible for the splendid pulpits in Pisa and Pistóia. It was in Toscana that the great family of the Della Robbia mostly produced their statuary in glazed terracotta. In the period of the Renaissance the architects of Toscana were renowned, and their work remains in the many fine palaces we see in and around Firenze today. Brunelleschi, Leon Battista Alberti, Rossellino, Michelozzo were among them. In painting, too, Toscana took the lead, with the works of Duccio and the Lorenzettis in Siena, Cimabue, Giotto and a host of others. Toscana in general, and Firenze in particular, was rich in all that has to do with art and architecture. Possibly the greatest sculptor of all time, Michelangelo, started his training as a lad under the patronage of Lorenzo de'Medici.

Nor did literature lag behind: the three 'greats' of the 13th century, Dante Alighieri, Francesco Petrarca and Giovanni Boccaccio, were all Tuscans.

Festivals Easter Sunday in Firenze: the *Scoppio del carro*, when an artificial dove, set alight, traverses a wire leading to the *carro*, a decorated float surrounded by popping fireworks. 1 May, also in Firenze, the *Calendimaggio*, when garlands are placed on monuments and around the necks of pretty girls. 24 and 28 June in the Piazza dei Signori in Firenze there is a rough-and-tumble football game in medieval costumes. 2 July and 16 August are important dates in Siena, for then is held the world-famous *Palio*, a horse race around the main square, all in costume and preceded by a parade of costumed dignitaries of the many *contradas* (divisions) of the city. In Arezzo on 4 September, the *Giostra del Saracino*, a colourful tournament dating back to the 13th cen-

tury. In Lucca on 13 September comes the *Festa del Volto Santo*, a solemn religious procession when the image of the Holy Face is taken from its place in a chapel in the cathedral and paraded round the city accompanied by priests and choristers.

Elba   L3

Elba is the largest island of the archipelago off the coast of Toscana. It has an area of 224sq km/86sq mi and a population of nearly 30,000. Its nearest point is only 10km/6mi from the mainland, and so it is easily reached from **Piombino** by steamer (70 minutes) or hydrofoil (20 minutes), which in the high season furnish 25 daily sailings. There is also a daily ferry service from **Livorno** (Leghorn).

To the British the island is familiar because of its Napoleonic associations. Though he spent only one year there, (1814–1815), he left many memories, and the Palazzina dei Mulni where he lived, and his summer residence, San Martino, are both now museums.

Elba was well known long before the days of Napoleon. The Greeks named it Athalia; later on the Etruscans knew and valued it for its iron deposits. When war raged between Pisa and the Florentine Medici family, it belonged first to one side and then to the other. The town we now know as Portoferraio was founded by Cosimo I of the Medici, who gave it its original name of Cosmopolo.

There is an excellent network of roads, over 170km/106mi asphalted, 90km/56mi macadamized. There are regular bus services and numerous good hotels. There are no fewer than 40 swimming pools, three 9-hole golf courses, 16 mini-golf courses, sailing schools, riding schools, a wealth of fine, sandy shore and an equable, mild climate.

Portoferraio on the northern side is the principal town, with many attractions and within easy reach of other centres. In Portoferraio make a point of visiting the old Medicean forts.

For those wishing to combine a holiday with some form of thermal treatment, there is an excellent thermal institute at **San Giovanni**, very near Portoferraio, where mud and seaweed therapy are said to be highly efficacious in the treatment of skin diseases, rheumatic and arthritic complaints and even cellulitis.

Marciana, also on the north coast, is a good centre and not far from the **Poggio thermal centre** for curative waters; it also has an excellent archaeological museum.

Porto Azzurro on the southern coast has good beaches and offers fine views.

Campo nell'Elba is very near the one airport and so is convenient for those wishing to make the short journey by air. It has many tourist attractions and good hotels, and is a good central point from which to reach smaller centres.

Those who have a passion for Pisan-Romanesque architecture will find many examples on the island, for example, the church of San Giovanni e San Nicola at San Piero not far from Campo nell'Elba, San Michele at Capoliveri on the southeastern peninsula, San Lorenzo at Marciana and Santo Stefano alle Trane in Portoferraio.

Food is excellent, the wines of Elba are justly popular and hotels are geared to welcome tourists.

Abetone   E4
(pop. 831) 1388m/4554ft above sea level. When one thinks of winter sports, one tends to think of the high mountains of the north, but there are quite a few centres in the Apennines where skiing and other winter sports are provided for. One such is Abetone, halfway between Modena and Lucca, in a splendidly panoramic position on the borders of Toscana and Romagna.

Extremely well-equipped with hotels, ski-lifts, a ski-school and a swimming pool of Olympic dimensions, it also offers excellent possibilities for interesting walks and for hunting.

Arezzo   I9
(pop. 73,176) Arezzo is of Etruscan origin; in the Middle Ages it was a flourishing *comune*, and it is now the economic centre of a large area of the province. It is rich in works of art, and one of Italy's greatest poets, Francesco Petrarca, was born here in 1304.

From the station, walk up Via Guido Monaco, turn right into Via Cavour, then left into Via dei Pileati, to reach the delightful Piazza Grande in which stands one of the town's most spectacular churches, Santa Maria della Pieve, constructed in the Romanesque style peculiar to Arezzo and the surrounding area. The façade is embellished with three tiers of columns which remind one of the pipes of a mighty organ; the bell-tower, set right into the façade, seems to float on its 40 double arches. As you enter the main door look up at the decorations of the barrel vault, representations of the months of the year, a very common form of ornamentation of 12th-century churches. At the extreme right-hand end is a particularly brutal carving representing December, showing a farmer killing a pig. Over the main altar is a delightful polyptych by the Sienese painter Lorenzetti (1320).

From the Piazza Grande behind the church, one has a splendid view of the exterior, the apse decorated with two rows of columns. This square is a treasure-house of architecture. Near Santa Maria is the fine Palazzo della Fraternità dei Laici, the lower part featuring huge 14th-century arches; the upper part is 15th century, the work of the Renaissance architect Rossellino. The fine arched Loggia is by Vasari, another famous citizen of the city, and around the other two sides of the square stand a range of tall medieval houses.

Continue up the Via dei Pileati past the Palazzo del Capitano on the left, and the house where Petrarca was born which has, alas, been almost entirely rebuilt. To the right is the large public park Il Prato with the remains of a former fortress of the Medici family; on the left is the cathedral with a Gothic façade, interesting frescoes and a striking marble altar, said to be the work of Giovanni Pisano. To the left of the altar is a funeral monument to a former Archbishop by an unknown Sienese artist, and near this monument is the famous *Madonna Tricolore* by Piero della Francesca. In one of the chapels, divided from the nave by fine wrought-iron gates, are two interesting terracottas, said to be Della Robbias.

Returning to the city centre by Via Cesalpino, one passes the Palazzo del Comune, farther down the Well of Tofano, mentioned by Boccaccio in the *Decameron*, and farther down again, the house of Guido d'Arezzo, who invented the tonic sol-fa, and who is remembered annually in August at a Polyphonic Congress held in the Petrarch Theatre.

At the junction of Via Cesalpino and Via Cavour, turn right to the great church of San Francesco, in the main chapel of which is the splendid series of frescoes by the Tuscan artist Piero della Francesca, painted between 1452 and 1464, and considered to be one of the three most important works of art in Italy – the other two are the Sistine Chapel in the Vaticano and the Cappella degli Scrovegni, Padova. One can gaze at these frescoes spellbound, then go away and return not once but many times, finding always something new, something of particular beauty. Of special interest are the *Meeting of the Queen of Sheba with Solomon*, the *Death of Adam*, and the *Dream of Constantine*.

In **Sansepolcro** (39km/24mi) are other works by della Francesca, notably the *Madonna della Misericordia*, and the fresco of the Resurrection. Also in Sansepolcro is the painter's house, reminiscent in miniature of the architecture of the Palazzo Ducale at Urbino. In the little village of **Monterchi** on the way (route 73) is the famous and unusual fresco of the *Madonna del Parto*.

Early in September Arezzo becomes very gay with the annual *Giostra del Saracino*, a colourful pageant held in the Piazza Grande. Various restaurants in and near the Piazza San Francesco serve delicious and rich Arezzo specialities, notably pork and lamb. *Firenze 85km/53mi, Perúgia 85km/53mi.*

Chianciano Terme   K8

(pop. 540) 540m/1772ft above sea level. Italy is famous for its many spas and thermal centres, one of the most frequented of which is Chianciano Terme in Toscana, not more than 30km/19mi from Lago Trasimeno, and reached along a good road through the very pleasant Umbrian and Tuscan countryside.

Its waters are recommended for those suffering from liver and biliary complaints, and it is a common sight to see patients strolling back from the thermal centre, bearing their own special glass or mug of the curative water.

The high season for such cures is from mid-April to the end of October, and during this period there is a fine programme of entertainments to relieve the tedium of the cure.

The old nucleus of the town is of Etruscan origin, for Chianciano lies in a part of Italy rich in Etruscan findings.

The Romanesque collegiate church has some fine decorations and sculpture by artists of the Sienese school, and in the small church of the Misericordia is a fresco said to be the work of Luca Signorelli.

An interesting excursion is to the town of **Chiusi** where there is a splendid Etruscan museum, the Museo Nazionale Etrusco, and from which one can visit some very interesting underground tombs, having obtained permission from the museum authorities.

Also nearby is the little town of **Pienza**, planned by Pope Pius II.

Cortona   J9

(pop. 26,720) This city, high on the hills above the station of **Terontola**, was of extreme importance in Etruscan days, and possesses a fine Etruscan museum, the Museo dell'Accademia Etrusca.

After a period of Roman occupation it was occupied in the 5th century by the Goths, and later followed the fate of the rest of Toscana.

In the Museo Diocesano is one of the finest Annunciations of Beato Angelico.

In the church of Santa Margherita, who died in Cortona, is the Gothic tomb of the saint (1362).

The cathedral still preserves traces of the original church of the 11th century, but has been many times restored.

A little way down the hill from the main city is the interesting church of La Madonna del Calcinaio, designed in 1485 by Francesco di Giorgio Martini; it was built on that spot as a result of the miraculous commands of the Madonna, despite the fact that the site is that of a landslide and therefore presents architectural difficulties, even at the present day.

The views from Cortona, apart from its architectural beauties, make a visit worthwhile.

Firenze (Florence)   G6

(pop. 428,955) The most important city of Toscana, Firenze spreads itself along both sides of the River Arno.

Founded by the Romans in the 1st century BC, it did not really expand until Carolingian days, developing between the 12th and 15th centuries into the greatest cultural centre of Europe. Despite internal strife between Guelphs and Ghibel-

Ponte Vecchio, Firenze

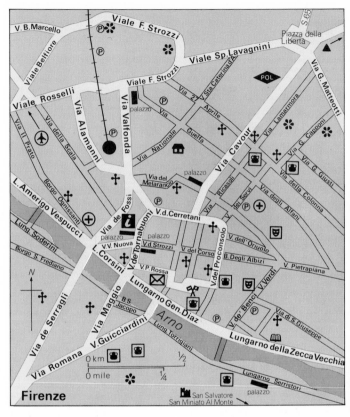

Firenze

lines, despite disputes with the Church state, Firenze forged ahead as a free *comune*. In the 15th century she enjoyed even greater prosperity under the *signoria* of the Medici family, wealthy bankers who eventually became the Grand Dukes of Toscana. Around the Court of Lorenzo de'Medici (the Magnificent) were such figures as Michelangelo, Raphael, Leonardo da Vinci. Lorenzo himself was a poet of no mean talent, and a great organizer of the spectacles and carnivals which were a feature of the age. During the late Middle Ages and the Renaissance, Cimabue and Giotto (two of the earliest masters of Italian painting), Brunelleschi, Donatello, Masaccio, Ghiberti, Beato Angelico, Filippo Lippi, Paolo Uccello, the Della Robbias, Verocchio, Pollaiolo and Botticelli were among the many pain-

ters, sculptors and architects working in and around Firenze, and today the city is a living monument to their lives and works.

The damage done by the floods of 1966 has still not been fully assessed, but the major works have been saved.

Benvenuto Cellini developed the art of the sculptor in bronze and silver to a high level. In the Galleria degli Uffizi, the Palazzo Pitti, the Bargello, the Convento di San Marco, the Accademia, the Medici Chapels and many other museums and palaces are housed treasures that testify to the genius of this city, as do the buildings themselves. See the Palazzo Vecchio, the nearby Uffizi (designed by Vasari), the Palazzo Strozzi, the cathedral with Brunelleschi's cupola, Giotto's bell-tower and the octagonal baptistery with its world-famous bronze doors, and the many churches – San Miniato al Monte, Santa Croce and the Cappella dei Pazzi among them.

The Italian language spoken today was born in Firenze at the end of the 13th century when Dante began writing in *Volgare* (the language of the common people). Romans declare that the purest Italian is *lingua toscana in bocca romana* (Tuscan spoken by Romans); Florentines are content with the first part of the phrase.

Today the city still plays a leading role in art and culture. May in Firenze is the month of musical events; at Easter, in memory of the victory of the First Crusade, the ceremony of the *Scoppio del Carro* is held in the cathedral square; a scene of fireworks and great excitement; in May and June football games in medieval costume are held in the Piazza della Signoria, preceded by a medieval pageant – football games which have to be seen to be believed. Shoppers find Firenze a paradise for leather goods, fine embroideries, and articles made of straw, either in the many elegant shops in such streets as Via de Tornabuoni, or in the famous Straw Market just off Via Calzaiuoli.

Here only the surface of Firenze has been touched; there is much more to see and to do; there are visits to **Fiésole** up on the hill, to **Pistóia**, **Lucca** and **Pisa**. Information is obtainable from the Tourist Information Offices inside the Central Station. *Bologna 104km/65 mi, Pisa 91km/57mi, Rímini 158km/98mi.*

Forte dei Marmi   F3

(pop. 9120) This is a lovely seaside resort within easy reach of **Pisa** (46km/28mi) and **Lucca** (44/27). It enjoys a splendid climate, protected as it is by the Apuan Alps, on the lower slopes of which are olive trees and pines. It has a large, sandy beach, and the many villas and well-kept, beautiful gardens along the shore give it an attractive appearance. It has good bathing, all kinds of water sports, fishing, boating, and there are delightful walks to be taken in the pinewoods.

In view of the town's excellence as a touring centre and resort, accommodation should be booked early.

Livorno (Leghorn)   H3

(pop. 165,000) Livorno is an agreeable resort lying in a fertile plain between hills and the sea. The promenade stretches for over 8km/5mi and in the bay is a modern reconstruction of the 14th-century lighthouse. The Medici fortress, the Fortezza Vecchia, was erected in the 14th century around a 9th-century building and was later (1521–30) reinforced by the architect

Sangallo. It is now transformed into conference rooms and restaurants. Everything in Livorno seems to be on a larger scale than normal: the statue of Ferdinando I de'Medici, erected to celebrate a victory over the pirates who once were the scourge of the Mediterranean; the extra-wide streets and spacious piazzas. The cathedral has been almost completely reconstructed since World War II, but preserves some fine paintings from the original edifice. Livorno's unique charm, its nearness to **Pisa** (21km/13mi), **Lucca** (42/26), and such seaside resorts as **Viaréggio**, suggest a stay of several days, possibly in combination with a week in Firenze (95km/59mi).

Lucca   G4

(pop. 88,428) Lucca is a charming little city with some splendid Tuscan-Romanesque architecture. Not far away are several villas which are numbered among the most beautiful in Italy, such as the **Villa Mansi**, and the **Villa di Marlia**, with charming gardens and fountains. About 17km/10mi to the north is the peaceful holiday resort of **Bagni di Lucca**, with lovely walks among the hills and along the banks of the river Lima, where there is a thermal establishment for the cure of arthritis. Lucca is pre-Roman, but it enjoyed its period of greatest splendour during the 12th and 13th centuries when it was a free *comune*. It is surrounded by ancient walls along the top of which is a pleasant tree-shaded drive. From a point in this drive can be seen the garden of a house described by Charles Morgan in his novel *Sparkenbroke*.

The cathedral of San Martino is a splendid example of Tuscan art and architecture, with the columned *loggettas* of its façade and its graceful bell-tower. Inside is a statue of the patron saint on horseback and a beggar, a group that was originally outside the cathedral but which has been moved inside to protect it from the weather. Also in the cathedral is the tomb of Ilaria del Carretto, the work of Jacopo della Quercia – notice particularly Ilaria's faithful small dog, lying at her feet. In the Cappella del Volto Santo (Chapel of the Holy Face), a highly venerated wooden statue of Christ is kept. Early in September every year is the *Festa del Volto Santo*. Services are held in the cathedral and during the evening the statue, arrayed in elaborate robes, is carried through streets, lit only by candlelight and torches, accompanied by a long procession of priests and choirs.

The church of San Michele houses a precious terracotta by Andrea della Robbia and a painting by Filippino Lippi. In the church of San Frediano, distinguished by a fine external mosaic, is the tomb of San Riccardo Ré d'Inghilterra, an English king of the 7th or 8th century who relinquished his right to the throne to become a saint. There is also a chapel devoted to Santa Zita, the patron saint of domestic servants, and a delightful baptismal font, the work of the 12th-century sculptor, Roberto.

Marina di Carrara
Marina di Massa   F2

(both pop. 12,000) These two well-appointed holiday resorts are within 7km/4mi of each other. Both have fine esplanades along a sandy shore and here and there little plantations of umbrella pines for those who prefer the shade to the blazing sun.

Behind them rise the Apuan Alps, white here and there, not with snow, but with the fine, white Carrara marble, which is exported from this area.

It is an easy bus or car journey up the mountain to Carrara itself; the city is a mere 80m/262ft above sea level, but the road continues upward beyond it until it reaches the quarries, the same quarries which were visited by Michelangelo when he wished to select personally the particularly fine white marble he wanted for his sculpture. These quarries have been worked for centuries, and there is still abundant marble. Along the way up the mountain one passes here and there small establishments where craftsmen fashion small statues, ashtrays and other objects.

There are camping facilities at both Marinas, and Marina di Massa also has a youth hostel; there are facilities for all kinds of marine activities, bathing is good, and the vegetation is lush and almost African in type.

Not far from **La Spezia**, **Lérici** or **Viaréggio**, either of these towns would make an excellent holiday base.

Pienza   K8

(pop. about 3500) This tiny but charming little city is well worth visiting if one is in the region of Chianciano, Montepulciano or Siena. It is a small, but exquisite, model of a purely Renaissance city, owing its beauty to the efforts of Pope Pius II, born here with the name Enea Silvio Piccolomini in 1405. On being elevated to the Papacy in 1458, it was his wish to transform the place of his birth into a model city, and for this purpose he engaged the Florentine architect Bernardo Rossellino, giving him a free hand. The project was carried out in three years (1459–1462) and still stands although, once Pius II had died, it was no longer the chosen 'off duty'

residence of Popes. The buildings calling for special notice include the cathedral, a very typically Renaissance edifice. On the timpanum of the façade will be noticed the crest of the Piccolomini family. The interior is divided into three naves of equal height, with a polygonal apse. In the crypt is a baptismal font, also the work of Rossellino. After the cathedral, Palazzo Piccolomini calls for attention, modelled largely on Alberti's Palazzo Rucellai in Firenze. The mansions one sees along Corso Rossellino were the dwelling places of the dignitaries of the Papacy.

The little town today is an agricultural centre where, among other products, it is possible to buy excellent cheeses.

Pisa   H3

(pop. 96,545) Pisa possesses one of the loveliest architectural groupings in Europe, in the Piazza del Duomo (or dei Miracoli), in which are to be seen not only the famous Campanile (Leaning Tower) and the cathedral, but the baptistery and the Campo Santo (burial ground), each a masterpiece of sculpture and architecture. The cathedral was begun in the 11th century, to the design of the architect Buscheto; it was completed in the following century, the organ pipe façade the work of another famous architect, Rainaldo. Among the treasures inside are the pulpit by Giovanni Pisano, the lamp on which Galileo Galilei based his theory of the swing of the pendulum, the splendid bronze doors of Ranieri, and some valuable paintings. The baptistery has an interesting cupola, which in fact consists of two: an inner one in the form of a cone which projects through the outer one – an idea taken from Arabian architecture. Because of its sea traffic during the Middle Ages, Pisa was in close touch with the Orient, and there is more than a flavour of the east in the architecture of the city. The decoration of the doors is particularly interesting, and the pulpit here is one of the last works of Nicola Pisano, father of Giovanni. The Campanile, work of Bonanno, was abandoned for 90 years when the slope was first noticed, but was eventually completed in the middle of the 14th century. In the nearby Campo Santo are famous frescoes by Gozzoli, Traini and Orcagno, recently restored after the devastations of World War II.

Pisa is a graceful city and the embankment of the Arno makes a particularly agreeable walk. Near the Ponte Solferino is another delightful little church, Santa Maria della Spina, jutting out right into the street; another veritable treasure-house is the church of Santo Stefano dei Cavalieri. *Firenze 18km/11mi, Livorno 19km/12mi.*

Pistóia   F5

(pop. 82,425) A little Tuscan city, within easy reach of Firenze and well worth a visit for those interested in sculpture and architecture.

The church of San Giovanni Fuorcivitas (12th century) is an interesting example of Pisan Romanesque, with a fine marble pulpit by Fra Guglielmo of Pisa. The cathedral (12th century) is also in similar style and has a fine bell-tower; it houses a famous *dossale* of San Jacopo, a

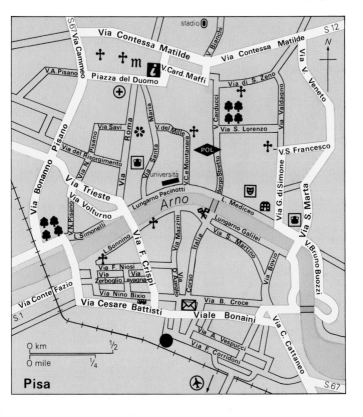

Pisa

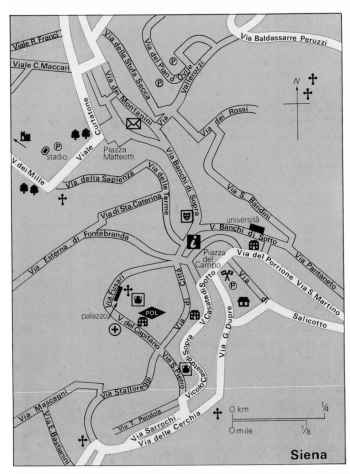

Siena

fresco by Lorenzo di Credi and a baptismal font of the end of the 15th century. The Ospedale del Ceppo, founded in the 13th century, has a magnificent coloured frieze, the work of Giovanni della Robbia, while in the church of Sant'Andrea is an exquisite pulpit by Giovanni Pisano.

Porto Santo Stéfano   N6

(pop. 8500) This is one of the more recent holiday resorts to gain popularity. Lying on the western coast of Toscana, its nearest railway station is Orbetello.

Originally a small fishing village, its wide, lovely bay and splendid sandy beaches have of late years attracted numerous tourists. Its buildings are largely post-World War II, as during that conflict the original village was completely destroyed. Because of its excellent port and good facilities for the repair and fitting-out of all kinds of sea craft, it attracts travellers by sea as well as by land.

In the season steamers ply easily and quickly to the nearby **Ísola del Gíglio** – a pleasant day's excursion.

The central point of the peninsula on which stands Santo Stéfano is **Monte**

Argentario, which provides interesting, if somewhat strenuous, walks.

Porto Santo Stéfano has all the charm of a small fishing village, combined with excellent modern facilities, including good eating-places.

Prato   G6
(pop. 121,200) Known to the woollen trade for its manufacture of cloth, this city also has several very famous monuments. Within easy easy distance of Firenze, it merits a visit of half a day if not more.

The cathedral (8th century, but enlarged in the early 14th century) has an elegant façade at the right-hand corner of which is the famous pulpit (pergamo del Sacro Cingolo) by Donatello, decorated with splendid reliefs. The choir is decorated by Filippo Lippi and the splendid gate leading to the chapel of the Sacro Cingolo dates back to the 15th century. On the fine altar (1478) is an exquisite statuette by Giovanni Pisano.

The battlemented castle is interesting, and another fine church is that of Santa Maria delle Carceri, a splendid example of Renaissance architecture.

San Gimignano   I6
(pop. 10,060) In medieval days, to have a tower to one's house was not only a means of defence, but also a status symbol. This little city is one of the few still possessing a fair number of the ancient towers that used to rise like tall trees above the horizon. Old prints show a veritable forest of towers, but nowadays the number is reduced to a dozen or so; nevertheless, approaching the city by road, the effect is still unusual. The main square, the Piazza della Cisterna, is surrounded by interesting palaces of the 13th and 14th century. The Palazzo del Podesta and the Palazzo Comunale (now the home of the civic museum with valuable paintings by Lippi, Pinturicchio and others) are both interesting, and in the Romanesque church known as the *Duomo* are examples of the work of Giuliano and Benedetto Maiano, Jacopo della Quercia and a fresco of Santa Fina – the patron saint of the city – by Ghirlandaio.

Siena   I7
(pop. 62,954) Siena is famous for its art and architecture, and noted for one of Italy's most colourful pageants, the *Palio*, the world's most tumultuous horse race.

The Gothic cathedral (off Via Fusari), originally planned to be much greater than its present size, has a splendid pavement, a fine pulpit by Nicola Pisano and members of his famous school of sculpture and, in the Libreria Piccolomini, a series of frescoes by Pinturicchio. In the main square is the impressive Town Hall, and nearby the graceful Torre del Mangia, with the one-handed clock that used to sound the hour of *mangiare* (to eat), and the charming Cappella di Piazza.

The Loggia della Mercanzia, the church of San Martino, and the church of Santa Maria di Provenzano are fine examples of Renaissance architecture, as is the Palazzo Piccolomini delle Papesse, designed by Rossellino. The 13th-century Gothic church of San Domenico is also interesting. The Museo dell'Opera del Duomo should be visited if only to see the famous *Maestà*, the *Noli me tangere* and *Gesù in Emmaus* by Duccio di Buoninsegna. Other works by Duccio, and by Dürer, Lorenzetti and Pinturicchio can be seen in the Pinacoteca in the Palazzo Buonsignori. The Casa di Santa Caterina, who wrote admonitory letters to the Popes during their residence in Avignon, is now a sanctuary.

Viaréggio   G3
(pop. 50,415) Viaréggio is an extremely popular seaside resort, surrounded by pinewoods and backed by the Apuan Alps, with a splendid beach. In February a Carnival is held, in which wonderfully decorated floats take part, with fireworks and similar attractions. Among its interesting buildings are the church of the Annunciation, the Palazzo Belluomini, and a 16th-century tower in the market square. *Livorno 40km/25mi, Lucca 24km/15mi.*

Volterra   I5
(pop. 17,137) By far the most dramatic approach to this ancient town is by road, when one has the sensation of almost flying over the eroded valleys that surround it. The picture gallery is housed in the 13th-century Palazzo dei Priori, decorated on the outside with numerous coats-of-arms. In the Pisan-Romanesque cathedral is a fine baptismal font by Sansovino and an exquisite *Deposition* carved in wood. The museum, with its fine collection of Etruscan funerary urns and other relics, is a joy, as are the Etruscan walls and the Porta all'Arco close to the cathedral. In Via Buonparenti are some interesting tall, narrow medieval houses. A pleasant walk through the town brings one to the grim fortress erected in 1472 by Lorenzo de'Medici, now used as a prison for those condemned to life sentences. Volterra is famous for its alabaster ornaments, and a visit to the various workshops is entertaining and not overly expensive. *Firenze 78km/48mi, Siena 50km/31mi.*

LE MARCHE

Occupying a position on the Adriatic side of the Apennines, the region consists of a series of high slopes parallel to the coast, decreasing gradually in height as they near the sea. The rivers run perpendicularly to the coast and are of a torrential nature, partly utilized for the production of electricity. The coast itself is rich in seaside resorts, where tourists are well provided for.

Wheat is grown, and there is considerable pasturage for cattle, pigs and sheep; tomatoes and cauliflowers are among the vegetable products, and there are numerous vineyards. Fishing is carried on all along the coast, the principal centre of this activity being San Benedetto del Tronto.

Around Pésaro sulphur is mined. The main industry is that of paper-making, centred on the city of Fabriano. Ceramics are made around Urbino, and Castelfidardo is famous for the manufacture of accordions.

One still sees ox-carts in use in this region, a relic of the long-distant Etruscan days.

In its earliest days the region was divided between the Gauls and the Piceni, and Romanization did not begin until the 3rd century BC, when it was first of all divided between the 5th and 6th Regions of Augustus and later united.

There are a fair number of Roman remains all over the area: the splendid Arco di Traiano in Ancona and Augustan arches in Fano and other cities.

The Longobards later dominated the part south of Ancona, while the northern part came under the Exarchate of Ravenna, and later under the Pope, who received it as a gift from the Franks. The word *marca* (march) was not used until the 10th century.

Feudalism and the ecclesiastical authority were both powerful until in the late 12th and early 13th centuries came the rise of free *comunes*, followed shortly by the *signorias*, which again wielded great power, as is seen in the history of the Montefeltro family of Urbino and the Malatesta in Rímini. Meanwhile the Church was striving to maintain and even to reinforce its one-time authority, in fact, under Cardinal Albornoz in the 14th century, many castles and cities fell under its domination. Little by little, following the short-lived rule of first the Sforza and later the Valentino dynasties from the middle of the 15th to the beginning of the 16th century, we see the Church ruling the entire area, except for the short Napoleonic era, until 1860, when Le Marche became a part of the Kingdom of Italy.

Building activity was considerable from the 11th to the 13th century, and there is an attractive blending of Romanesque with Byzantine styles as, for example, in the dramatically-sited church of Santa Maria at Portonovo near Ancona, or the cathedral in Ancona itself, badly damaged during the recent wars and by various earthquakes and an alarming landslide. Restoration work is always in progress.

The Gothic period left evidences in Ancona, showing signs of strong Venetian influence, as in the Loggia dei Mercanti in that city and in the church of San Nicola at Tolentino, a church well worth a visit not only for its architecture but for a fine series of frescoes reminiscent of Giotto and for a 15th-century portal by Nanni di Bartolo.

For Renaissance architecture at its finest one cannot do better than visit Urbino with its splendid Palazzo Ducale, and the sanctuary town of Loreto where, in the Santuario della Santa Casa are examples of the work of some of the finest sculptors of the period: Bramante, Laurana, Pontelli and Sansovino. These cities possess priceless paintings by Piero della Francesca, Melozzo da Forlì, Signorelli and others. The Museo Nazionale in Ancona has paintings by the Venetian Crivelli and in the Palazzo Comunale at Recanati is a fine Lotto.

Other arts find expression in the majolica to be seen at Urbino, Pésaro and other centres. The town of Castelfidardo is noted not merely for two great victories, that of Rodolfo da Varano against the Ghibellines in 1355 and that of General Cialdini in 1860 against the Papal troops, but also for accordion making.

Literature owes a debt to Le Marche, for in the little town of Recanati was born

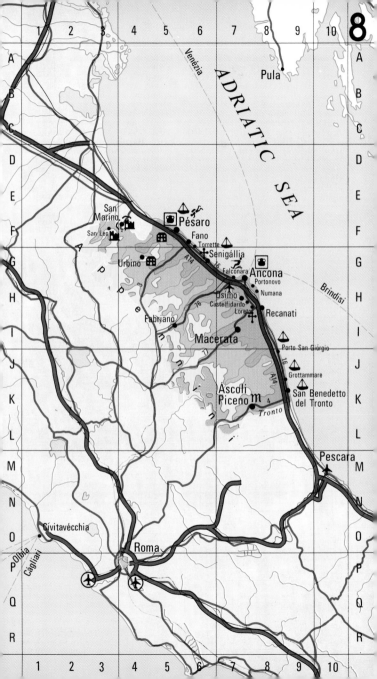

the poet Giacomo Leopardi (1798–1837), a near-contemporary of Keats and Shelley. **Festivals** The first Sunday in August sees the colourful *Quintana* (a tournament in costume) in Ascoli Piceno. There is a parade through the streets, headed by the Mayor, after which cavaliers from every quarter of the town present themselves to their ladies to receive the traditional handkerchief to bring them good fortune, before engaging in combat to defeat the figure of a Moor. Fireworks follow in the evening, and all ends with the singing of a triumphal hymn in honour of the winner. In Fano at the beginning of August is the summer carnival, with a long file of allegorical carts, song, dancing and a Pantagruelian feast, ending with a huge bonfire in which the *Pupo*, representing the spirit of Carnival, is burnt.

Ancona   G7

(pop. 98,175) This busy Adriatic port is one of the most interesting cities of the Marches. Its origins go back to 400 BC. First Greek, then Roman, at the fall of the Roman empire it became one of the five marine cities dependent on the Byzantine overlords of Ravenna. It then fell under the domination of the Church state, was in turn besieged by Frederick Barbarossa and occupied by the Malatestas, once again became a part of the Church state, and was finally united with the Kingdom of Italy in 1860.

The city rises sharply from sea level, and though it suffered grave damage during World War II, it is well endowed with pleasant squares – Piazza Cavour and Piazza Roma – and the streets in the new part are spacious and well planned. The really interesting part of the city is, however, the older section, over towards the headland from the heights of which the Romanesque cathedral looks down upon a tangle of narrow, twisted, cobbled streets. Here hide the Palazzo degli Anziani (the University, with a fine *Virgin and Child* by Titian and another by Crivelli); the Museo Nazionale, rich in treasures of antiquity; the church of San Domenico with a Titian *Crucifixion*; the quite charming church of Santa Maria della Piazza, a mixture of early Christian and Romanesque architecture that is well worth a visit; and in a nearby street the elaborate façade of the 15th-century Loggia dei Mercanti. Ancona has three interesting arches, the Arco Traiano and Arco Clementino below the cathedral, and the baroque Porta Pia nearer the harbour. In the harbour, too, is the flat, rectangular Lazaretto (seamen's hospital) designed by the 18th-century architect Vanvitelli who also designed the Arco Clementino.

Ancona is an excellent centre from which to visit the inland towns of **Recanati** – birthplace of the poet Leopardi and the singer Gigli – the pilgrimage town of **Loreto**, and **Osimo**, **Castelfidardo**, **Macerata**, all charming hill towns rising from the fertile tablelands. Those preferring seaside amusements may go by steamer to the nearby beaches of **Passetto**, **Portonovo** and **Numana**, while motor coaches travel south along the Via Adria to the more distant resorts of **Porto San Giórgio**, **Grottammare** and **San Benedetto del Tronto** (excellent camping facilities; 90km/56mi). Nearby beaches to the north are at **Torrette**, **Palombina** and **Falconara**, the airport for Ancona. *Pésaro 63km/39mi, Pescara 152km/95mi.*

Ascoli Piceno   K8

(pop. 51,600) This is a pleasant city situated on the plain where the Rivers Tronto and Castellano converge; it is a

San Leo

centre that attracts lovers of Roman remains and medieval monuments. There is a charming little Roman gate, Porta Gemina, dating back possibly to the 1st century BC. Beyond it can be seen a portion of the Roman wall.

Piazza Arringo is interesting for here stands the cathedral, the 16th-century Bishops' Palace, and the Palazzo Comunale, behind the baroque façade of which are the former palaces of the Commune and of the Arringo. Here is housed the local picture gallery which has paintings by Titian, Giordano, Reni, Magnasco and others.

Loreto   H8

(pop. 8565) This pilgrimage town is about 28km/17mi from Ancona. Its great interest for visitors is the Santuario della Santa

Casa, the alleged house of the Madonna which, according to the legend, was brought to Loreto by angels. The sanctuary rises at the end of a lovely square in the centre of which is a fine 17th-century fountain. The façade is late Renaissance, and the three bronze doors bear splendid reliefs; inside the church is a veritable museum of works by Signorelli, Sansovino, Raffaello de Montelupo and many others, while the Palazzo Apostolico, the work of Sangallo and Sansovino, houses a museum. There are a number of hotels, but, as Loreto is a pilgrimage town, accommodation is not easy to find and is apt to be expensive.

Pésaro   F5
(pop. 70,500) This is another of the popular seaside resorts along the Adriatic coast, but it is also a busy centre of commerce, which, after having been a Roman colony in its early days, was burned to the ground during the Gothic invasions, then rose to eminence again under the *signorias* of the Malatesta, Della Rovere and Sforza families.

Not surprisingly, with this historical background, Pésaro has many interesting buildings. The 15th-century Palazzo Ducale is among them, as is the church of San Francesco and a fine Romanesque cathedral of the 13th century. The Musei Civici, including a collection of majolica said to be the finest in Italy, are housed in the Palazzo Toschi-Mosca and are very well worth visiting. In addition to these, there is a fine picture gallery.

The music lyceum, the Conservatorio Rossini, bears the name of the composer, who was a native of the city. His house still stands and holds a small museum. The theatre (1637) also bears his name.

The splendid esplanade at Pésaro extends for 3km/2mi along the shore, and inland there are many panoramic walks to be taken.

Pésaro is well-served by road and rail services, and has numerous good hotels.

San Leo   F3
San Leo occupies a commanding position on a height in the Apennines, about 12km/7mi southwest of San Marino. It is crowned by a fortress, built originally in medieval days but enlarged in the 15th century by Francesco di Giorgio Martini. One famous prisoner in this fortress was the Palermitan Giuseppe Balsamo, better known to the world as Cagliostro, one of the world's best-known 'confidence men'. Here he was imprisoned and here he died in 1795. It is possible to visit his grim prison where there is a museum of arms and a small gallery of pictures.

The cathedral, said to have been erected on the ruins of a Roman temple, is a fine Romanesque-Gothic edifice.

The view from San Leo is extensive and very interesting.

Senigállia   G6
(pop. 36,500) This agricultural, commercial and industrial city, 15km/9mi north of Ancona on the Adriatic coast, combines the industry of shipbuilding with that of tourism, fishing and all the possibilities of amusement that make for a splendid seaside holiday. It has a long stretch of sandy beach that slopes gently to meet the Adriatic.

Founded originally by the Gauls, later it became a Roman colony, passing into the possession of the Longobards when they invaded Italy. Later for some time it was a free *comune*, after which it passed under the *signoria* of the Malatesta family, and from that, under the jurisdiction of the Papacy.

There are some fine paintings to be seen in the 18th-century cathedral, and in the church of Santa Croce.

A pleasant excursion takes one to the church of Santa Maria delle Grazie, where there is a fine painting by the Umbrian painter Perugino.

Senigállia is becoming very popular with tourists, and there are numerous good hotels as well as camping facilities.

Urbino   G4
(pop. 20,550) The great Palazzo Ducale, the 'city in the form of a palace', was begun in the year 1444. In 1468 the architect Luciano Laurana took charge of the work for the illustrious *signore*, Federico da Montefeltro, who founded there one of the greatest cultural centres of his time. The palace rises on a hill and the two tall towers of its façade look down over the valley in truly ducal fashion. The interior courtyard is simple and elegant, and the whole palace is a series of splendid halls and rooms in which are displayed art treasures of great beauty and considerable value, for the palace now houses the Galleria Nazionale delle Marche and has works by Raphael, Piero della Francesca, Titian and many others. A whole morning or afternoon is barely sufficient to see and savour everything.

The 14th-century church of San Domenico boasted until recently a fine terracotta by Luca della Robbia in the lunette above the main portal, now under restoration. The 15th-century house of Raphael, the Casa di Raffaello, can also be visited. *Pésaro 36km/22mi.*

UMBRIA

Umbria, Holy Umbria, the green heart of Italy, is one of the favourite regions for Italians as well as for foreign visitors. Situated in the centre, it is the only peninsular region entirely surrounded by land. Largely mountainous, bordered on the east by the Apennines, its main water-courses are the upper basin of the Tévere (Tiber) and the Nera. In the northwest lies Lago Trasimeno, the largest of Italy's peninsular lakes, famous in history as being the site of Hannibal's defeat of the Romans in 217 BC, familiar to art-lovers as appearing in the background of many paintings by Perugino and other Umbrian painters.

There are three islands on Trasimeno: Maggiore, rich in memories of St Francis of Assisi, Minore and Polvese. Steamers ply across the lake from Passignano to Castiglione del Lago, touching Maggiore en route. It is a pleasant day's outing to cross the lake mid-morning, visiting the church at Castiglione del Lago, where hangs a reputed Raphael of the Madonna with the Christ-child, then taking lunch in a *trattoria*, or eating a *tosto* at a bar before making the return journey.

Not far from the industrial city of Terni in the south of the region is the spectacular Cascata delle Marmore (waterfall), the harnessing of which has proved a rich source of hydroelectric power.

Umbria was Etruscan before it was Roman and both civilizations have left their mark; Perúgia has no fewer than three Etruscan arches and a very interesting tomb, discovered in 1983 in the suburb of Monte Lupo. Orvieto also boasts Etruscan tombs, and Roman remains are to be seen in such unexpected spots as the little hill town of Spello, as well as in such cities as Gúbbio, Spoleto and Nórcia.

It is said that more than twenty thousand saints have been born in Umbria; three at least are outstanding, San Benedetto di Nórcia and his twin sister Scolastica, born in 480 AD, and St Francis, born in Assisi in 1181.

Life in Umbria has always had strong religious and Papal associations. During the 13th century both Orvieto and Perúgia sheltered exiled Popes. Perúgia has been the scene of five Papal conclaves; four Popes have died there. Small wonder that Umbria is a region of splendid religious buildings, Romanesque and Gothic, and of painters such as Perugino and Pinturicchio, who have excelled in religious art.

The Middle Ages seem still alive today as one walks around the narrow, tortuous streets of Perúgia, Bevagna, Todi, Nórcia – in fact, in almost any town of the region. In Gúbbio medievalism seems to blend with other-worldliness, making it different from all other Umbrian cities. Here is a little city where many houses in the older part have 'doors of the dead' – extra doors, close to the front door but at a higher level, walled up, except when a corpse is taken out of the house for burial.

Many of the cities are in themselves museums of art and architecture: the great fountain in front of the cathedral in Perúgia is the combined work of Nicola and Giovanni Pisano; the huge basilica of St Francis in Assisi has magnificent frescoes by Cimabue, Giotto and Simone Martini; the cathedral in Orvieto, with external reliefs by Maitani and frescoes by Signorelli inside, springs upon the vision like an exotic flower in a cottage garden; Todi, Bevagna and many other provincial centres have municipal squares that are a miracle of perfection. Nature, too, has showered riches upon Umbria; from the bastions of its hill towns one looks out upon scenes of unforgettable beauty. Not far from Spoleto is another example of Nature at its loveliest, in the Fonti del Clitunno (Springs of Clitumnus), sung by poets from Virgil to Byron and Carducci.

Festivals The festivals of Umbria are many and picturesque: Assisi – *Calendimaggio*, 1 May, the celebration of the Return of Spring; the main square is the scene of the choosing of the *Madonna Primavera* from among the prettiest girls of the city, all in fancy dress. Gúbbio – Festival of the *Ceri* (Candles), 15 May, which are not candles, but huge pillars of decorated wood on which are mounted the three patron saints of the city. Spello – *Corpus Domini*, streets are carpeted in flowers arranged in picturesque designs. Orvieto – *Corpus Domini*, a caged dove is flown on a wire over the heads of the

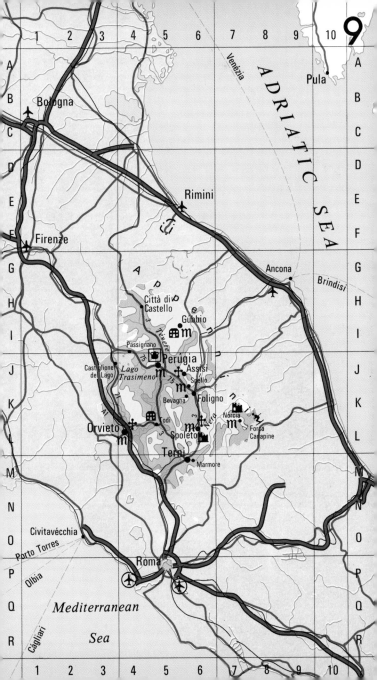

spectators in the main square before the cathedral; the cage is surrounded by fireworks which are ignited before the flight begins. Foligno – The *Quintana*, September (2nd Sunday), a parade in costume followed by a tournament of riders whose aim is to take a ring from the outstretched hand of the figure of a Moor.

Assisi   J6

(pop. 25,372) The city of St Francis seems impregnated with the spirit of that gentle saint who died at the age of 44 in 1226. True, Assisi has other memories; beneath the Temple of Minerva, now transformed into the church of Santa Maria sopra Minerva, are the remains of a Roman forum, but the ever-present thought in the minds of visitors is of the beloved San Francesco.

The first great monument to visit is the Basilica di San Francesco, begun in 1228. In the lower church are frescoes by Simone Martini in the chapel of St Martin; there are also charming stained-glass windows, possibly to the design of the same artist. In the upper church are frescoes by Cimabue, the master of Giotto, and the splendid series, the *Story of St Francis* by Giotto and his school. The body of the saint, not discovered until the beginning of the last century, is in the simple crypt beneath the lower church.

Another interesting church is that of Santa Chiara, the founder of the Order of the *Clarisse* (Poor Clares). This is a Gothic building of the second half of the 13th century, with impressive arched supports on the exterior, a huge rose window, the crucifix which according to the legend spoke to St Francis, and a painting on wood of Santa Chiara (1283). The church of San Rufino, where St Francis was confirmed, is a splendid example of Umbrian Romanesque architecture; the façade contains three rose windows, a beautifully decorated central door and two side doors. Unfortunately, the interior was rebuilt in a manneristic style that did not blend well with the exterior; however, changes are now being made.

Leaving the town by the Porta Nuova (east), and descending sharply for a mile or so, one comes to the first convent of the Poor Clares, **San Damiano**, where St Francis was converted. The tiny church is unspoiled and tranquil, and more than any other place in Assisi speaks of the spirit of the Saint. Some 2–3km/2mi west of the town lies the great **Basilica di Santa Maria degli Angeli** (16th-century) which houses the humble little church, the Porziuncola, St Francis' first church, and the spot where he died, '*nudo sulla terra nuda*' ('naked on the naked earth').

The **Carceri**, the site of the solitary hermitage where he used to pray, is 8km/5mi from Assisi. Another walk or short drive is to **Rivotorto** where a sanctuary rises over two huts, once lived in by the saint. *Perúgia 24km/15mi.*

Gúbbio   I5

(pop. 34,606) This is one of Umbria's many interesting cities, particularly in mid-May when the *Festa dei Ceri* is held, an ancient pageant in which young men, dressed in costume, race through the narrow streets in three teams, each team bearing an enormous wooden platform on which is mounted the figure of a patron saint of the city. After a banquet in the Palazzo dei Consoli, they race up the steep hill to the sanctuary of Sant'Ubaldo, where the figures are deposited until the following year. There is a magnificent view from the sanctuary, which can be reached by cable railway.

In the Palazzo dei Consoli is a fine collection of works of art, and the famous Tavole Eugubine, seven bronze tablets covered with lettering and dating back well over 2000 years. The Palazzo Ducale, the Municipio and the Palazzo del Bargello are all worth visiting, as is the cathedral. One wall of the church of San Francesco was the wall of a house in which the saint once found refuge. In the church of Santa Maria Nuova are some charming frescoes by the Umbrian artist Nelli. The city also has a Roman theatre in which open-air performances of Shakespeare and other dramatists are given during summer evenings. *Assisi 57km/35mi, Perúgia 40km/25mi.*

Nórcia   K7

(pop. 7629) This is a good winter sports centre. On the road from Spoleto the scenery becomes grander and grander, hills become mountains, and the little stream that runs beside the road turns into a mountain torrent. It is an ancient city, home at one time of the mother of the Roman emperor Vespasian; in more recent days the birthplace of San Benedetto (480–546 AD) and his twin sister, Santa Scolastica. It was San Benedetto who founded the religious Order of the *Benedettini*, and in the principal square of the little town is a statue of the saint. The small fortress was built in 1554 for Pope Julius III; in the same square is the church of San Benedetto, 7th-century with a 13th-century façade. The crypt once formed part of a Roman palace, allegedly where the saint and his sister were born. The church of Sant'Agostino is one of the most interesting in this area, with altars in local baroque – unpainted –

and with some delightful, well-preserved frescoes of the Umbrian school. In a niche behind the altar is a precious statue in wood of San Sebastian, a favourite in country churches for his power against the plague.

Forca Canapine (13km/8mi) is a splendid winter sports centre, and the hotel of the same name is excellent, as is its restaurant. *Spoleto 50km/31mi.*

Orvieto   L4

(pop. 25,090) This is one of the most picturesque cities of Umbria; built on a mound of tufa rock, it is breathtaking, whether one approaches it by rail or by road. In recent years there have been threats of subsidence of the tufa and strengthening works have had to be undertaken.

Several times Orvieto has been the refuge of Popes, and it has always been closely linked with Papal affairs. The magnificent cathedral bursts upon one's vision as one makes one's way through the medieval streets. The building was begun in 1260. The splendid Gothic façade is superimposed upon a typical basilica; the architect is thought to have been Fra Bevignate, but some authorities are inclined to regard it as the work of Arnolfo di Cambio. In 1309 a Sienese architect, Lorenzo Maitano, took over the work and changed the concept of the structure. His façade is a splendid example of Pisan Gothic, terminating in pinnacles clearly inspired by the French. The four pilasters

The Duomo, Orvieto

decorated with bas-reliefs are superb. The mosaics are mostly 17th-century; the only remaining 14th-century ones are in the Victoria and Albert Museum, London. The interior is rich in works of art. In the Cappella di San Patrizio is a splendid series of frescoes (1499–1504), the work of Signorelli. The chapel on the other side of the cathedral houses the Miraculous Host, which prompted the building of the cathedral when it oozed blood on the hands of a doubting priest. The new bronze doors by the sculptor Greco caused considerable controversy when first hung, but are now accepted by most critics.

Another interesting church is that of San Domenico, probably the first church dedicated to the founder of the Order of Dominicans, of which, thanks to a building project early this century, only the transept remains. However, the lovely funeral monument to Cardinal de Bray, the work of Arnolfo di Cambio, is still there. The oldest church in the city is that of San Giovenale (1004). *Arezzo 119km/74mi, Roma 126km/78mi.*

Perúgia   J5

(pop. 116,710) Perúgia is well situated, and is an excellent centre from which to visit other cities of this agreeably green heart of Italy. Almost 500m/1640ft above sea level, surrounded by the foothills of the Apennines, it rarely becomes uncomfortably hot in the summer months. Perúgia was originally an Etruscan city, and in its museum is a fine collection of relics of that time; the Arco Etrusco is a magnificent portal at the foot of Via Rocchi and Via Bartolo, the two steep streets running downwards from behind the cathedral. This archway is also known as the Arco d'Augusto, for it is a composite construction, with not only a Roman arch superimposed upon the original Etruscan, but also a Renaissance *loggetta* which was added during the 16th century.

The principal street, Corso Vannucci, runs from the Piazza IV Novembre down to the delightful gardens, Giardino Carducci, overlooking the fertile valley and the low surrounding hills. The cathedral is Gothic of the late 14th and 15th century, with some excellent stained glass; in its museum are some fine works of art by Umbrian and Tuscan artists, but the focal point in this square is the magnificent Fontana Maggiore, constructed in the late 13th century to celebrate the completion of an aqueduct bringing water to Perúgia from Montepulciano, and decorated with bas-reliefs of striking beauty by Nicola and Giovanni Pisano. The enormous Palazzo dei Priori occupies the other side of the square and was built over a period of more than three centuries; the oldest part is that facing the square, the newest is in Corso Vannucci, and the whole is a harmonious blending of the various styles. The palace also houses the Galleria Nazionale dell'Umbria – a splendid collection by Perugino, Pinturicchio, Duccio and others. Farther down the Corso is the Collegio di Cambio, frescoed by Perugino.

A pleasant walk from the square is down the steep Via dei Priori, a typical medieval street, which sweeps round into an open piazza in which are situated the delightful Oratorio di San Bernardino, with a façade decorated in bas-reliefs by Agostino di Duccio, and the huge ruined church of San Francesco al Prato. To the right is Via A. Pascoli, tree-lined and pleasant, which leads to Palazzo Gallenga, now the seat of the University for Foreigners, where students from all nations come to study the language, art, literature and music of Italy. From Piazza Fortebraccio in front of the university, a walk up the steep Corso Garibaldi brings one to the charming little church of Sant'Angelo, worth visiting also for the views beyond. Another church that demands a visit is San Pietro, reached through the Porta San Pietro (another example of the work of Agostino di Duccio). The church is a museum in itself; note particularly the 16th-century courtyard, the unusual bell-tower, the magnificent choir stalls and the paintings.

These are just some points of interest in a city that has much more to offer to those who have time to wander lazily through its streets. An absorbing half-day excursion is to Ipogeo dei Volumni, an Etruscan tomb in the suburb of San Giovanni. Another Etruscan tomb was recently discovered in the suburb of Monte Lupo.

Spoleto   L6

(pop. 36,769) Spoleto is high above sea level and is dominated by a 14th-century fortress, with a spectacular viaduct nearby. Its civilization has developed from Umbrian, Etruscan and Roman origins and a Roman theatre, Roman walls, gates and a Roman house, allegedly once lived in by the mother of the emperor Vespasian, remain as witnesses of its early splendour. When the Longobards invaded Italy in the 6th century, the city became one of their dukedoms, and eventually it formed part of the Church state. Many of its streets still have a medieval aspect. The splendid cathedral of Santa Maria Assunta, a Romanesque building of the 13th century, has a marvellous mosaic high up on the west front, and an attractive portico of more recent date. The interior is baroque, with a bronze above

the main portal by Bernini. There is a fine pavement, and behind the main altar a famous fresco by Filippo Lippi, begun in 1467. In the sacristy is a famous crucifix painted on parchment stretched on wood, the work of Alberto Sozio (1187). In the first chapel on the right as one enters are frescoes by Pinturicchio. The cathedral stands at one end of a sloping piazza in which, during the annual Festival of the Two Worlds (July), open air performances of such works as Verdi's *Requiem* are given.

Another lovely Lombard-Romanesque church is that of Sant'Eufemia nearby, with a charming ladies' gallery and a valuable and anonymous triptych.

One has to obtain keys and permission to visit the Roman house and the little, disused church of Santi Giovanni e Paolo, but both are worth the trouble, particularly the latter as among its many frescoes is an extraordinary one depicting the murder of Thomas à Becket. Farther from the centre of the city are two other extremely interesting churches, that of San Pietro with its wonderful Romanesque façade, and the church of San Salvatore, constructed at the end of the 4th or the beginning of the 5th century (this church is just beyond the cemetery). The 13th-century Palazzo Pubblico is now the home of the art gallery, and another fine 14th-century palace, the Palazzo della Signoria, houses the Museo Civico.

A pleasant excursion is to **Fonti del Clitunno** (springs), 12km/7mi along the main road to Foligno. These springs have been sung by poets through the centuries and half an hour is well spent wandering in the shade of the poplars and weeping willows; a pair of swans glide over the waters, and all around is peace. Farther along the road is a tiny 5th-century church. *Perúgia 57km/35mi, Roma 133km/83mi.*

Todi   L5

(pop. 20,659) Todi stands on a height, like many Umbrian towns; it is encircled by three sets of walls – Etruscan, Roman and medieval. The main square is an almost perfect example of medieval architecture, with a Romanesque cathedral and three palaces: the Palazzo del Popolo and the Palazzo del Capitano del Popolo, both 13th century, and the Palazzo dei Priori (14th century). It has other interesting churches: San Fortunato, Gothic with delightful choir stalls, and at the foot of the entrance steps, a statue of Jacopone da Todi, the 13th-century writer; and a charming little church, built to a design by Cola di Caprarola, the Tempio di Santa Maria della Consolazione. *Perúgia 47km/29mi.*

LÁZIO

Lázio received its name from its earliest inhabitants, the Latini, at a time when it consisted of the Tyrrhenian coast south of the Tévere (Tiber), embraced by the Lazial and Tiburtine Hills, a territory that merited its name, which apparently indicated 'plainland'.

With the passing of time the area dominated by Roma increased and in the Middle Ages the name was abandoned, while the various additions took on different designations. In 1870, however, Papal power ceased and the united province around Roma was established under its ancient name of Lázio, which nowadays extends north and east as far as the Apennines, south to the northern bank of the River Garigliano, with the Tyrrhenian forming its western boundary.

Mountains, hills, plain, one-time marshes (now mostly reclaimed) and a lengthy coastline – Lázio has a little of everything. South of the Tévere, the once volcanic nature of many of the hills has rendered the soil rich enough to encourage intensive cultivation. Progressing north and east towards the Apennines, one encounters first of all low, calcareous hills, rising to great heights along the northeastern boundary of the region.

Lakes are mostly of volcanic origin. Lago di Bolsena, Lago di Bracciano and the small Lago di Vico all come into this category, as do the little lakes, Albano and Nemi in the Colli Albani (Alban Hills).

Lying between the two Papal strongholds of Orvieto and Viterbo is Lago di Bolsena, in the heart of Etruscan territory, near such centres as Tarquínia of the many towers where there is a fine Etruscan museum, and nearby some splendid painted tombs; Vetralla where there are unexplored rock tombs; and Tuscánia with its lovely Romanesque churches.

The town Bolsena, too, has its history, for here is the church where, in the year 1243, in defiance of the doubtings of a sceptical celebrant, the Host dropped blood on the corporal and even down to the pavement before the altar. The corporal that featured is kept in a special reliquary in the cathedral of Orvieto.

Coming to less weighty matters, near the southeasterly corner of this lake is the little town of Montefiascone, long famous for its wine, the very wine that features in a sad little tale of the German Bishop Fugger of olden times, a gentleman who appreciated good wine so much that he was wont to send his servant ahead of him on journeys to test the wine, and, if he found it good, to mark the place with the word *Est*. When he arrived at Montefiascone, the servant found the wine so superior to all the others that he wrote *Est, est, est*. When the bishop arrived, he called for the wine, sampled it, and was so entirely in agreement with his servant's verdict that he drank far too much of it, and did not live to tell the tale. Travellers have been warned – the wine *is* good, but if tempted to over-indulge, remember the fate of poor Bishop Fugger.

Another pleasant lake is Bracciano, about 35km/22mi northwest of Roma. The eighth Italian lake in size, its waters abound in fish and in the town above is the splendid six-towered Orsini castle of the 15th century.

After a busy but exhausting time in Roma, a visit to Lakes Albano and Nemi in the nearby Alban Hills, is agreeable. The former, elliptical in shape, is near the little town of the same name, which alas, is not best equipped to welcome visitors. It is well to proceed to Nemi nearby. This is a smaller lake, almost completely circular, lying far down within a surround of wooded slopes. There is a strawberry festival here in June, but it is usually possible to find exquisite strawberries as late as September. Both these lakes are of volcanic origin.

Down on the shore stands a museum in which are housed two Roman ships. Be warned, it is a good 2km/1mi down the slope, and on the return journey the distance seems to have grown considerably! You may have asked in the town where to find the museum, and been told 'Down there'. But if you have neglected to ask 'Is it open?', no one will have mentioned that probably it is not! The walk back is pleasant, but very long.

If one is driving and has a day to spare while in the vicinity of Roma, there are many interesting places within reach.

Travelling from Roma along the Via Casilina and branching off to the left after about 37km/23mi, one comes first of all to Palestrina, a picturesque city of about 10,000 inhabitants, 515m/1690ft above sea level and presiding over a wide valley, typical of the scenery of this not very well-known part of Italy. Here in 1525 was born the famous composer who took his name from that of the city. There is an interesting museum and the immense temple of Fortuna Primigenia (8th century BC) and among the treasures in the museum is a wonderful mosaic depicting Egypt at a moment when the River Nile was in flood.

From Palestrina, retracing one's tracks one can branch off again from Via Casilina, this time to the right, to take a look at Segni, interesting for its surrounding walls. Back once again to Via Casilina one should travel on to Anagni (pop. 15,500) a medieval city with a fine Romanesque cathedral that has a splendid mosaic floor and lovely Byzantine-type frescoes of the 13th century. It was in this cathedral that Pope Alexander III pronounced the excommunication of Barbarossa. It was once the favourite dwelling place of Pope Boniface VIII, whose palace, now converted to other uses, still stands, and it was here in the year 1303 that William of Nogaret dared to slap the face of the aged prelate, a blow from which he never recovered.

From Anagni, a winding road to the left brings one to the thermal town of Fiuggi, where those who wish may pause awhile to 'take the waters'. Leaving Fiuggi and taking Road No. 155 – which is fairly winding – when one arrives at the turning for Collepardo, it is as well to proceed beyond this point and uphill until arriving at the Certosa (Charterhouse) of Trisulti, which comes surprisingly into view in the midst of a small forest of oak trees; a huge concentration of religious buildings around the ancient church of San Bartolomeo. There is much to visit here, the great and small cloisters, the chapter house and an enchanting 17th-century chemist's shop. One can also buy an excellent liqueur distilled from the locally-grown herbs.

From Trisulti and down the winding road again, one goes on to Alatri, of about 21,000 inhabitants, a city more than 500m/1640ft above sea level and famous for its massive cyclopic walls which date back to the 4th century BC. The central part of the town has preserved a medieval aspect.

Driving back to Roma, you will probably feel that your day's excursion has been rewarding.

The climate in Lázio varies from typically maritime along the coast, to temperate with colder winters in the river valleys, then, as one nears the mountains, it becomes continental with severe winters and, along the slopes of the Apennines, the possibility of heavy rain. Roma has rain on an average of 80 days per annum, and an average annual rainfall of 760mm/30in, the wet periods reaching their peak usually from October to December, with the minimum in July.

Festivals Good Friday in Sezze, about 15km/9mi from Latina, has a procession in costume respresenting, among other things, the re-awakening of the dead – on the men's costumes are painted extremely realistic skeletons. *Corpus Domini* is celebrated in many provincial towns, Genzano di Roma for one, by 'paving' the streets with pictures composed entirely of tiny flowers. In Viterbo 3 September sees the Processions of Santa Rosa, in memory of a young girl who in 1243 saved the people of her town from the tyranny of Frederick II; on the eve of the festival a huge papier-mâché edifice in the form of a bell-tower, with a niche containing the image of the saint, is borne through the streets by 80 men in white.

Città del Vaticano
(Vatican City)   **J4**
Città del Vaticano, the seat of the Pope and his court of ecclesiastical and civic dignitaries, is an independent State, an enclave with its own coinage and stamps and its own radio transmitting station. Constituted on 11 February 1929, under the Lateran Treaty between Italy and the Holy See, it comprises the Basilica di San Pietro in Vaticano, the Vatican Palace and precincts, while the three basilicas of Santa Maria Maggiore, San Giovanni Laterano, San Paolo fuori le Mura are included in its extra-territorial rights.

Rome (Rome)   **J5**
(pop. 2,364,727) Roma, true heart of Italy, is not only capital of the Republic but, in the Città del Vaticano, capital of the entire Catholic world. Throughout Italy are representations of a she-wolf suckling twins, and on the left-hand side of the slope rising to the Campidoglio (Capitol – 1), in a cage let into the rock, is another she-wolf, a reminder of the mythical founding of the city. Ancient Roma was famous for its power, its architecture, its statuary, its culture and its cruelty. The Colosseo (2) was the scene of gladiatorial fights; the catacombs of San Callisto, Sant'Agnese and others are a tragic reminder of the privations suffered by Christians until the Edict of Milan (313

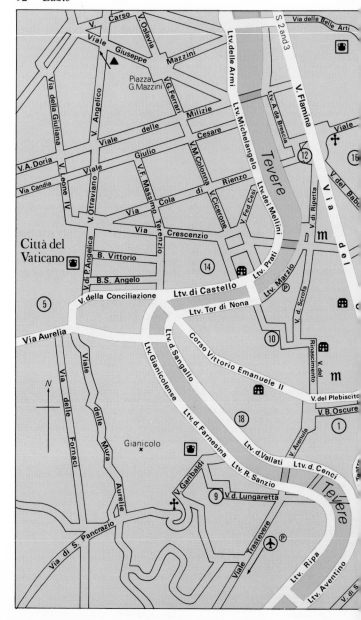

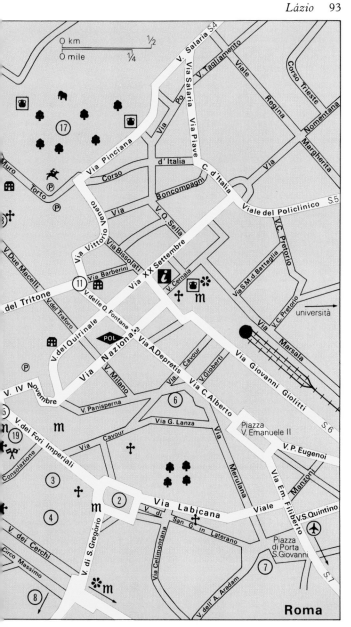

Roma

AD) allowed them freedom to worship openly. Sacked twice during the 5th century AD, Roma was reduced to a travesty of its former glory; Pope Gregory, writing nearly 50 years after the second disaster, speaks of a city with more empty spaces than houses, more sheep in its streets than human beings. But as the power of the Empire declined, that of the Church state grew, and Roma flourished. For about 70 years following the year 1305, the Papacy established itself in Avignon, with a corresponding reduction of the population and standard of living in Roma; the Papacy returned, and once again Roma rose triumphant. In 1527 it was sacked by the combined forces of Spain and the Austrian Empire – it has survived to become a city which one cannot hope to know completely in a lifetime.

Imperial Roma Relics of the ancient city are to be seen primarily in the region of the Foro Romano (3) and Colosseo where one may walk for a considerable time (preferably in the early morning or evening) tracing the outlines of the imperial city, the arches of Titus, Constantine and Janus, the Ara Pacis (Altar of Peace), the columns of Trajan and Marcus Aurelius, the Terme di Caracalla. From the Palatine Hill (4) with remains of Roman palaces one can wander down the Via Appia with its umbrella pines and tombs of famous Romans.

Christian Roma The present Basilica di San Pietro (5) was designed by Bramante (16th century) and built on the site of the previous basilica erected by Constantine on his conversion. The dome was the creation of Michelangelo, as was the lovely *Pietà* in the interior. The canopy over the altar and the circular colonnade in the Piazza are by Bernini, who also designed the Royal Staircase in the Vaticano. The baroque façade was designed by Maderno. The Vaticano is full of treasures: the frescoes of Michelangelo in the Sistine and Pauline chapels, the sculptured group of Laocoon (50 BC) in the Museo Pio-Clementino, the suite of rooms decorated by Raphael, the Pinacoteca, the Borgia Apartments. All these museums are open only 0900 to 1400.

The church of Santa Maria Maggiore (6) is 4th century, restored in the 16th century, with some fine mosaics of the 5th and 13th century. The main façade was designed by Fuga in the 18th century. San Giovanni in Laterano (7) has lovely cloisters, and nearby is the chapel containing Scala Santa, the stairs down which Christ supposedly walked at the Passion. They were brought to Roma by Elena, the mother of Constantine. The Basilica di San Paolo fuori le Mura (8), rebuilt 1823, has a beautifully sculpted Easter candle by Fuga, a confessional altar by Arnolfo di Cambio, and lovely Romanesque cloisters. Santa Maria in Trastevere (9) is a Romanesque building with fine medieval mosaics in the apse.

Squares Roma is a city of lovely squares. The Campidoglio was designed by Michelangelo; the bronze equestrian statue of Marcus Aurelius dates from 176 AD. In Piazza Navona (10) is the Fountain of the Rivers, designed by Bernini, who also designed the Fontana del Tritone in Piazza Barberini (11). Piazza del Popolo (12), with the churches of Santa Maria dei Miracoli and Santa Maria di Montesanto, was planned after the sack of Roma in 1527, but the 19th-century architect Valadier is largely responsible for its classical appearance. One of the most picturesque combinations of square and architecture is the great staircase designed 1725–26 by de Sanctis, which leads from Piazza di Spagna (13) to the church of La Trinita dei Monti. In a house to the right of these stairs Keats died in 1821.

Other Sights The bulk of Castel Sant' Angelo (14) was a Roman sepulchre that was transformed into a fortress in the 10th century. Popes have fled to it for safety; Benvenuto Cellini was one of the few prisoners who managed to escape from it. The huge white monument to Vittorio Emanuele II stands near the Piazza Venezia (15) and contains the Tomb of the Unknown Soldier. One of the loveliest parks is the Pincio (16) which forms, with the Zoo, part of the great expanse of green surrounding Villa Borghese (17). This is now a museum which includes Titian's *Sacred and Profane Love*, Canova's statue of Pauline, Napoleon's sister, and Raphael's *Deposition*. The Palazzo Farnese (18) and the Museo Capitolino (19) should also be visited.

Excursions In addition to the magnificent fountains of the Villa d'Este, **Tivoli**, there are fabulous natural cascades in the Via Gregoriana and in the cathedral, a splendid 13th-century *Deposition* in wood, consisting of five figures. Not far from Tivoli is **Hadrian's Villa** (2nd century BC) where there are the remains of various buildings copied from those the Emperor had seen or heard about. **Castel Gandolfo**, in a delightful position above Lake Albano, is the summer residence of the Pope. **Nemi** (4km/2½mi) is mirrored in its lake, and is famous for its delicious strawberries and wines. **Frascati** is a town of superb villas, parks and fountains. Its name dates back to the time when it was an insignificant village and the roofs of its houses were covered with *frasche* (small boughs). **Ostia Antica** can be reached by metropolitan railway. Excavations have uncovered a city of the 4th century BC with a theatre, forum, flour mills, a delightful fountain of Amore and Pysche and some mosaic pavements, relics of a great port with a population of some 100,000. Not far away is the modern resort of Ostia.

Information Roma is so vast that it is essential to take one or more of the tours organised by CIT, Piazza Esedra. Other useful addresses are: Ente Provinciale per il Turismo, 11 Via Parigi; Comune di Roma, Assessorato per il Turismo, 68 Via Milano; Rome Automobile Club, 261 Via Cristoforo Colombo.

Tarquínia   H2

(pop. 12,000) Visitors following the traces of Etruscan civilization may well find themselves travelling to Tarquinia. Inland not more than 5km/3mi from the Tyhrennian Sea, this small town gives one the idea of being remote, not just from the sea, but from the entire world.

Originally Etruscan, it became important in Roman times, but when Roma fell, the Tarquinians retired to the upper part of their hilly city and reinforced their safety with walls and a stronghold. In the Middle Ages many of the houses erected high towers of the type generally associated with the Tuscan city of San Gimignano, many of which remain to this day. There are three interesting Romanesque churches, Santa Maria di Castello, where there is a charming cosmatesque pulpit, San Pancrazio and San Francesco, but the chief attraction of Tarquinia is the Museo Nazionale, which is housed in the 15th-century Vitelleschi palace. Here are to be seen Etruscan remains of extreme interest; the collection of vases is splendid. It is advisable to check opening and closing times.

Near the city are Etruscan tombs in the necropolis which date from the 7th to the 2nd century BC. Among the finest of these painted tombs is that of the Auguri (end of 6th century BC), the Tomb of the Baron (end of 6th century BC) and the Tomb of the Leopards (end of 5th century BC).

There are many interesting walks and the **Lido di Tarquínia**, about 5km/3mi away, has a fine stretch of sand.

There is good accommodation to be had, but this is limited, so book early.

Tivoli   I6

(pop. 33,200) If staying in Roma, a visit to Tivoli makes a welcome break from the bustle of the city.

Of ancient origin, Tivoli was much liked by the Romans as a holiday centre. The Temple of Vesta goes back to the last years of the republic, as does the Temple of the Sybil.

The poet Horace loved Tivoli and had a house in or near the city.

The Emperor Hadrian (2nd century AD) had a villa built nearby, in the grounds of which were erected replicas of the monumental delights he had enjoyed seeing during his many travels.

The Villa Gregoriana is one of the great attractions of the city, not least because of the celebrated waterfalls within its grounds, and the Villa d'Este, a 16th-century transformation of an ancient convent, with splendid gardens and fantastic fountains, is another of the sights not to be missed.

The cathedral has works in the sacristy attributed to Bernini, and there is also a splendid *Deposition* in wooden statuary. The Romanesque church of San Silvestro merits a visit, too.

Viterbo   G3

(pop. 48,120) This city, of Etruscan origin and later a Roman colony, developed greatly during the 10th century. It was a seat of the Popes during the period of dissidence between the Popes and Roma, and was the seat of the first Papal conclave. After a period of contestation between Popes and emperors, in 1375 it came finally under the domination of the Papal state.

Traces of Pelasgic walls still remain, and there is much evidence of the one-time medieval splendour; the whole district of San Pellegrino, for instance. The Palazzo Papale (13th century) is a fine example of Gothic Viterbese architecture, and has an exquisite loggia.

The cathedral of San Lorenzo, originally built in 1192, but later restored in 1681, has a fine 14th-century bell-tower, a baptismal font of the 15th century and the tomb of Letizia Bonaparte.

In the church of San Sisto (11th to 12th century) is a Roman baptismal font.

The fountains of the city are famous, particularly the Fontana Grande (1279) and those in Piazza della Morte and Piazza Pianoscarano.

There are thermal curative establishments, and around the city are delightful walks to such interesting places as the ruins of Ferentum, the Villa Lante at Bagnaia, a fine Renaissance building by Vignola with statuary by Giambologna, and the Cistercian abbey of San Martino al Cimino.

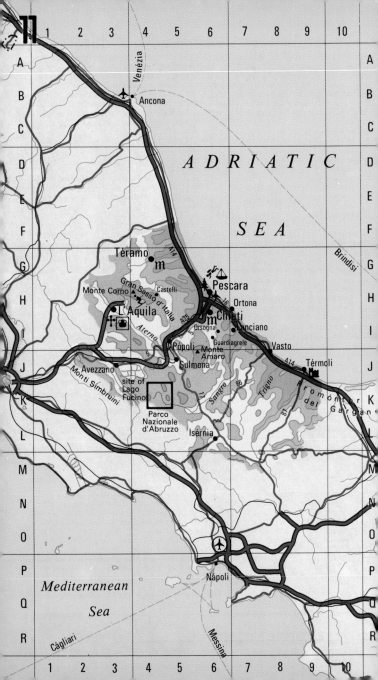

ABRUZZI AND MOLISE

Here are two more regions which are associated, with a coastline that runs from the mouth of the River Tronto southwards to just above the Gargano peninsula; on the west and south the area is bordered by Lázio, Campania and the northern boundary of Púglia.

Historically the two regions are distinct; there is the Abruzzi proper, which includes the provinces of Chieti, Téramo, Pescara and L'Aquila, and Molise, which occupies the territory of Campobasso.

The highest peaks of peninsular Italy rise in the heart of the Abruzzi. There is the Gran Sasso which in Monte Corno arrives at 2914m/9560ft above sea level, and La Maiella where Monte Amaro is 2795m/9170ft. These chains of mountains, together with the Simbruini and della Meta mountains, make up a vast region of high peaks, with occasional large valleys.

Molise extends south of La Maiella; its physical aspect is not unlike that of the Abruzzi, and as one draws nearer to Campania the mountains become less lofty.

The rivers run perpendicularly to the coastline. Some, such as the Aterno, near Pescara, cut deep gorges down the mountain sides.

In spite of the high percentage of mountainous country, there is a good amount of forest and agricultural land. One of the major crops is potatoes, followed closely by wheat and maize; along the coast vegetables grow well. There is a certain amount of vine growing and olive groves; sugarbeet is also grown. Oddly enough the Abruzzi stands high in apiculture; but saffron, which at one time grew in considerable quantity around L'Aquila, is now declining.

Among the rich forests stands out the Parco Nazionale d'Abruzzo (National Park of the Abruzzi), instituted with the idea of protecting the region's wildlife.

Sheep-grazing has always thrived, the mountains providing summer pastures, the plains a milder winter climate; some fishing is carried out along the coast.

In spite of its resources of water, which have led to the installation of a considerable number of electric networks, there is a lack of great industries, except for sugar-refining in the region of the one-time Lake Fucino and some chemical industries. There are, however, a fair number of smaller industries: pottery-making, particularly at Castelli in the province of Téramo, distilleries – the liqueur Aurum is a local product – and the making of 'confetti' (sugared almonds).

Tourism is well provided for all along the coast, and in the interior there are excellent opportunities for winter sports.

Both regions were inhabited in ancient times by fierce war-like tribes, but in the time of Augustus became part of the 4th Region.

There are relics of ancient Roma to be found all around; Chieti possesses a theatre, baths, temples, Téramo a theatre and an amphitheatre, and these are but two of numerous sites.

It was from the Longobards in the 6th to 7th centuries AD that first inklings of the present name appeared: to them the part around Téramo was known as Apruzzo.

At this time Molise was added to the Duchy of Benevento, and what is now Abruzzi fell to the lot of the Duchy of Spoleto, a condition that continued under the Franks, though in 843 AD an autonomous region, Marsia, developed in the interior.

In the 12th century the Pope ceded the region to the Normans, but this domination was sensed only in Molise until Frederick II came to the throne, when Abruzzi sided with him against the Church, at which time the city of L'Aquila came into being. Later, under the Angevin and Aragonese, the region followed the lead of Nápoli.

During the Middle Ages the art of architecture developed in the region in numerous cathedrals and abbeys. At this time L'Aquila began to enrich itself with churches which, while they followed the examples of Lombardia and Púglia, maintained a certain individuality of style, mainly seen in square façade with rectilinear balustrade, as in the church of Santa Maria di Collemaggio.

Following about 200 years of Spanish domination, and a short intervention by Austria, the region passed under the Bourbons of Nápoli; in 1860 it became part of the new Kingdom of Italy.

Molise largely follows the pattern set by Abruzzi, but mention must be made of a series of 9th-century frescoes in the crypt of the church of San Lorenzo in San Vincenzo al Volturno, apparently unique in the world of art.

Festivals First Thursday in May at Cocullo in the province of L'Aquila, a festival that might repel many, that of the *Serpari* (snake-catchers). The origins of this festival go back a long way; even Pliny makes mention of it. It has to do with the cult of the pagan goddess Angizia, nowadays substituted by San Domenico, whose statue on the day of the festival is adorned by living snakes and then carried in procession through the streets of the little hill town (870m/2854ft above sea level) accompanied, one is happy to add, by local snake-catchers.

Easter morning in Sulmona sees a statue of the Madonna borne through the streets on the shoulders of youths in costume.

On the Tuesday after Easter, Orsogna in the province of Chieti holds the Festival of the *Talami*, when local children enact Biblical scenes.

L'Aquila   H3

(pop. 58,420) This is a delightful medieval city situated on a wide plateau surrounded by a circle of the Apennines. It is a fine centre for walks through breathtaking scenery, and is within easy reach of the lovely pinewoods of Róio and the skiing resort of **Campo Imperatore** on the Gran Sasso, the highest part of this section of the Apennines. The church of Santa Maria di Collemaggio, a 13th-century Romanesque-Gothic edifice with a charming façade in pink and white marble with three elaborate rose windows – the façade was added later – lies just outside the southeast walls of the town. The entrance doors are elaborate, and inside is the tomb of Pope Celestino V, a Renaissance work by Gerolamo da Vicenza. This huge church has also one of the few *porta Santa* (holy doors) used only in the years of a papal jubilee. Returning along the Viale Francesco Crispi one comes to the Corso Vittorio Emanuele, lined with *portici* (arches), under which it is pleasant to sit and take a cup of coffee or an apéritif and watch the world go by. Behind this street is the lovely Basilica de San Bernardino.

In the Public Library are two volumes printed in 1482 by Adamo di Rotwil,

disciple of Gütenberg, and a fine collection of plain-song manuscripts. At the northern end of Corso Vittorio Emanuele is a large park, in one corner of which stands the striking castle built by the Spanish in the 16th century, nowadays the home of the Abruzzi National Museum. The cathedral has been largely rebuilt since it was first constructed in the 14th century, and architecturally the nearby Chiesa del Suffragio (18th century), which has a delightful cupola by Valadier, is far more interesting. These two churches stand in the Piazza del Duomo, the scene of a busy market on most mornings. Not to be missed is the Fountain of 99 Channels, close by the station.

While in L'Aquila an excursion worth taking is to the **Gran Sasso**. One can take a bus in the square, which passes through a series of charming little villages until it reaches the terminus of the cable railway which travels in two stages to the summit, from which the views are spectacular. *Ascoli Piceno 109km/68mi, Pescara 104km/65mi.*

Pescara   H6

(pop. 94,000) In addition to being the capital of its province and a very busy industrial city, Pescara is also one of the important seaside centres of the mid-Adriatic coast. It has excellent hotels and restaurants and extremely good road and rail communications.

Standing on the site of the ancient city of Alternum, Pescara was conquered by the Romans in 214 AD and later destroyed by the Longobards during the course of the Barbaric invasions. Nowadays it presents the appearance of a well-planned, completely modern city. The Italian poet Gabriele d'Annunzio was born in Pescara.

There are many small beaches in the vicinity, and a lovely pinewood; excursions to the **Gran Sasso**, the great National Park of Italy, are not difficult to arrange.

Térmoli   J9

(pop. 11,000) This is an active port near the peninsula of the Gargano, that spurlike promontory at the north of Púglia on the Adriatic coast.

A busy little town, one of its interests for tourists is that it is one of the points of embarkation for the fascinating **Trémiti** islands. It has a good beach, and though hotels are not numerous, there are good camping facilities.

It boasts a 13th-century castle, built by Frederick II, and a very interesting 12th-century cathedral. Fishing is good at Térmoli, and there is plenty of hunting inland during the autumn.

CAMPANIA

This region, to many foreign visitors, is the 'real' Italy, the region of the Tarantella, of sunshine, frivolous gaiety, of a sense of 'living for the day'; certainly, it has much of natural beauty to offer, and its inhabitants display an engaging desire to please.

Bounded on the west by the Mare Tirreno (Tyrrhenian Sea), its coastline offers a chain of delightful seaside resorts, vying one with another in natural beauty and in excellent tourist facilities. Coastal plains yield soon to the slopes of the Apennines, with here and there deep valleys. At times, for example around the Sorrento peninsula, the rocks rise sheer after a mere strip of blackish volcanic sand. The region is not lacking in volcanic manifestations: one has only to remember the not infrequent eruptions of Vesúvio, the bubbling witches' cauldron of the Solfatara near Nápoli and the buried cities of Pompei and Ercolano, plus the ever-present possibility of earthquakes. Because of its volcanic nature the soil is fertile, yielding three or four crops annually, even though the terrace cultivation of hilly regions demands much hard work and tenacity of purpose.

The area was once so racked with malaria that the Greeks abandoned the plain on which stand the magnificent ruins of Paestum; fortunately that same fear kept away many who might have raided the temples and used their stone for other buildings. Malaria has now been conquered; the menace today, where Paestum is concerned, is that of the speculating builders who, contrary to the law, run up concrete excrescences nearer and nearer to the glory that was Greece.

Beauty, history and climate combine to render Campania congenial and attractive, and one should not content oneself with visits to the 'obvious' tourist spots. For instance, from Vico Equense it is possible to go by bus or car to the summit of Monte Faito, to ramble among the woods there and to eat in one of several good restaurants. Similarly, from Amalfi, it is almost a 'must' to travel up the hill – preferably by slow-motion *carozza* – to visit Ravello, with frequent pauses on the way to rest the horse and admire the view, and once arrived to admire the beauties of the cathedral with the pulpit by Nicolò da Foggia, the other lovely church of San Giovanni del Toro, the Palazzo Rufolo and Palazzo Cimbrone; from the belvedere of the latter one has a marvellous view.

Visiting Vanvitelli's Royal Palace at Caserta, it is well to allow time to drive up to Vecchia Caserta, 7km/4mi away, an almost-forgotten little town of Longobard origin with a Norman Romanesque cathedral of the 12th century.

From Nápoli itself there are numerous 'extras'; apart from the obvious Pompei and Ercolano, there are the Campi Flegrei (Phlegrean Fields), the Lake of Avernus, and near Pozzuoli is the so-called extinct volcanic region of the Solfatara, where recent earth tremors (bradyseism) make one doubt the suitability of the adjective 'extinct'.

Ninety per cent of Campania is given over to agriculture: vines, tomatoes, citrus fruits. Olives are grown on the calcareous slopes, vines on the volcanic soil, and the wine from these grapes is extremely good. Fishing and the preservation of fish is a big source of income, and the corals from the region are worked in many establishments. Probably the best pasta (macaroni, spaghetti *etc*) comes from Campania, said to be the true home of pasta. Around Sorrento it is possible to find excellent inlaid woodwork, and the working of cameos is another trade at which local craftsmen are expert.

The islands off the coast, Capri, Íschia and Prócida, attract great numbers of tourists for their great beauty of scenery and their pleasing climate.

Capri So much has been written about this island that many people feel themselves familiar with it even before going there. If one is spending a holiday in the area of Nápoli, a visit to this island should be included.

Boats ply daily from Nápoli, Sorrento and Amalfi. Once arrived, a lift takes one speedily up the cliff into the town. The main street winds pleasantly upwards, lined with restaurants, bars and tourist shops, to a hillside dotted with houses.

Capri was probably originally settled by the Phoenicians, but it first achieved notoriety under the Romans. The emperors Augustus and Tiberius both knew it. The latter had a 'stately pleasure house' on Capri, and tales of his orgies form a part of the folklore of the island. One is shown the precipitous rock from which he is said to have cast discarded favourites.

It is thought that Norman Douglas used the background of Capri for his novel, *South Wind*. Dr Axel Munthe has rendered it familiar to all who have read his appealing *Story of San Michele*, and one can still visit the house the building of which is described in the story.

One should visit the villa where Munthe lived, the 17th-century church of Santo Stéfano, the heights of Anacapri, or walk to the cliff where once stood the villa of Tiberius. Then, down again on the shore, it is possible to take a boat to fairyland, alias the Blue Grotto. Once arrived, you will change into an even smaller boat, and will probably be bidden to lie flat while this little cockleshell makes its entrance into the grotto, but once inside, the reward is great. Water, walls, everything one sees is of a deep pellucid blue; one puts one's hand into the water and it appears to be covered with silver.

It is possible to spend an entire holiday on Capri, but because of its great popularity, very early booking is necessary. **Íschia** is larger than Capri, and while it is no less beautiful, its beauty is simpler.

There are numerous boat services to Íschia, and in addition to natural beauty, the island offers a wide variety of water sports, hunting and fishing.

Not only a holiday resort, it is also a spa, with curative springs at Fornello and Fontana, which produce strongly radioactive water at a temperature of 65°C/148°F.

The late Renaissance baptistery of the church of dell'Assunta is interesting, as is the 15th-century Aragonese castle and the botanical garden.

There are numerous excellent hotels and restaurants, so visitors are well provided for.

Prócida lies between Nápoli and Íschia and is a pleasant little island, reminiscent of an oriental village with its white houses. It provides for tourists in that there are lovely walks to be taken, with many picturesque viewpoints on the way. In the abbey of San Michele there is a fine ceiling painting by Luca Giordano.

There are only two hotels, but Prócida is within easy reach of both Nápoli and Íschia by boat.

Near Nápoli is a trio of lakes, the fame of which has come down in mythology. Homer and Virgil both sang of Avernus, Lucrinus and Fusaro, and Roman emperors and the aristocracy of their day revelled in the splendours nature offers there. Avernus presents a somewhat alarming aspect; here one stands amid the ruins of the villas, thermal establishments,

Capri

temples and tombs of the time when Roma was at its greatest. This lake, once thought to be the entrance to the Nether Regions, has become even more awe-inspiring, for something seems to have gone wrong with part of the drainage system, and effluent that ought by rights to go far out to sea, has been known to arrive there.

Lucrinus still attracts holiday-makers to the narrow stretch of sandy shore dividing it from the sea; Fusaro, almost entirely circular, is separated from the sea by a pinewood; it is famous for the production of oysters. Nearby stands the Royal Casino built in 1782 by Vanvitelli for the Bourbon King Ferdinand II.

The 8th century BC saw the Greeks established along the coast, at Paestum, Nápoli and Cuma. These were menaced in the 6th century by the Etruscan founders of Cápua, then in the year 330 BC we see that city united with Roma against the Sannites who advanced from the interior, from which time the Romanization of Campania proceeded until under Augusttus it formed, with Lázio, part of the 7th Region. Then, under Domitian, it became a province in its own right. This territorial unity held good under the Ostrogoths and the Byzantines, but fell apart when the Longobards arrived and established first of all a principality at Cápua and then in 900 AD extended this to Benevento, which became a Longobard duchy, while the Byzantines still maintained power in the Duchy of Naples. In the 9th and 10th centuries AD Amalfi broke free and, establishing its autonomy, became a great naval power, the rival of Pisa and Génova – the Amalfitani Naval Code was of infinite importance during the Middle Ages.

The fact that the region was divided into many sections made it an easy prey to the Normans who, stemming from the region of Aversa in 1030, gradually spread until, by 1077, they not only held Cápua but annexed Salerno and in 1139 Nápoli. Campania became identified with the Kingdoms first of Sicilia then of Nápoli and later what was known as the Kingdom of the Two Sicilies. In the 12th and 13th centuries it formed a part of the Norman-Swabian dynasty, then at the beginning of the 16th century, under the Angevins and the Aragonese, it became important, with Nápoli as the capital city. For over 230 years it suffered Spanish domination, and a viceroyalty was established. It received its autonomy under the Bourbons and this lasted with small interruptions under Napoleon until 1860, when Garibaldi sealed its unity with the Kingdom of Italy.

Campania is a region richer than many in relics of antiquity. Paestum is pure Greek; Cuma, Pompei, Ercolano are Roman. Pozzuoli is rich in remains of Imperial Roma; some part of the one-time Temple of Serapis is now under water, and for that reason more fascinating to see. Recently the phenomenon of bradyseism – a slow up and down movement of the earth's crust – has been affecting the area. Benevento has a Roman triumphal arch, Bácoli huge cisterns, while Cápua boasts several villas, and almost everywhere it is possible to find bridges and sepulchres which speak of Roma. Paleochristian art, too, can be seen; Nápoli has the baptistery of San Giovanni in Forli and the catacombs of San Gennaro extra Mœnia.

The Longobard period is remembered in monuments at Cápua and Benevento, and the churches that rose between the 11th and 13th centuries were splendid combinations of Classical, Byzantine, Arabo-Norman and Lombard style. Then came a period during which were constructed the splendid pulpits and bronze portals to be seen in many churches, for example the bronze doors of the cathedrals of Amalfi and Atrani, brought from Constantinople. In the Palazzo Rufolo at Ravello are examples of charming Arabo-Sicilian stonework. Under the Angevins and the Aragonese came the Gothic and Spanish influence in cities such as Cápua.

During the Renaissance and baroque periods the region as a whole echoed Nápoli, for example Vanvitelli's 18th-century Royal Palace at Caserta. In the 17th century a great school of painting centred upon Nápoli, with such representatives as Salvatore Rosa, Ruoppolo and Ribera.

Festivals Hardly a 'festival' but a serious affair at Nápoli and Pozzuoli is the commemoration ceremony of San Gennaro when the blood of the saint liquefies – or does not – in the church of San Gennaro in Nápoli before a wildly excited crowd of the faithful. The more solemn of the two annual occurrences is on 19 September, the anniversary of the saint's martyrdom, the other takes place on the eve of the first Sunday in May. Because of the intense crowds, it is not easy to witness either.

On 29 June of every year in the little village of Cetara, not far from Amalfi, the statue of San Pietro is borne through the streets, followed by a procession.

The most festive of the festivals of Nápoli – which has several – is that of *Piedigrotta* on 8 September of every year, when a gaily-caparisoned procession leaves the church of Piedigrotta and parades through the streets to the accompaniment of fireworks, music and general revelry. The following morning, in the vicinity of the Aquarium is held what might be termed a children's *Piedigrotta*, a parade of young children, whose fancy dress must be made only of crêpe paper – a little festival well worth a visit.

Amalfi   L5

(pop. 6803) This is one of many fine seaside resorts along the coast between Nápoli and Salerno. In the Middle Ages it was an important Marine Republic, ranking with Venezia in volume of trade with Constantinople and the Orient. The Marine Laws of Amalfi were the codex of marine commerce until as late as 1570, and the original Tavole Amalfitane can still be seen in the Municipio.

The splendid cathedral, standing at the top of a long flight of steps, is eye-catching façade crowned by a mosaic of Christ enthroned, recalls its medieval glory. It dates back to the 9th century, but it was rebuilt in 1103, when the lovely Paradise Cloisters were added. In 1066 the splendid bronze doors were brought from Constantinople. The cathedral is dedicated to Sant'Andrea, whose remains are buried beneath the altar. There is an interesting fountain in the square, and it is amusing to walk in and around this square and the narrow streets to enjoy the busy life of the town and the open air market. Also worth visiting are the restored Arsenal, where at one time boats were built, and a former Capuchin convent.

One of Amalfi's attractions is a boat trip to the Grotta di Smeraldo, where the light gives the water an almost unbelievably beautiful colour. In the cathedral of **Atrani** with its magnificent bronze doors, the former dukes of Amalfi were proclaimed. If you are spending some days in Amalfi, a pleasant leisurely excursion – preferably by horse-drawn carriage – is up the steep, winding hill to **Ravello**.

There are numerous hotels, two of which were originally convents, which have been beautifully converted and offer excellent – but not cheap – hospitality. One can breakfast in what were once cloisters. One of these convents is across the road from a one-time watch-tower, a relic of the days of Saracen invasions, and this has been converted into a most agreeable bar and tearoom, with stairs leading down to the hotel's excellent private beach.

From Amalfi, another pleasant walk along the cliffs is to the small coastal towns of **Minori** and **Maiori**, once too insignificant to merit a mention other than as fishing villages, but now rapidly developing into good tourist centres.

Nápoli (Naples)   K4

(pop. 1,150,390) It would be hard to find a city more beautifully situated, a huge bay, houses rising up in terraces to the hills behind, with Vesuvius, ever watchful, ever menacing, in the background. Climatically, Nápoli is fortunate, mostly sunny, often extremely hot, but with a freshness from the sea that prevents it from becoming unbearably sultry. A rich, florid city with an almost oriental splendour in its buildings, it is over-populated, vociferous and kindly. Apart from the more obvious sights, the tourist should also walk down some of the crowded side streets, the *Bassi*, where whole families live in one large room in the basement of a tall palazzo, and much of the day's work is done in the street. Modern Nápoli has wide streets and up-to-date houses, but the real Nápoli is the city of the *Bassi*, the palaces that remind one of bygone glory.

The waterfront is extremely beautiful. The huge Castel Nuovo, built in the time of Charles I of Anjou (1280) and reconstructed during the 15th century, has an interesting triumphal arch and the rooms of the Bourbon kings, one of which leads to the Tower of the Beveretto, looking out to sea. There is a fine museum in the castle. Follow the waterfront to the Palazzo Reale in Piazza Plebiscito; on the other side of the square is the 19th-century church of San Francesco di Paola, designed by Pietro Bianchi. Again on the front are some of Nápoli's famous restaurants. Continue along the bay to the fishing section at Mergellina, passing through the green, shaded Villa Comunale, pausing to visit the Aquarium. Close by is the church of Santa Maria di Piedigrotta, a 14th-century building, which is illuminated during the *Festa di Piedigrotta*.

Back in the city centre, at the junction of Via E. Pessina and Via Foria, the Museo Nazionale has a splendid collection of archaeological treasures, mosaics, sculpture and paintings. Walk north along the Corso Amedeo di Savoia to the Parco di Capodimonte where Charles of Bourbon used to hunt game. The palace is now a museum, with a fine collection of paintings by Bellini, Titian, Parmigiano and Correggio. By the Sanità bridge are the church and catacombs of San Gennaro; the catacombs (2nd century AD) are on two levels, and contain wall paintings. The lighting is not good.

Another walk starts from the church of Santa Chiara (east of Via Monte Oliveto). Although badly damaged in 1943, the church has been restored, and the cloisters with majolica columns are in a charming setting. Farther along is the church of San Domenico. St Thomas Aquinas taught in the adjoining convent. Along Via Duomo

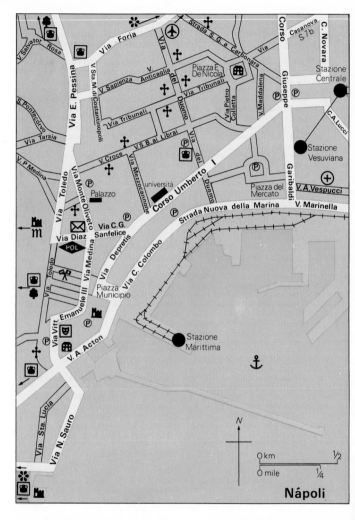

Nápoli

is the church of the Gerolomini, centre of Father Borelli's work to help the poor of the city, and across the road lies the 13th-century cathedral. Here is celebrated the Miracle of the Liquefaction of the Blood of the Patron Saint (first Sunday in May). Upon the degree and speed of liquefaction depend the fortunes of Nápoli for the following year. To the north of the nave,

one may descend to the church of Santa Restituta, the first Christian basilica of Nápoli. The low screens (*plutei*) dividing the presbytery from the nave have some absorbing bas-reliefs.

Excursions are many. Coaches go to **Vesúvio**, or one can take the Circum-vesuvian Railway to **Pugliano** from which buses connect with the chairlift.

This particular trip could be combined with a visit to **Ercolano**, which was submerged under a wave of molten lava in 79 AD. During the reign of the Bourbons, the district was a resort for wealthy families, and there are still some delightful villas, parks and gardens. It was at this time that excavations began to reveal much of the old Roman city which now offers a fascinating insight into Roman life.

There are also daily coach tours to **Pompei**, which was buried under a blanket of dust at the same time as the Ercolano disaster. Here, the services of a guide are essential, if one is to appreciate the amazing temples, forums and private houses. The museum contains many works of art from this city, once a pleasure resort of wealthy Roman citizens. **Caserta** (27km/17mi) is a busy provincial town where Vanvitelli built the 'Versailles of Italy' for the Bourbon king. This elegant palace, surrounded by delightful gardens, contains a private theatre, a series of wonderfully-furnished rooms, and a fine portrait gallery. There is an excellent restaurant in the park.

It is also well worthwhile travelling a further 7km/4mi uphill to the old city, **Vecchia Caserta**, of Longobard origin, where one finds a scattering of ancient houses that give one the feeling of having stepped back into the Middle Ages. There is also a splendid Norman-Romanesque church, built in the local black and yellow tufa rock, and boasting a fine pulpit and some early mosaics.

The building of the Royal Palace of Caserta, and the consequent demand for local labour, led to the almost complete desertion of the old city for the new.

Ravello L5

(pop. 2530) Ravello, on the spur of a mountain dividing two valleys, has a good climate, several hotels and some splendid panoramic views. The cathedral has two magnificent pulpits, one of 1272, and an earlier one of 1130. The latter is decorated with a head and two profiles, the work of Nicolò da Foggia, and the columns of the pulpit rest on 'perambulating' lions. The Palazzo Rufolo, in the gardens of which are splendid examples of Moorish architecture, and the Palazzo Cimbrone, also with lovely gardens and a breathtaking panoramic view from the belvedere, are two lovely villas. There are charming Romanesque cloisters in the church of Sant'Antonio. Two pleasant walks are to **Scala** (1km/½mi), or down the long hill to **Minori** where there is a Roman villa. *Amalfi 4km/2½mi.*

Salerno L6

(pop. 110,995) The Roman city became part of the Longobard Duchy of Benevento in the 6th century; then, in the 9th century, an independent principality, falling eventually into Norman hands in 1076. The famous Salerno School of Medicine, founded in the 9th century, flourished until the beginning of the last century. The old town rises up towards the hills behind the bay; along the shore is the modern part, with gardens and a promenade. The city offers all kinds of seaside amusements, and there are pleasant walks to be taken in the district. In the old part is the cathedral of San Matteo, an 11th-century building with an attractive courtyard and covered forecourt. The interior is richly decorated and houses many treasures including a splendid pulpit and, in the crypt, two statues of the patron saint whose bones are buried there. The Museo del Duomo also has many precious exhibits including a famous 12th-century *Exultet*. In the church of San Giorgio are frescoes by Solimena; the Chiesa dell'Annunciata was designed by Vanvitelli. Salerno also has another interesting museum, the Museo Provinciale.

The ancient Greek city of **Paestum** (40km/25mi) is reached easily by rail or road. Here are the temples of Neptune and of Ceres, and a fine basilica dating from the 6th century BC. There is also a fascinating museum, and city walls that cover over 4km/2½mi with four city gates. In the vicinity are medieval coastal towers erected as a means of defence against Saracen raiders.

Sorrento L4

(pop. 11,768) This is one of the loveliest seaside resorts in the vicinity of Nápoli. At Easter the streets are gay with orange trees and flowering almonds, and there is an interesting and very solemn procession on Good Friday when the statue of Christ reclining is borne through the streets by black-robed, cowled figures, to the accompaniment of funeral music. The main square has a monument to the poet Torquato Tasso who was born in Sorrento in 1544. In this square, too, are *carrozzas* (little carriages) with plumed horses, and numerous shops selling the lace, embroidery, and inlaid woodwork for which the town is famous. In the tree-lined Via Correale is the Museo Correale with a fine collection, and with a splendid view from the belvedere. The bathing beach is small, and the sands, being volcanic, are blackish, but bathing is good. There are boat trips to **Capri** and **Amalfi**, and interesting walks.

PÚGLIA AND BASILICATA

Two more regions usually associated, occupying the southeastern extremity of the peninsula from a little north of the spur-like peninsula, Gargano, down to the 'heel' of Italy, cut off from Calábria by the spine of the Apennines.

Taking first of all **Basilicata**, known also since 1932 as Lucania, this western section is largely mountainous; its few rivers are unpredictable, floods and landslides are not infrequent and, except in the north where grapes are cultivated, agriculture is difficult. Lack of good roads and hydroelectric power combine to render the region backward as regards heavy industry, though native craftsmanship reaches a high level. Since the end of World War II, state intervention has provided schools, hospitals and aqueducts, roads are being improved, conditions are better, but the old traditions die hard. A region once notorious for brigandage, this is now one of the least turbulent regions of the south.

Potenza, the main city, 822m (2697ft) above sea level, is the highest capital in peninsular Italy; the air is good, but windy. **Melfi** merits a visit for its fine cathedral, and another important city is **Matera**, built mainly on the edge of an abyss in the rocky plain.

When in the 8th and 7th centuries BC the Greeks founded colonies along the Ionic coast at Metapontum, Siri and Eraclea, this region enjoyed the fruits of a high civilization, dispersed in the 6th century BC when the Lucanians from the interior advanced and gradually established themselves.

Under Roma, Basilicata was included in the 3rd Region, but was not regarded as being very important.

The museums of Matera, Potenza and Metapontum have much to show by way of prehistoric remains, but there is little evidence left of the Greek period except for the splendid Tavole Palatine (Doric columns) at Metapontum. An amphitheatre at Venosa remains from Roman times.

Under the Barbaric invasions, aided by increasing epidemics of malaria, the population was considerably reduced. A part of Basilicata was added to the duchy of Benevento, then in 847 AD it became part of the principality of Salerno. Next came the Byzantines and by the middle of the 11th century the beginning of Norman domination. Not until the 12th century was the name Basilicata used.

The Middle Ages saw a great flowering of architecture, modelled on that of Púglia, Sicília, Campania and even France. The last is manifest in the great cathedral of Acerenza and the abbey of the Sacred Trinity at Venosa. While the cathedral of Matena is purely Pugliese, that of Melfi is redolent of Sicília, especially as regards the bell-tower.

The Normans, and later the Angevins, liked Basilicata and under them it enjoyed a period of prosperity, but from the 14th century onwards Nápoli became the centre of power and Basilicata fell into a decline, living in political isolation, troubled by quarrels between the various dynasties and feudatories. Faraway events had little effect on the torpor into which the region had sunk.

From 1815 onwards the ferments of the *Risorgimento* began to circulate, but it was not until 1860 that Basilicata became recognized as a part of the Kingdom of Italy.

The influence of Venezia is seen in that such painters as Vivarini and Cima da Conegliano are represented in the churches of Matera and Migliónico.

Festivals *Corpus Domini* is celebrated in Potenza by a procession during which flowers of *ginestra* (broom) are thrown by the crowds. In Accettura near Matera, 29 May sees a great procession in honour of the patron saint Giuliano. Matera on 2 July holds the *Festival of the Madonna della Bruna*. A statue of the Madonna is taken through the streets accompanied by a parade in costume. In the evening the papier-maché cart is pulled to pieces and the spectators take pieces home for good luck.

Púglia has few high mountains. Monte Calvo in the Gargano rises to 1056m (3464ft) above sea level, Montecornacchia, in the eastern Apennines, to just over 1100m (3609ft); otherwise, the region is flat. A wide stretch of plainland, the Tavoliere Capitanata, follows the coastline from north to south, backed by the so-called Terra di Bari, which peters out south of the town of Francavilla, giving way to the slightly higher Murge Tarantine, Murge Salentine and Terra di Otranto, which constitute the Salentine peninsula.

There are few rivers, so most of the necessary water comes from an aqueduct, fed by the River Sele in Campania, but even this is insufficient. Forests, except for the magnificent Foresta Umbra on the Gargano, are practically non-existent. Scarcity of water has enforced specialization in crops demanding little: vines, which produce grapes equally good for eating and for wine-making; olive trees, which grow to a fantastic size and yield excellent oil; almond trees, the nuts from which are world-famous. Thyme, sage and rosemary flourish, and on the Salentine peninsula peas, beans and tomatoes are grown, and there is some cultivation of citrus fruits – otherwise, agriculture is limited to cereals and forage.

Fishing supplies local needs, and is carried on not only along the coast, but in the two lakes, Lésina and Varano, north of the Gargano. The bay of Táranto has long been famous for large, succulent oysters and mussels.

As regards industry, the only bauxite mines in Italy are situated in the Gargano; the salt marshes of Margherita di Savoia, to the north of Barletta, are the most important in Europe. Along the coast are several large refineries.

Bari and Brindisi have long been important for communications with the east; Táranto is one of Italy's two naval bases, La Spezia in Liguria being the other.

From the 8th century BC a flourishing Greek colony had Táranto as its capital; then followed a period of prosperity under the Romans until the Fall of Rome, after which came attacks by the Byzantines, the Longobards and the Franks, and also by Saracen raiders along the coast.

In the 9th century AD the Byzantines established command. From the 11th century marine trade with Amalfi and the Dalmatian and Levantine ports was carried on.

Next came Norman domination of the region. The Crusades and trade with the east brought prosperity. When the Swabians took over from the Normans, Púglia was not only rich, but had a period of splendour in art and literature.

Later, under the Angevins and the Aragonese, decline set in. Venezia as-

sumed much of the marine commerce. Turkish raids, particularly around Ótranto, made the condition of coastal cities desperate. The decadence was aggravated by famines, malaria and the plague that raged over Europe. The Spanish period (1503–1707) served only to aggravate a sad case.

Under the Bourbons things improved. For one thing they were horse-lovers, and during their domination the Tavoliere around Fóggia was used for pasturage, until the city and its surroundings seemed like an Italian Wild West. (This pasturage was abolished by law in 1860). The decade 1805–15 saw Púglia once again prosperous. In 1860 it was added to the newly-formed Kingdom of Italy.

The region is rich in prehistoric dolmen and menhirs. Greek vases found in various necropolises can be seen in the museums of Táranto, Bari, Lecce and Ruvo. There are two great archaeological complexes at Canne della Battaglia and Egnázia. Roman remains are plentiful, among them the one remaining column of the two that originally marked the end of the Via Appia (Appian Way). In Lecce there is a fine Roman amphitheatre.

From the 11th to the 14th century came the erection of splendid cathedrals and churches in which the native Romanesque is embellished with oriental elements. In Táranto and Ótranto the cathedrals adhere to the Roman basilical form, and the latter has a fine mosaic floor. Many such buildings contain sculptural elements of great beauty, episcopal thrones, pulpits, bronze doors, portals and windows displaying Byzantine and oriental motifs. France and the Holy Land were mainly responsible for the Gothic influence noticeable from the 12th century onwards. During the 13th and 14th centuries numerous castles were built, among them Castel del Monte near Ándria, the hunting lodge of Frederick II.

There is little Renaissance architecture, and the influence of Venezia can be seen in the art of the region.

In the 17th century a particular type of baroque appeared in Lecce, peculiarly suitable to the easily-worked local stone which assumes a warm, golden hue with the passage of time. During this period, too, a local school of painters developed, strongly influenced by Nápoli, but with a certain individuality; in the 19th century the painters Altamura and Toma were much admired.

There is an odd little architectural enclave not far from the world-famous caves of Castellana, the region of the *trulli*. The small centres of Fasano and Alberobello possess groups of small houses, circular in form, white-walled, with conical stone roofs. The origin of the form is lost in the mists of antiquity, but the houses to be seen today date back to 1555 when the peasants of Conversano asked the local feudator, Count Acquaviva, if they might establish themselves in the territory. Permission was granted, but only on condition that any buildings should be built entirely of stone, without the aid of mortar or plaster. The most spectacular group of *trulli* is at Alberobello, where there are over a thousand.

Festivals Bari, 17 May, the *Festival of San Nicola* whose relics were brought from the monastery of Mira in 1097. The effigy of the saint is borne out to sea in a fishing boat to receive the homage of the faithful who go out in boats to visit it. Ostuni, last Sunday in August, a parade of 'well-dressed' horses with a prize for the best. The trappings are most elegant, with ribbons and flowers; final touches are administered not in the stables but in the houses of the owners. Hardly a 'festival',

but the Trade Fair of the Levante held every September in Bari is of great importance in relations with the Orient. On 26 September the patron saints of Bitonto, Cosma and Damian, are borne in procession; pilgrims arrive from near and far, and the most devout carry lighted candles on their shoulders.

The Trémiti (Tremites)   A8

These isles are off the coast of the Gargano, that spur-like promontory that juts out from the coast at the northern extremity of Púglia. To reach them, one can take a steamer from the little port of Rodi on the Gargano, or from Térmoli at the southern end of the Abruzzi, or travel by the swifter hydrofoil.

In order of size the group comprises San Domino, San Nicola, Capraia and Pianosa. There is a small hotel on San Domino and there are camping sites on San Nicola.

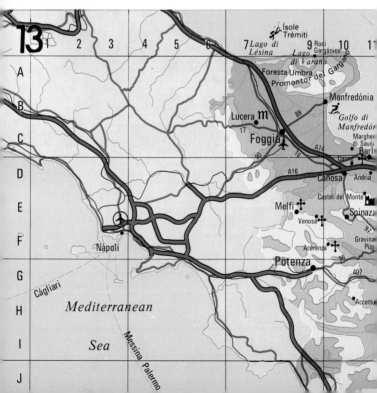

Bari D13

(pop. 323,060) Bari is one of the busiest commercial cities of the province, trading with the East and Middle East. In the middle two weeks of September is the international trade fair, the *Fiera del Levante*, one of the most important in Europe; in May there is an International Festival of Military Bands. On 17 May, a solemn procession recalls the transference to Bari of the bones of its patron saint, San Nicola. The next day a procession of pilgrims and sailors carries an effigy of the saint shoulder-high to the Piazza Mercantile; after a mass in the open air, the effigy is mounted on a sloop and taken out to sea, where it is visited by pilgrims and brought back to land in the evening.

The city is divided into two parts, the modern commercial centre, and the old city. Here, the church of San Nicola, a Romanesque building of the 11th and 12th centuries, has a delightful façade, one of the richest in this region. In the cathedral is preserved a valuable *Exultet* (the

prayer recited on Easter Sunday during the blessing of the Easter candle).

Not far from Bari are the famous caves of **Castellana** (40km/25mi), and it is within handy reach of the little town of **Alberobello** (67km/42mi) with its outlandish *trulli*, small white stone houses with conical roofs. A pleasant bathing resort which complements the facilities of Bari is **Torre a Mare**. Seafood in this area is excellent.

Barletta C11

(pop. 69,000) This is a city of pre-Roman origin, first known as Canusium, later as Barulum and finally Barletta. It lent its name to one of the famous events in Italian history, *La Disfida di Barletta*, when Ettore Fieramosca, a soldier of fortune, issued a challenge to one of the attacking French – the room in which the challenge was uttered is still to be seen in Barletta.

The cathedral (1267) is splendid inside and out, appearing smaller than it is in actual fact, because of the surrounding

buildings. Another treasure of the city is the Colossus, an Imperial bronze statue, 5m/16ft high, dating back to the 4th or 5th century and brought back from the Orient in the 13th century.

Having looked carefully at these and other architectural beauties Barletta has to offer, come back along the coastal road and make your next stop at **Trani**, 14km/8mi away; a small but flourishing maritime and commercial centre up to the 15th century, when it passed into the hands of Venezia. Trani is famous for bell-founding, among other things.

It is a quiet little place nowadays but has a beautiful cathedral with a bell-tower beside it for which the adjective 'beautiful' is hardly adequate. Standing as it does, right on the shore, one can look through the portal and passageway at its base and see some of the most charming seascapes imaginable.

The next stop should be at **Biscéglie**, after another 8km/5mi, and here is another marine centre with yet another interesting 11th-century church, that of Sant'Adoeno, erected by the Normans and dedicated to the saint of Rouen. There is a splendid font here.

After another 8km/5mi you come to lovely **Molfetta**, where at Easter is held one of those solemn religious processions so dear to the people of southern Italy.

The interesting part of Molfetta is the medieval section, down towards the sea, where stands the old cathedral (not to be confused with the nearby new cathedral, a 17th-century edifice). This older, Romanesque building is fortunate in having remained both inside and out as it was originally. It is recognizable from the outside by its three imposing cupolas, rather the shape of open Japanese parasols.

The little harbour of Molfetta is enchanting, and after such a tour as has been suggested, one returns to Bari with the feeling of having spent one's time well. *Bari 55km/34mi.*

Bitonto   D12

(pop. 38,500) Bitonto is an extremely interesting city of Apulia for those who admire Romanesque architecture, of which its cathedral is one of the outstanding examples. The entire façade, and particularly the right-hand side, might well be called a poem in stone. Inside there is a splendid pulpit (1240) the work of Master Bonifacio, and the crypt with its thirty columns, no two of which are alike.

The church of San Francesco has a fine 13th-century Gothic portal and the very old abbey of San Leo has interesting 15th-century cloisters. Another architectural

jewel is to be found in the Loggia of Sylos Calò, and it is rewarding to walk through the 15th-century Gothic portal of the Sylos Labina mansion to see the lovely Loggia in the courtyard.

Bitonto is within easy road and rail distance from Bari and well worth a visit.

Bríndisi   G17

(pop. 73,000) This has been a major port throughout its history which goes back to pre-Roman days. Virgil, born near Mántova, died at Bríndisi in 19 BC. The old – and interesting – part of the town contains several monuments. Not far from the port is the one remaining of the two columns that marked the end of the ancient Via Appia. Nearby is the 12th-century church of San Giovanni al Sepolcro, now a museum. The cathedral was rebuilt during the last century, and little remains of the earlier edifice. About half a mile from the city is the imposing Castello Svevo, begun in 1227 by Frederick II, later enlarged by Ferdinand of Aragon and at present the seat of the Comando Militare Marittimo.

There is a splendid beach at the thermal resort of **Torre Canne**. Grapes, dried figs and melons are especially good at Bríndisi, and there are numerous restaurants where one may enjoy marine food.

Lecce   H18

(pop. 76,305) This is an agricultural, industrial and good tourist centre about 41km/25mi from Bríndisi, 14km/8mi from the pleasant seaside resort of **San Cataldo**, and one of the finest Italian baroque cities, centred round the Piazza del Duomo. The cathedral is 12th-century, and was altered in the 17th century by the architect Zimbalo, who added a fine bell-tower from which there is a lovely view of the city. The Vescovado (Bishop's Palace) and the Seminario Vescovile complete the composition. The church of Santi Nicola e Cataldo, to the north of the city, has a stupendous baroque façade; another highly decorative church by Zimbalo is that of Santa Croce, undergoing restoration. The local yellow-brown stone lends itself beautifully to the intricacies of this particular style of architecture. The town also possesses a Roman theatre and amphitheatre, and a 16th-century castle.

Matera   G12

(pop. 40,000) This town is well worth a visit. It is a busy commercial centre but also has lovely buildings, such as the fine Apulian Romanesque cathedral (1268–70), and the churches of San Domenico and San Francesco.

Possibly the greatest attraction, however, lies in the houses and churches excavated in the rock on which the upper city stands, particularly the little church of Santa Maria de Idris which has a walk leading to another hypogeum (underground church) with Byzantine frescoes of the 12th century.

Ótranto   I19

(pop. 4070) This busy agricultural and commercial centre of Roman origin was an important city during the Middle Ages. It has a fine Romanesque cathedral, restored in 1481, but possessing a splendid mosaic floor, featuring among other characters King Arthur of Round Table fame (1166). There is also a charming Byzantine church, San Pietro, with a cylindrical dome and three semi-circular apses.

Added to which, fish in Ótranto is excellent, so that a visit to this little part of Púglia is by no means a waste of time.

Potenza   G9

(pop. 44,490) This city, 823m/2700ft above sea level, is the highest city in peninsular Italy. The air is good, but it is a windy city. Parts are old and shabby, but there is also an elegant section and it has a fine cathedral and two Romanesque churches (San Michele Archangele and San Francesco). Note the wooden portal of the 12th-century convent of the latter church. In the Town Hall is the Roman sarcophagus of Rapolla, said to have inspired Jacopo della Quercia when he designed the much-admired tomb of Ilaria del Carretto in the cathedral in Lucca.

Ruvo   D12

(pop. 23,500) 260m/853ft above sea level. This is a city scorched now and again by a stifling *scirocco* that seems to take away all wish or power of movement; nevertheless, it is one of the 'musts' of Apulia.

Within easy reach of Bari by train, it boasts yet another of the lovely Apulian Romanesque cathedrals, with a charming rose window and a bell-tower that started life as a cylindrical defence tower in Norman days.

In the period when Apulia was Magna Grecia, it was famous for the making of pottery vases, which were exported to the mother country, Greece. During excavations in Ruvo, a vast number of these vases were brought to light, objects of great beauty, decorated with heroic and mythological scenes, coloured and glazed, and in almost perfect condition. Needless to

say, many of these found their way into various museums all over the world, but the little Museo Jatta in Ruvo still has over 1800 pieces, things of a rare beauty that should be seen by anyone visiting the city.

Apulia is dotted with castles built by the Norman kings, and from Ruvo one can go by car or taxi to visit the most famous – **Castel del Monte**. Enquire in advance about opening times, as it may be necessary to get special permission to visit the interior of the castle. Not only is this castle one of the showpieces of Norman architecture, it is one of the architectural masterpieces of the whole world. Needless to say, the king who had it erected was Frederick II, who used it as a hunting lodge. The architect was one Nicola da Foggia, whom many believe to have been that Nicola who, when Frederick II died and his court was dispersed, travelled through Italy until he came to Pisa and became known as Nicola Pisano.

Táranto   H15

(pop. 193,000) This city, tucked away under what one might call the 'instep' of Italy, is a busy industrial centre, but also a very interesting town to visit.

Originally it was one of the most flourishing cities of Magna Grecia, in the days when the southeast coast of Italy was heavily settled by Greeks.

It consists of the old city and the new and, not surprisingly, the most interesting architecture is to be found in the former. There is the 12th-century cathedral of San Cataldo which rose on the site of an earlier 4th-century edifice; there is a castle which was largely rebuilt in the late 15th century by Ferdinando of Aragon, and a fine 19th-century Municipio (Town Hall).

At one time Táranto was famous for wool and for the dyeing of wool with a purplish dye made from a certain kind of mollusc peculiar to the district. It is also said that the inhabitants of Táranto were responsible for the introduction of cats into Europe.

Nowadays one of the chief industries of Táranto is the cultivation of oysters, said to be the finest in Italy. The writer Norman Douglas was of the opinion that the inhabitants of Táranto were of a sluggish nature, thanks to their overeating of mussels, which are also found in considerable quantities.

Táranto has two ports, a military one and a civil, and its two cities, old and new, are united by a drawbridge.

The Museo Nazionale is one of the finest in Europe for its collection of precious prehistoric relics.

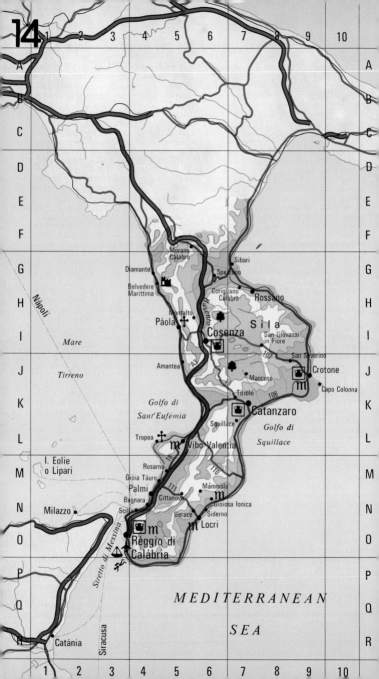

CALÁBRIA

Calábria occupies what we might call the 'toe' of Italy, bordered by Campania on the north, by the Mare Tirreno (Tyrrhenian Sea) on the west, the Ionian on the east, and on the map looks as though it had just kicked Sicilia into the Mediterranean.

Largely mountainous, on the west the mountains drop precipitously down into the sea and coastal strips are narrow; on the east, the plateaux of the Sila intervene before wider coastal strips are reached, especially in the north and central parts of the region. In the far south rise the wooded heights of Aspromonte, Montalto, the highest point, 1956m/6417ft above sea level.

There are numerous bays around the coasts and the fine sands – some of a pinkish hue because of the presence of coral – are an attraction to tourists, as are the chestnut woods of the Sila, for about one-fourth of Calábria is under forest, in spite of de-forestation in former days by the poorer members of the population who regarded trees as 'thieves of the soil'. Many people see in the mountains of Calábria a strong resemblance to those of the north rather than to the typical southern landscape.

There are three great plains, that of Sant'Eufémia on the bay of the same name, the Plain of Rosarno behind Gióia Táuro, and finally the area around Réggio, all on the Tyrrhenian side, while on the Ionian there is the Plain of Sibari in the north, and the March of Crotone.

The few rivers are liable to flooding and swift-running, which gives rise to shortage of the water essential to agriculture. One river, the Busento, which divides the older part of Cosenza from the newer, is said to be the river whose stream was diverted around 410 AD so that the treasure of King Alaric of the Visigoths might be buried safely in its bed. Many have hunted this fabled treasure, but so far it has not come to light.

Calábria has many natural beauties. The rock Scilla, which, with the whirlpool Charybdis, was sung of by Homer and Dante, lies 15km/9mi north of Réggio. Between Catanzaro and Crotone, the landscape seems more lunar than terrestrial; the Ionic coast is splendid in its great desolation; this is the coast deserted by the Greeks who fled, and by the local population who took to the hills to escape the scourge of malaria, a danger now eliminated but which served to drive away even the raiding Corsairs.

There are numerous lovely bays along

the Tyrrhenian coast from which can be seen the Isole Eólie and at times Monte Etna in Sicilia.

At least two famous men were born in Calábria; in 1508 the philosopher Telesio was born in Cosenza; in 1613 the painter Mattia Pipeti was born in Mancuso in the Sila, now a holiday centre. In another town of the Sila, San Giovanni in Fiore, there is the tomb of the mystic Gioacchino di Fiore mentioned in the third book of Dante's *Divine Comedy*.

Here and there are apparently untouched medieval towns such as Corigliano Calabro, 219m/718ft above sea level.

In the 16th century a group of Albanians fled their own country and settled in a few Calabrian towns, among them Spezzano, where even today their native language, customs and songs persist.

The Tyrrhenian coast is lined with huge olive groves, plantations of citrus fruit, bergamot in particular, the foundation of many essences. Figs grow well and are a source of income.

Tuna and swordfish are caught in large numbers along this coast.

Calábria is still a poor region, and lack of suitable employment has led to much emigration. Things are improving, however, and efforts are being made to attract tourists; good hotels are springing up in the larger centres and there are a fair number of camping sites.

Under the colonizing Greeks in the 7th to 6th centuries BC Calábria enjoyed a period of great splendour, especially in Réggio, Crotone and Sibari. Hostile to Roma in the wars against Pyrrhus and Hannibal, the region became subject to her after the second Punic War and, in the 2nd century BC, colonies were founded and the road from Cápua to Réggio traced out. When the Empire fell, Calábria lapsed into a state of misery. Some help was given by Theodoric in the period 494 to 526 AD then, with the incursions of the Longobards, the territory was divided and the area of Cosenza was assigned first to the duchy of Benevento, later to the principality of Salerno.

Saracen raids imposed a heavy tax on the inhabitants, but the Normans brought peace and security (11th to 12th century AD). In later years Calábria shared the destiny of the south, and Angevins and Aragonese impoverished the region.

In 1848 there was a peasant rising against the Bourbons, suppressed by Garibaldi, and in 1860 Calábria became a part of the United Kingdom of Italy.

There are many relics of ancient civilization in the museums of Réggio, Catanzara, Cosenza and Crotone. Excavations at Locri still reveal evidences of the past. In the museum at Riace (inland a few kilometres from coast road 106 south of Monasterace Marina) can be seen the two much-discussed bronze statues rescued from the sea-bed in the early 1980s. On Capo Colonna near Crotone one column remains of the one-time Temple of Giunone. Near Vibo Valentia and along the coastal esplanade at Réggio are remains of imposing Greek walls. The Roman period left baths in Réggio, a theatre at Gioiosa Iónica.

Byzantine art and architecture were widely diffused up to the Middle Ages: Rossano preserves a splendid Greek Gospel, its red pages written on in letters of silver; in the Episcopal Palace in Cosenza is a Byzantine cross of exquisite workmanship. The architecture of the baptistery at San Severino, the church of the Cattolica in Stilo, the church of San Marco at Rossano is pure Byzantine, and the cathedrals of Tropea and Gerace, the Roccelletta near Squillace are examples of this allied with Romanesque. The Gothic did not begin to penetrate until the early 13th century. The influence of the Renaissance is stronger in painting than in architecture. Réggio possesses a fine example of the work of Antonello da Messina, Morano Calabro boasts a Vivarini. Sculpture by Laurana and Gaggini is fairly widely dispersed. During the 17th and 18th centuries came a period of fervid building to replace earthquake damage.

One may wonder at the 'newness' of Réggio di Calábria, bearing in mind that it was founded in the 8th century BC. Much of the original city perished in the earthquake of 1908.

Festivals At Easter-time in Réggio, Karacolo, Mammola, Tiriolo and Vibo Valentia comes the rite of the *Affruntata*, a procession during which there is an encounter between the statue of the Madonna and that of the risen Christ. In the early days of May in Tropea comes the *Festival of the Camel*; in the evening following a day of jollifications, a young man places on his shoulders the image of a camel constructed of fire-crackers, which are then ignited as he courses through the streets accompanied by a band of drums and tambourines.

Palmi on the last Sunday in July celebrates the festival of the Madonna with a long procession of decorated boats.

Also in Palmi on 16 August, a procession of the faithful who, for grace received, cover themselves with prickly branches.

Belvedere Marittima   G4

(pop. 10,500) For those wanting a really quiet yet delightful holiday along the coast of Calábria, Belvedere would be ideal. There is but one hotel, quite moderately comfortable, but the owner also has a series of fairly well-equipped seaside bungalows which he rents out during the season.

The small town is tranquil; its main interest is the daily departure and return of the fishing fleet. Swordfish are found here and make an appetizing dish, as do the local sole.

On a hill above the town is the frowning bulk of an Angevin/Aragonese castle, and a couple of churches. Little narrow streets wind in and out of this upper part.

A pleasant walk takes one along the shore to the nearby town of **Diamante**, even smaller, but again with possibilities for sea bathing and with some lovely panoramic views.

Both these places have a long way to go before they qualify as regular tourist resorts, but they are well worth exploring.

Belvedere Marittima is on the main railway line to Réggio di Calábria, and the station is busy. Communications to other coastal cities farther south, such as **Páola**, **Amantea**, **Tropea** and so on, are facilitated by this railway line, and it is even possible to go as far as **Cosenza**, though this last is less easy, because after turning inland to approach the hilly city, one travels on a rack type of railway and progress is decidedly slow and jerky.

Páola   I5

(pop. 15,000) This is an agricultural centre, the main products of which are oil and wine, but it has a good stretch of sandy beach, but with the growing importance of Calábria as a resort province, is rapidly taking on the aspect of a holiday centre.

An interesting excursion by bus or car from Páola is to the **Santuario di San Francesco**, which is set in an extremely

Scilla

picturesque position at the mouth of the River Isca.

Réggio di Calábria   O3

(pop. 152,350) This is the capital of the province and is a busy tourist centre, important for its export of citrus fruits and various essences manufactured from these, particularly that of bergamot.

Its climate is excellent, it has a fine coastline and is a good centre for excursions, either on the mainland or over the Stretto di Messina and into Sicilia.

In the days when Greece had established southern Italy as Magna Grecia, Réggio was of great importance, which did not cease when the region fell under Roman rule. During the Middle Ages it was repeatedly sacked, but enjoyed a further flowering under the Normans. It has suffered the ravages of several serious earthquakes, the most recent in 1908 when it was almost completely devastated and many relics of the past destroyed.

Part of the ancient castle remains, and is now the seat of the geophysical observatory.

There are interesting walks, and from the slopes of Aspromonte can be enjoyed a fine panorama. Réggio is in the midst of the so-called 'violet' coast embracing the centres of **Scilla**, **Bagnara**, **Palmi** and **Monte Sant'Ella**. The site of the ancient city of **Locri** is within easy distance.

Siderno   N6

(pop. 15,500) This is a charming seaside resort on the eastern coast of southern Calábria. It has its own port and is a fairly busy industrial centre set in an agricultural and olive-growing district.

Hunting and fishing are good and bathing is excellent and well provided for.

There is a long, wide stretch of sand separated from the main part of the town by attractive gardens.

9km/6mi away is an excellent camping site.

Siderno is on the Ionian sea coast, and the inhabitants take pride in the fact that the Ionian is not among the seas that have suffered pollution from modern industry.

Tropea   L4

(pop. 7000) This town, which lies at the southern end of the Golfo di Sant'Eufémia in Calábria, is a very picturesque tourist centre with its own port.

During the 9th century AD it was captured by the Saracens, but later came under the rule of the Angevins and later again of the Aragons.

It has many interesting buildings, including the 9th-century cathedral which, in addition to some fine 16th-century bas-reliefs, has a lovely marble ciborium among its treasures. The 12th-century church of San Francesco and its chapel of a century later are interesting to visit, and in the church of the Annunciation there is a charming 16th-century group of marble statues.

Tropea has an excellent beach, and fishing and other nautical sports are well provided for. Photographers will doubtless wish to 'snap' the picturesque church of Santa Maria dell'Isola which stands out against the sky from its position atop a high cliff.

Tourism, which is fairly new to Calábria, is fast developing and hotels are springing up at the various beauty spots along the coast.

SICÍLIA

Sicília is the largest island in the Mediterranean, lying between the southern extremity of the peninsula and the African coast. It has a special statute and enjoys particular forms of autonomy, which are shared with the Ísole Eólie, the Egadi, the Pelage, Ustica and Pantelleria.

Mostly mountainous, its heights culminate in the great volcanic complex of Monte Etna. There is a large fertile plain inland from Catánia, others in the southwestern corner of the island and around the Bay of Gela, while behind Palermo lies the fertile and beautiful area known as the Conca d'Oro (Golden Valley).

The climate is typically Mediterranean. Summers are very hot and dry and the rainy season of the winter months is so short that finding sufficient water for crop irrigation is an ever-present problem. The rivers alternate between dry, stony beds in the summer and raging torrents in winter.

In spite of this difficulty, Sicília is an agricultural region. Once the granary of Italy, in spite of reckless deforestation it still produces large quantities of wheat and oats, and its production of citrus fruits represents almost four-fifths of the national yield. Vines give good-quality wines of high alcoholic content; Malvasia is the special wine of the Ísole Eólie, Marsala comes from the district of the same name, and the wines of Pantelleria are well known. Among other products are almonds, olives, walnuts, figs, carob beans and pistachio nuts; tomatoes and artichokes are also grown in large quantities.

Sheep, cattle and goats are raised, and fishing prospers, especially for tuna, which supplies a sizeable canning industry.

Sulphur and rock salt are mined, and oil drilling has proved successful near Ragusa and Gela, which supply the refineries at Augusta on the east coast.

Much of the attraction of Sicília comes from its checkered history and the many monuments that record the various dominations. This history, plus superlative coastal scenery, climatic conditions and hotel accomodation, combine to bring visitors in their thousands.

It is not difficult to reach Sicília; steamers from Nápoli travel to Palermo and Messina; there are air services to Palermo, Trápani and Catánia, and a ferry from Réggio di Calábria.

Siracusa (Syracuse) was great and powerful under the first Dionysius, who died in 388 BC. In his day was built the Castle of Eurialus, still extant and regarded as one of the finest examples of military architecture. When the Romans attacked Siracusa in the 2nd century BC, their defeat was due to the ingenuity of the famous mathematician Archimedes, who designed the large cranes that overturned many vessels, and destroyed others by means of 'burning glasses' which set them on fire.

Although small groups of Spanish and Italian colonists arrived, not to mention the Phoenicians who founded the city of Palermo, they were outnumbered by the Greeks who occupied first the eastern shores and then gradually forged their way along the southern coast, where they founded the city of Agrigento.

Relics of Greek civilization still stand in the Valley of Temples near that city, in the theatres in Siracusa and Taormina, and in the now deserted sites of Segesta and Selinunte.

Following the defeat of Carthage, the Romans tried again, this time successfully; first Siracusa and later the entire island fell under their power. It was they who discovered and exploited the rich deposits of sulphur and other natural resources.

In memory of their stay there is a Roman theatre at Siracusa, and near the city of Piazza Armerina, 50km/31mi southeast of Enna, stands the 5th-century Villa di Casale with attractive and well-preserved floor mosaics.

Following the Barbaric invasions of the mainland, Sicília came under the domination of Byzantium, and from about 535 AD Greek was once again the official language and the church adopted the Greek ritual.

By the 8th century AD Mohammedanism was endeavouring to eradicate

Christianity, and Sicília was one of its points of attack. In 827 the Moslem Arabs invaded; in 831 they captured Palermo, in 878 Siracusa was destroyed. Under their rule commerce prospered, taxes were lowered, religious toleration of a sort existed. They installed an excellent irrigation system; citrus fruits and mulberry trees with their attendant silkworms were introduced. Arab weights and measures are still in use today, and many Arab words have remained in the language, for example *maggazzino* (warehouse).

In the 1030s a Byzantine force landed in Messina, among them Harold Hardrada, later one of the invaders of England. In 1060 came Roger d'Hauteville, first of the Norman kings who were the rulers of the island for over 200 years.

Under the Normans, particularly Roger II and Frederick II, Sicilia rose to an unprecedented peak of splendour. These two kings were outstanding in every way. Roger, though a Christian, was crowned in a mosque in Palermo, and in the church of the Martorana in that city there is a mosaic depicting him wearing the cloak and stole of an apostolic legate, with a Greek crown being placed on his head by Christ himself; yet he was reputed to maintain a harem. He it was who initiated the building of the great cathedral at Cefalù. When, for lack of male heirs to William II, the crown went to the Hohenstaufen dynasty, Frederick II of Swabia proved to be one of the greatest emperors of all time. Even today, looking at the tomb of this great ruler in the cathedral of Palermo, one feels one is in the presence of royalty. His court at Palermo attracted men of culture; poets, artists, musicians, scientists. He lived in regal luxury, more Oriental than European, and it is rumoured that he, too, maintained a *seraglio*.

With the passing of the Normans the picturesque history of Sicilia ends, with the possible exception of the incident known as the *Sicilian Vespers* of 1282. The allegedly too-friendly relations between a French soldier and a Sicilian woman sparked off a war which ended with the defeat of the invading French.

From this time on the history of the island was one of foreign domination on the part of Italy, France and Spain. In 1347 it was swept by the Black Death, a plague said to have caused the death of a good third of the population.

Internal revolts from time to time led to banditry and Sicilia gained the not entirely undeserved reputation of being a turbulent island, for which its past history might well furnish an excuse, and yet at the same time explain the enchantment

that lingers over the one-time *Trinacria* of Virgil.

Sicília has something of everything to offer. Vestiges of the past remain, not only in art and architecture, but in the very features and characteristics of the people. The gay, painted carts that are such a feature of rural Sicília depict legends that go back into mythology; the puppets one enjoys at street-corner 'theatres' are by no means of recent origin.

Among its lesser joys are the out-of-this-world pastries of Palermo, and that delicious ice-cream cake known as *Cassata Siciliana*.

The little terracotta statuettes are the product of local craftsmen who have inherited their skill from past generations. The embroidered blouse you admire, and which is not your size, can be copied within twenty-four hours in exquisite handwork.

Festivals Holy Week is celebrated in every city of Sicilia with processions in costume. *Palio dei Normanni* (Horse race in costume) 13 August, at Piazza Armerina. In Messina 15 August sees the *Procession of the Vara*, a great float surmounted by a pyramid of angels with the statue of the Virgin at its peak.

Ísole Eólie o Lípari
(Aeolian or Lípari Isles)   A14

This group of islands lies between Nápoli and Sicilia and is passed by steamers travelling between Nápoli and Messina.

In the *Aeneid*, Virgil refers to them as *Aeolia*, the kingdom of the god of storms and winds, Aeolus, but in spite of this reputation, the climate of the islands is so mild and agreeable as to recommend them for winter holidays. This refers particularly to Lípari, the ancient Meligunis and the largest island of the group which comprises seven in all: Lípari, Filicudi, Alicudi, Salina, Vulcano, Panarea and the fearsome Strómboli which, despite its ever-active volcano, boasts three hotels.

Approach is easy by steamer and the speedier hydrofoils from Nápoli, Palermo, Catánia, Taormina and Milazzo near Messina.

All seven islands have good hotels and camping possibilities.

There is no end to the attractions for visitors; walkers find countless beauty spots to be explored; all the islands have wide, sandy beaches, stupendously tall, rugged cliffs, grottoes and floating islands, and there are possibilities for excursions of all types, from yachting and motorboating to a trip on one of the large fishing vessels, while underwater fishing is popular. One of the most popular attractions is a night visit to the crater of Strómboli. Fishing is carried on in a big way, and it is pleasant at nightfall to watch the local fleet going out to sea with the *lampare* alight. (These are lights facing down into the water to attract passing shoals of fish.)

Pantelleria   J2

Pantelleria is an extremely interesting little island, lying off the shores of Trápani on the western coast of Sicilia. It is not the easiest place to visit, since boats call only twice weekly, nor for accommodation, as there are only two hotels and those of fourth category.

Nevertheless, for the hardy traveller Pantelleria presents many attractions. Extremely mountainous, rising in the centre to more than 800m/2625ft above sea level, it is of volcanic origin, and the many eruptions have tortured its cliffs into fantastic shapes. It is also of great archaeological interest, being the ancient Cossyra. Among the treasures to be explored are

the *Sesi* (prehistoric tombs), a neolithic village and the Phoenician acropolis.

Hunting and underwater fishing can be enjoyed, and the wines, particularly the local *passito* (not unlike Moscato) are extremely good.

Agrigento   G9

(pop. 47,000) This city, on the southern shores of Sicília, is built on two hills, from which one can see the Mediterranean. **Porto Empédocle**, the coastal town, and a centre for deep-sea fishing, is only about 5km/3mi away.

Agrigento had its beginnings almost 600 years before the birth of Christ, when it was a Greek colony. Its original name, Girgenti, by which it was known until 1927, is reminiscent of the Arab domination of the island.

It is a fascinating city to visit, and since it possesses remains of no fewer than twenty Greek temples, most of them situated in the lovely Valley of the Temples between the two hills, it is a mecca for

archaeologists. The most famous of the temples is that of Hercules, recognizable by the tapering of its remaining eight columns; twenty-five columns still stand of the Temple of Giunone Lacinia (5th century BC), and it presents a most evocative vision of what the Valley must have looked like in its early days. The remains of the great Temple of Olympic Jove and that of Castor and Pollux are also impressive, while the almost perfect Temple of Concord is one of the loveliest to be found in that part of Italy and Sicilia known as Magna Grecia. These are but the highlights of the stupendous collection to be found in the Valley, which in the month of February becomes even more beautiful, the flowering almond trees decking the temples with a shower of blossom. February is an ideal month in which to visit Agrigento and to take part in the Festival of the Almond Trees.

Coming nearer, but not very near, to the present day, Agrigento also boasts a fine Romanesque-Gothic church, that of San Nicola, and the 14th-century cathedral has a sepulchre, that of DeMartinis, which is a treasure of art.

Not surprisingly, the Civic Museum of History offers a fine collection of treasures of archaeological interest, while, in the museum of the cathedral is the sarcophagus of Phedra, dating back to the 2nd century AD.

Hotels are various, a few excellent, others mediocre; there is a camping ground nearby, and several restaurants and trattories where the food is good.

The modern bathing beach of **San Leone Bagni**, near Porto Empédocle, is well equipped.

Catánia   F14

(pop. 363,000) This city, standing in the middle of the east coast of Sicilia, occupies an extremely picturesque position below the towering height of Monte Etna.

Conquered by the Romans in 263 BC, it enjoyed alternating periods of great prosperity and equally great depression, but

under the Emperor Augustus it was regarded as the most flourishing city in Italy, and under the Saracens and Normans it continued to prosper until it suffered considerable damage in the earthquake of 1169. It soon recovered itself and began again to flourish under the Aragon rulers until another earthquake in 1693, from which time many of the buildings we admire today were constructed.

The central part has agreeable 18th-century architecture, but as a town it is not well-kept, and during the past 20 years it has grown rapidly and without any definite town planning.

It is criss-crossed by streets all of which seem to be climbing up towards Etna; one of the most famous streets is Via Etnea, which runs in a perfectly straight line for a length of 3km/2mi.

The cathedral, originally of the 12th century, was rebuilt after the earthquake of 1693. (The painter Vincenzo Bellini is buried in the chapel of Sant'Agata.) In Piazza Duomo, the square in which the cathedral stands, is a famous Elephant statue; the elephant is the symbol of Catánia and it is said that in paleolithic days elephants roamed the island of Sicilia. The Ursino Castle, now the seat of the Civic Museum, was one of the many erected by Frederick II halfway through the 13th century.

For those who like baroque architecture, Catánia offers many examples, such as the Biscari Palace.

Catánia lies in a rich agricultural district and its main sources of wealth are agriculture and oranges. Forests of chestnut trees line the slopes of Etna and add to its picturesque aspect. Etna is lovely to see but dangerously unpredictable: as recently as 1983 there was an alarming eruption. February is the best month to see the temperamental volcano in all its glory, when almond trees are blooming, snow still covers the slopes and the sea is of an almost unbelievable blue.

Going from Catánia to Taormina along the coastal road one passes many interesting little places; **Aci Castello**, where there is a black castle which once belonged to (yes, you are right!) Frederick II; then a few miles further along the same road you come to **Aci Trezza**, the setting for Verga's famous novel *I Malavoglia*. Out in the sea stand the Cyclops, huge rocks which according to legend were those thrown by the giant Polyphemus in an effort to hit Ulysses.

Proceeding even further one reaches one of the most interesting towns in this part of Sicília, **Acireale**, an almost entirely baroque city, the jewel of which is the church of San Sebastian. This is said to be a very 'close' town, a place where folks keep themselves to themselves, and are extremely jealous of the traditions of this little place.

Cefalù   D10

(pop. 13,000) One can go to Cefalù for a seaside holiday, and a most enjoyable one, for it is a well-equipped place, but to visit the city without paying homage to the 12th-century cathedral is to miss one of the great churches of the Middle Ages.

This massive building stands on a height in the rear of the town. It is approached by a flight of steps and presents an austere façade flanked by two square towers. Internally there is a fine presbytery, and the bowl of the apse is dominated by a huge mosaic representing Christ, the Pantocrator.

Behind the cathedral are the remains of a megalithic temple to Diana, and nearby is the very interesting Mandralisca Mansion, with a fine collection of paintings.

A short, steep bus or car ride from Cefalù takes one to the sanctuary hill town **Gibilmanna**, 800m/2625ft above sea level, where even today you can see the village women fetching water from the well, bearing the vessels on their heads.

Lying midway between Palermo and Messina, Cefalù is easily reached from either by road or rail. Not far away is a well-run tourist village.

Palermo   C8

(pop. 585,000) Spectacular is the adjective for this very busy and very beautiful city, whose checkered history has endowed it with a wealth of varied architecture.

Palermo was originally founded by the Phoenicians, but became Roman about 250 years BC. After the rout of the Byzantines by the Saracens in the year 831 AD, it knew a period of great prosperity, which continued even after the arrival of the Normans, who made it the capital of the island. King Roger II and King Frederick II were the monarchs who brought Palermo to the height of its splendour.

In 1282 Sicília rebelled against French rule in the incident that has come down in history as the *Sicilian Vespers*, after which the French were expelled from the island. Then, until Garibaldi conquered Silicia in 1860, it passed successively through the hands of the Angevins, the Aragons and the Bourbons.

It is still a busy port and has an excellent and much-frequented tourist section. A city of great natural beauty, it has also some of the finest public parks in Italy.

The things and places one ought to visit are numerous. The most famous and spectacular meeting point is that of the

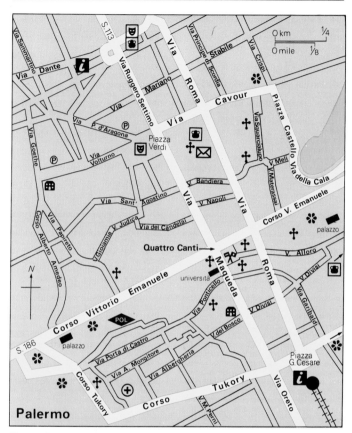

Palermo

Quattro Canti (Four Corners), which is a good point of location when wandering around the city. The 12th-century cathedral (north of Corso Emanuele) is breathtaking; in it are the tombs of the Norman kings. The 11th-century church of San Giovanni degli Eremiti has interesting Arab cupolas; in the church of the Martorana (Santa Maria dell'Ammiraglio) are wonderful mosaics. In the Oratorio della Compagnia del Rosario di San Domenico is a painting by Van Dyck; the Oratory of the Company of San Lorenzo has a precious Caravaggio.

The erstwhile palace of the Norman kings was restored in the 18th century and of the original 12th-century fabric remains only the Pisana Tower and the Palatine Chapel, which latter must be added to the sightseer's list for its wonderful mosaic decoration and its marvellous wooden ceiling. The castle known as La Zisa is a fine example of 12th-century Muslim architecture. Palermo has a fine National Museum, an astronomical observatory and an interesting Botanical Garden.

Having seen all these, a visitor can spend literally days before exhausting the many other interesting churches and buildings around Palermo, such as the nearby Convent of the Cappuccini, the not-to-be-missed cathedral of Monreale – note particularly the lovely cloisters and the mosaics that line the interior walls of this cathedral. Yet another interesting church is that of San Giovanni dei Lebbrosi (11th century).

From 13 to 15 July of every year there is the colourful Festival of Santa Rosalia, patron saint of the city.

Hotel accommodation is good and plentiful and there are many excellent restaurants.

Siracusa (Syracuse)   H15

(pop. 83,000) This city, not surprisingly, when one thinks of its history, has much to offer visitors.

Its excellent port is built partly on the mainland, partly on the island of Ortigia, the site of the original town, now joined to the mainland by a bridge.

Founded by the Greeks almost 800 years before the birth of Christ, Siracusa had a long reign of glory, having become, by 485 BC, the principal Greek city in Sicilia. Its outstanding rulers were Dionysius the Tyrant, and his not much less tyrannical son, Dionysius the Younger.

Roman occupation led to the decline of its power, and Siracusa never again rose to its one-time heights of prosperity, but it possesses today relics of that past splendour that gives us an insight into what it must once have been.

A little outside the city itself, looking towards Africa, which it is said can be seen on a very clear day, is the great military fortification of the older Dionysius, the Castle of Eurialus. Siracusa has also a fine semi-circular Greek theatre of the 4th to 3rd century BC, and even earlier is the pagan altar nearby, dedicated to Gerone. Still in the same area is a Roman amphitheatre of the time of the emperor Augustus. All these are to be found not far from the one-time huge lime-quarries, now transformed into public gardens. Here, too, is the so-called Ear of Dionysius, a cave the formation of which resembles that of the human ear.

There is also the Spring of Arethusa around which is woven the charming legend of the nymph of that name who, pursued by the river god Alpheus, implored the aid of the goddess Diana, who responded by changing her into a spring.

King Frederick II left his mark in Siracusa by way of remodelling the 11th-century Maniace Castle.

The National Archaeological Museum is interesting; among its many exhibits is what must surely be the coyest statue of Venus extant.

Archimedes, the great mathematician, was a native of Siracusa, a fact commemorated by a handsome fountain in the square of the same name.

In the convent attached to the church of San Giovanni are interesting catacombs, and the cathedral, in spite of its 18th-century façade is, internally, the 5th-century reconstruction of what was formerly the Temple of Athena.

A few years ago work was begun on what was intended to become a modern cathedral, dedicated to the miracle-working Madonna delle Lacrime, a holy image whose eyes at certain times were seen to be filled with tears. A lot of poor property was demolished in order to accommodate this new building, which is being built out of the offerings of the many poor parts of the city.

Siracusa is well equipped with hotels, and from it there are many interesting excursions to be made.

Taormina   D15

(pop. 8000) 206m/676ft above sea level. In a country where many lovely places abound, it is pointless to indicate any one in particular as the most beautiful, but certainly Taormina ranks very high on the list. Lying on the eastern shores of Sicilia, midway between Catánia and Messina, the coastal road to either of these offers panoramic views.

The French writer Roger Peyrefitte wrote of this lovely city that 'Taormina is to Sicily what Sicily is to the world'; the poet Horace felt that it was a place 'where one would wish to live, forgotten and forgetting'.

Taormina seems to offer something of everything: panoramic beauty and a wonderful climate first of all; semitropical vegetation, clumps of prickly pear here and there, lining the little lanes leading down the ravines to the soft, sandy beaches and the deep, blue sea; a wealth of hotels and restaurants to suit all pockets, and camping grounds too. Walking through the town one passes medieval mansions, several Romanesque-Gothic churches, and the austere 16th-century cathedral, the old convent of San Domenico (now a luxury hotel), with its lovely old cloisters. In Taormina are the remains of a large Graeco-Roman theatre with Monte Etna forming a spectacular and permanent backdrop. There is the arena which was once the scene of mock sea-fights, and these are but a few of the many interesting sights to be seen.

The tourist in search of souvenirs will find an abundance in the little craftsmen's shops along the narrow streets. Glance at the women sitting in cottage doorways, embroidering exquisite silk blouses, and you will see that hardly one is wearing glasses.

Taormina is a definite 'must' for anyone visiting Sicilia.

SARDEGNA

Sardegna is the second largest of the islands of the Mediterranean. Its geological foundations go back to the paleozoic age. Prevalently mountainous, its highest peak is in the Gennargentu range, and there are plains and tablelands to vary the landscape, while the coastline is an invitation to all who love the sea.

A mere 180km/112mi from the mainland, it is fairly accessible by boat and plane; in fact, there are more than 100 flights daily, and modern ferries capable of transporting not only people, but caravans and boats. Once arrived, there is an excellent network of roads. Nevertheless, because of the popularity of the island, there are sometimes tiresome hours of waiting for available transport.

Sardegna is divided into four provinces, Cágliari, Sássari, Núoro and Oristano, each furnished with reliable tourist information offices (see Useful Addresses, page 19).

The climate is mild and around the coast there is little possibility of rain. Tourism is developing rapidly, especially in the north, along the far-famed Costa Smeralda (Emerald Coast), paradise of the 'jet set', the Golfo dell'Asinara (Bay of Asinara), the archipelago of La Maddalena and Santa Teresa di Gallura. In all of these one has the choice of a host of well-run hotels, but very early booking is essential.

The south, east and west are somewhat less well-geared for tourists, but even there a fair choice of reliable, modern accommodation exists.

There are camping sites around the coast and inland, youth hostels at **Alghero**, **Arzachena**, **Bari Sardo**, **Calasetta** and **La Maddalena**, to mention but a few. The exotic and expensive Club Mediterrane has a tourist village on La Maddalena.

Everyone has heard praises of its coastal joys, but Sardegna offers inland treats as well, which throw some light on its strange, almost mysterious history. Though the origin of the population is uncertain, it is known that during the neolithic age navigators used to land in Sardegna, followed from the 7th century BC by Phoenicians, Greeks, Etruscans, Carthaginians, Romans, Vandals and Byzantines, all of whom have left their mark.

From the 7th century AD onward, the Byzantine empire having gone into a decline, a form of self-government arose in the form of four *Giudicati* centred on Cágliari, Porto Tórres, Arborea and Gallura. Later, during the 11th century, began the conquest of the island by the maritime republics of Pisa and Génova. Then, during the 13th and 14th centuries, we see Sardegna under Spanish domination until about 1700, when there was a short period of Austrian rule. Following this it was given to the House of Savoy, and thus came into being the Sardinian/Piemontese Kingdom, from which in 1861 King Victor Emmanuel II was called to be the first king of United Italy. Now, although within the limits of the Italian Republic, Sardegna is more or less self-governing.

Going around the island one notices a particular characteristic of its most ancient civilization, the *nuraghi*, cone-shaped megalithic structures, the stones piled one atop the other without the aid of mortar or cement. The purpose of these has puzzled archaeologists through the ages; some imagine them to have been fortresses, others see them as places of worship; others again regard them as dwellings. There are about seven thousand on the island, and one is unlikely to pass one's holiday without encountering a few. They date back at least as far as 1500 BC.

Then, too, the island has the reputation of being inhabited by the 'little people', the fairies, who are said to have had their habitations in the *domus de Janas*, grottoes cut into the rock and consisting of small windowless chambers, though many believe these to be tombs.

Coming to more recent antiquities, there are the Roman towns of **Nora**, **Antas**, **Tharros**; **Cágliari** has a fine Roman amphitheatre, and there are numerous Romanesque churches, Spanish castles and towers.

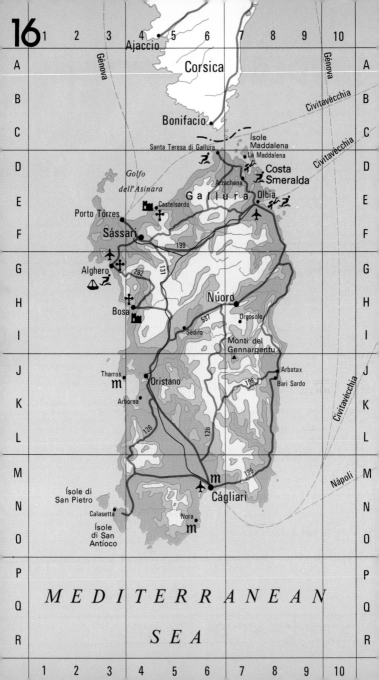

All of Sardegna is interesting; Alghero, in addition to its fine beach, grottoes and a necropolis, has a fine Aragonese-Gothic cathedral, and nearby are *nuraghi*. Here you can see the working of coral, for which the island is famous, and there are stupendous views for camera enthusiasts; **Bosa** has the remains of the Malaspina castle and a fine Romanesque church; in **Castelsardo**, in addition to the Doria Castle and the 16th-century cathedral, you can see the local basket-makers at work.

To add to your knowledge of where to go and what to see, the Assessorato al Turismo della Regione Sarda, Viale Trento 69, Cágliari, publishes an excellent little handbook, *Sardegna Guida*, in Italian, French, German and English.

Thinking of souvenirs to buy, Sardinian handwork has its origins in the traditions of the past; there are carpets woven on hand looms, and this craft has been extended to include wall hangings and upholstery fabrics, the designs of which are traditional and unusual. Because certain regions are rich in china clay, there is considerable production of ceramics, particularly in Cágliari and Sássari. Handworked embroideries on scarves or household linen are exquisite, but difficult to find.

Silverware, articles in gold and corals are obtainable in a variety of types, as are basket-work, carved wood and articles made of the local cork.

Where eating is concerned, the ham of the wild boar is exquisite as are the eggs of mullet and tuna fish, preserved as only the Sards know how. Sucking pig is another speciality, and sweets are particularly good – try *sebada*, a fritter stuffed with cheese and seasoned with bitter honey.

Vernaccia, a dry wine, is the favourite wine; if you prefer a sweet wine, try Malvasia or Moscato.

Some excellent little ports cater especially for tourists travelling in their own boat, **La Maddalena**, **Porto Tórres** and **Arbatax** among them.

Festivals Orgósolo – 16 January *Sant'Antonio* – bonfire and procession. Last Sunday in May, Sássari – *Sardinian Cavalcade*. Sédilo – 6–7 July, *palio* in costume around the medieval walls. Sássari – 14 August, large, heavy votive candelabra carried in procession by Sards from all over the world who have managed to come home for the festival.

KEY WORDS

academy – accademia
airport – aeroporto
arch – arco
armoury – armeria
baker's shop – panetteria
baths (spa) – terme
beach – lido, spiaggia
bell-tower – campanile
bridge – ponte
butcher's shop – macelleria
camp site – campeggio, camping
castle – castello
cathedral – duomo
chapel – cappella
chemist's shop (pharmacy) – farmacia
convent – convento
dairy – latteria
exchange – cambio
ferry – traghetto
fortress – fortezza
forum – foro
fountain – fontana, fonte
gallery – galleria
gardens – giardini
greengrocer (fruit and vegetable market) – erbivendolo
hospital – ospedale
hotel – albergo
house – casa
information office – ufficio informazioni
inn – locanda
library – biblioteca
market – mercato
monastery – monastero, certosa (Carthusian)
motel – autostello, motel
museum – museo
palace – palazzo
park – parco
parking – parcheggio, posteggio
parking meter – contatore per parcheggio, parchimentro
picture gallery – pinacoteca
police – polizia
policeman – poliziotto
police station – commissariato, ufficio di polizia questura
railway station – ferrovia, stazione ferroviaria
restaurant – ristorante, trattoria
shore – spiaggia
sports stadium – stadio
square – piazza
station – stazione
supermarket – supermercato
swimming pool – piscina
telephone – telefono
theatre – teatro
tobacconist's – tabaccheria
town hall – municipio
tunnel, gallery – galleria
zoo – zoo, giardino zoologico

INDEX

All main entries are printed in heavy type. Map references are also printed in heavy type. The map page number precedes the grid reference.